TERM PAPER RESOURCE GUIDE TO AFRICAN AMERICAN HISTORY

TERM PAPER RESOURCE GUIDE TO AFRICAN AMERICAN HISTORY

Caryn E. Neumann

GREENWOOD PRESS
Westport, Connecticut · London

Library of Congress Cataloging-in-Publication Data

Neumann, Caryn E., 1965–
    Term paper resource guide to African American history / Caryn E. Neumann.
        p. cm.
    Includes bibliographical references and index.
    ISBN 978–0–313–35501–1 (alk. paper)
    1.   African Americans—History—Study and teaching. 2.   African Americans—History. 3.   African Americans—History—Bibliography. 4.   Report writing—Handbooks, manuals, etc.   I. Title.
    E184.7.N47 2009
    973'.0496073—dc22   2008051972

British Library Cataloguing in Publication Data is available.

Library of Congress Catalog Card Number: 2008051972
ISBN: 978–0–313–35501–1

First published in 2009

Greenwood Press, 88 Post Road West, Westport, CT 06881
An imprint of Greenwood Publishing Group, Inc.
www.greenwood.com

Printed in the United States of America

The paper used in this book complies with the
Permanent Paper Standard issued by the National
Information Standards Organization (Z39.48-1984).

10 9 8 7 6 5 4 3 2 1

Contents

Acknowledgments

I would like to thank my colleagues at Miami University–Middletown for their support. I am grateful to my editor, Wendi Schnaufer, for her interest in the project and her patience. Elizabeth Claeys, a superb copy editor, saved me from considerable embarrassment. I have used Greenwood Press books for many, many years. It is an honor to be part of the family.

Introduction

African American history is one of the most exciting fields to study. To a large degree, the history of blacks is the story of the triumph of the human spirit. African Americans rose from the depths of slavery and the terror of lynching to win an equal place at the table of American democracy. Along the way, African Americans created a rich history of political thought, artistic achievements, and cultural contributions. Until the flowering of the civil rights movement in the 1960s, however, much of the African American past remained unexamined. A disturbing number of prominent white scholars did not believe that blacks had a history worthy of study. They blocked the efforts of younger scholars to uncover this history. Without scholarly and institutional support, researchers could not easily proceed. The result is a relative weakness in the number of books devoted to topics in African American history. As books serve as the foundation for Web sites and documentary films, there is a related scarcity of these sources. As more scholars enter the field, this shortage will be corrected.

This book has been created to help high school and college students identify exciting and interesting research topics. It addresses 100 of the most significant historical events in African American history, from the slave trade in the sixteenth century to the Katrina Hurricane in New Orleans in 2005. Where sources are scarce, some topics have been combined, such as the Chicago race riot of 1919 and the Tulsa race riot of 1921. The guiding philosophy underlying the choices for inclusion is to ensure that the breadth of African American history is covered. The people and events listed in this book are the ones that are typically covered in a college-level survey course of African American history. Every attempt has been made to find term paper topics that students would find to be both exciting and intellectually challenging to research. The books should be readily available through libraries or Amazon.com.

The topics cited in this book are listed chronologically, but not all include specific dates. Historians disagree about when exactly the Great Migration began and ended. The Harlem Renaissance, generally associated with the 1920s, began about 1915 with the Great Migration. Topics in African American history can attract a considerable amount of political commentary. Sites exist that present slanted views of slavery, the Ku Klux Klan, and welfare, among other hot button topics. Some works that address political topics have been created to promote a particular political point of view. Every effort has been made to list fair and balanced books, Web sites, and films. If a student elects to search for Web sites that are not listed in this guide, the CRAAP test is recommended by a number of universities as a guide to evaluating Web sites. It can easily be found through a Google search or at http://www.csuchico.edu/lins/handouts/evalsites.html. The test asks a series of questions to determine the Currency or timeliness of the information, the Relevance of the information, the Authority or source of the information, the Accuracy of the information, and the Purpose of the information.

USING THE GUIDE

Each entry begins with an overview of the event that is designed to encourage student interest in the topic. The overview is followed by Term Paper Suggestions that feature traditional research questions that students may adopt or alter for research papers. Questions listed under Alternative Term Paper Suggestions provide students with creative ways to present their research, such as by creating a Web site, podcast, series of letters, graphic novel, or artistic project. The remaining categories are presented alphabetically as follows:

Primary Sources—The range of primary sources is not especially broad in African American history because of the lack of importance once attached to the black past. The primary sources provided may take the form of memoirs, essays, photographs, and laws.

Secondary Sources—These materials include interpretations of primary sources by historians, sociologists, and other scholars.

World Wide Web—Relevant internet sites are provided for each entry. All are considered to be valid and stable. They were operative at the time of publication.

Multimedia Sources—Videos are provided for most topics, with some entries also including audio components.

1. Atlantic Slave Trade Expands to North America (1581)

The history of slaves in America begins in the 1430s in Europe. The Moors of North Africa, Europe's main supplier for slaves of all races, charged exorbitantly for slaves. Prince Henry of Portugal, known as "The Navigator," aimed to save the financial resources of his country by finding a way around these middlemen while also exploring the vast wider world. Henry established a school for cartographers, explorers, and ships' pilots to help the Portuguese investigate the shores of Africa and Asia.

The Portuguese sailors who ventured into the unknown discovered gold, silk, spices, and, most significantly, African slaves. In 1444, Portugal imported African slaves into the colony of Madeira, off the coast of Morocco, to work alongside slaves from eastern Europe. When the Turks captured Constantinople in 1453 and shut off the slave ports of the Black Sea to western European ships, western Europe shifted to reliance upon African slave labor. By 1500, about 5,000 Africans per year were exported as slaves, a number that jumped dramatically over the next decades. Some of these slaves began to arrive in the New World, probably in 1501 but possibly earlier. In 1581, at the order of King Philip II of Spain, 500 slaves were sent to St. Augustine in Spanish Florida. These slaves were the first documented slaves in North America.

The vast majority of slaves came from one of four regions: West Central Africa, the Bight of Benin, the Bight of Biafra, and the Gold Coast. Once captured by African warriors, African men, women, and children were chained to one another, sometimes in groups of up to 100 individuals. They would walk to the sea, where they would be held in slave pens for sale to Europeans. Many of the slaves were force-marched, often from great distances, to the ships, leaving them both exhausted and traumatized. Captured Africans sometimes died on the march or perished in the pens while waiting for slave ships to reach port. They were often poorly fed and poorly treated. The loss of life before slaves walked onto ships is estimated at 10 to 15 percent.

About 12 million Africans boarded slave ships for the Middle Passage to European colonies in the Americas, but only 10.5 million lived to see landfall on the other side of the Atlantic. Slave ship captains aimed to make as much money as possible by shipping Africans as quickly as possible to arrive at ports in saleable condition. Though slave traders did choose slaves carefully, sick Africans often wound up on ships. Diseases would rapidly spread through the confined and crowded spaces aboard ships. Ships to North America carried about 200 slaves, with this number increasing to 289 by 1800.

TERM PAPER SUGGESTIONS

1. The slave trade had economic benefits for the Africans who sold slaves and the Europeans who traded slaves. Discuss the economic considerations of the slave trade for Africa or a European country.

2. Examine the role played by Portugal in the development of the slave trade.

3. Examine the role played by Great Britain in the development of the slave trade.

4. Explore life on board a slave ship for a slave or a crew member.

5. Compare and contrast views of slavery in the Quran and the Bible.

ALTERNATIVE TERM PAPER SUGGESTIONS

1. Create a piece of art that illustrates the passage of an African into slavery in the Americas.

2. Perhaps using David Eltis's *The Trans-Atlantic Slave Trade: A Database on CD-ROM,* create an interactive map that shows the areas of Africa from which slaves were taken and the areas where they went.

3. Assume that you are an African who has been captured, sold into slavery, and taken on the Middle Passage to the Americas. Write diary entries about your experiences.

4. Compose a song that illustrates a slave's perspective of the Middle Passage and post a performance of your song on YouTube.

SUGGESTED SOURCES

Primary Source

Equiano, Olaudah. *The Interesting Narrative of the Life of Olaudah Equiano.* New York: Penguin, 2003. Kidnapped from Africa at the age of 10 in 1755,

Equiano spent 10 years working on British slave ships until purchasing his freedom and becoming an outspoken opponent of slavery.

Secondary Sources

Burnside, Madeleine, and Rosemarie Robotham. *Spirits of the Passage: The Transatlantic Slave Trade in the Seventeenth Century.* Key West, FL: Mel Fisher Maritime Heritage Society, 1997. A lavishly illustrated history of the slave trade that was created to accompany the museum exhibit of the English-owned *Henrietta Marie,* a slave ship that sank in 1700.

Davis, David Brion. *Inhuman Bondage: The Rise and Fall of Slavery in the New World.* New York: Oxford University Press, 2006. Written by a Pulitzer Prize winner, this book traces American slavery back to its ancient roots and discusses the world history of antiblack racism.

Falola, Toyin, and Amanda Warnock, eds. *Encyclopedia of the Middle Passage.* Westport, CT: Greenwood Press, 2007. More than 200 entries cover the gamut of topics on the Middle Passage.

Gomez, Michael A. *Reversing Sail: A History of the African Diaspora.* New York: Cambridge University Press, 2005. An excellent history of Africans in the New World from slavery through the Cold War.

Klein, Herbert S. *The Atlantic Slave Trade.* New York: Cambridge University Press, 1999. Surveys the West and East African experiences in the slave trade as well as the social impact and economics of slavery in the Americas.

Lovejoy, Paul E. *Transformations in Slavery: A History of Slavery in Africa.* New York: Cambridge University Press, 2000. Provides a world history of the enslavement of Africans from the fifteenth century to the early twentieth century.

Northrup, David. *The Atlantic Slave Trade.* New York: Wadsworth, 2001. Aimed at the college market, this collection of essays focuses on debates about aspects of the slave trade.

Rediker, Marcus. *The Slave Ship: A Human History.* New York: Viking Adult, 2007. Examines the relationships between the captain and crew, the crew and slaves, and the captives themselves on a slave ship.

Smallwood, Stephanie E. *Saltwater Slavery: A Middle Passage from Africa to the American Diaspora.* Boston: Harvard University Press, 2007. Explores what it was like to be an African slave traveling to the Americas.

Thornton, John. *Africa and Africans in the Making of the Atlantic World, 1400–1680.* New York: Cambridge University Press, 1992. Explores the contributions made by Africans to the New World.

Walvin, James. *Atlas of Slavery.* New York: Pearson Longman, 2006. Uses maps to explore the historical geography of Atlantic slavery.

Walvin, James. *Black Ivory: Slavery in the British Empire.* New York: Harper Collins, 1992. Focuses on the daily lives of slaves in Great Britain and the British colonies in North America and the Caribbean.

World Wide Web

"Africans in America." http://www.pbs.org/wgbh/aia. This PBS Web site includes "The Terrible Transformation, 1450–1750." It contains primary sources, secondary sources, a resource bank, and a teacher's guide.

"African Slavery Primary Sources." http://www.historywiz.com/africanslavery .htm. Includes a diagram of a slave ship as well as primary documents, such as Olaudah Equiano's narrative and a 1788 document about conditions aboard an English slave ship.

"The Role of Islam in African Slavery." http://africanhistory.about.com/od/ slavery/a/Slavery101.htm. Traces the long history of slavery in Islamic Africa.

"The Transatlantic Slave Trade." http://africanhistory.about.com/library/weekly/ aa080601a.htm. Gives an overview of the transatlantic slave trade complete with maps, demographic data, and analysis.

"The Transatlantic Slave Trade." http://www.metmuseum.org/toah/hd/slav/hd _slav.htm. The Heilbrunn Timeline of Art History, sponsored by the Metropolitan Museum of Art, illustrates slavery through the arts.

Multimedia Sources

The Africans. Washington, DC: WETA/Washington, D.C. and the BBC, 1986. 9 DVDs. Includes a one-hour segment on the "Tools of Exploitation" including the colonial economic system and the development of slavery.

Africans in America. Boston: PBS, 1998. 2 DVDs. This six-part documentary includes chapters on the spread of slavery to the New World.

Eltis, David, et al. *The Trans-Atlantic Slave Trade: A Database on CD-ROM.* New York: Cambridge University Press, 2000. Contains the records of 27,233 transatlantic slave ship voyages made between 1595 and 1866 by Europeans. The software allows users to select data according to time period or geographic area. Data can be downloaded into other software.

Roots—Anniversary Edition. Los Angeles: Warner Home Video, 2007. 4 DVDs. Popular 1977 miniseries about the history of an African American family; includes a vivid depiction of the Middle Passage.

Wonders of Africa—Slavery and Colonialism in Africa. Wynnewood, PA: Schlesinger Media, 2002. DVD. Shows the impact of the African slave trade upon Africa and includes a visit to a slave fortress in Accra where slaves were held pending transport to the Americas.

2. Slavery Is Introduced to Virginia (1619)

In 1619, a Dutch man-of-war ship arrived in Jamestown, Virginia. In exchange for supplies, the Dutch captain set ashore 20 captive "Negars," the first Africans known to have set foot in the British colonies in the North America. These Africans from Angola were used to work plantations of tobacco, a crop that required enormous amounts of labor to produce. While the first Africans were apparently treated as indentured servants and released after a period of service, the pressing need for tobacco workers gradually led to the establishment of African slavery in North America.

The English settlers who arrived in 1607 in Jamestown, the first successful English colony, came to get rich. They were instructed by the Virginia Company, the organizer of the colony, to find a good source of wealth, preferably precious metals or a passage to the Pacific and the riches of Asia that lay beyond. Unable to find gold or the route to Asia, they did stumble upon another source of riches—tobacco.

Tobacco, part of the nightshade family, could be found only in the Americas. It came to Europe via contact with Native Americans. The English started using tobacco in the late sixteenth century. Considered an herbal remedy for a wide range of ailments, tobacco also counteracted weariness, induced relaxation, and relieved hunger. The English consumed tobacco in snuff, by chewing it, and by inhaling it. Smoking proved the most popular style, by far, of tobacco use, perhaps because it is also the most efficient and potent way of absorbing nicotine. The English obtained tobacco through capture, trade with foreigners, or smuggling, making tobacco both scarce and expensive.

With a vast market for tobacco in Great Britain, the Virginians latched on to the plant as the key to survival and prosperity. Native Virginian tobacco proved too strong for the European market, so Jamestown colonist John Rolfe began experimenting with other strains in 1612. Rolfe planted some seeds of *Nicotiana tabacum* that he had obtained from Trinidad, in the Caribbean. In 1616, Rolfe took the first commercial shipment of Virginian tobacco to London. Rolfe's tobacco ensured the success of Jamestown. By 1638, tobacco and Jamestown had become synonymous, and most new arrivals aimed to get rich by planting tobacco. To succeed, they ultimately decided that they need slave tobacco workers.

TERM PAPER SUGGESTIONS

1. Write an essay exploring "what if" African slaves had never come to Jamestown. Would the colony still have survived? Would tobacco have become as common?

2. John Rolfe gleefully reported the arrival of the first Africans in Virginia and developed the tobacco that would result in the lifetime enslavement of Africans. Who was Rolfe? Investigate his life.

3. We know very little about the first Africans in British America. Anthony Johnson, who presumably started in the New World as a slave, is one of these pioneers, and he is the only one who left a substantial paper trail. Investigate Johnson's life.

ALTERNATIVE TERM PAPER SUGGESTIONS

1. Look at the official Jamestown Web site. Design a new Web site that emphasizes the history of African Americans at Jamestown.

2. Did Africans in Jamestown have substantially different lives from white settlers? Write a short story exploring the life of an African in Jamestown.

3. James I of England wrote a "Counterblaste to Tobacco" in 1604 in which he attacked the "stinking weed." The document can be found at http://www .laits.utexas.edu/poltheory/james/blaste/blaste.html. Write a document in similar style in which you blast tobacco for contributing to the rise of slavery.

SUGGESTED SOURCES

Primary Sources

Johnson, Charles, and Patricia Smith. *Africans in America: America's Journey Through Slavery*. New York: Harcourt Brace, 1998. Includes the journal account in which John Rolfe reports of the Dutch warship that stopped in 1619 to sell Africans.

Southern, Ed, ed. *The Jamestown Adventure: Accounts of the Virginia Colony, 1605–1614.* Winston-Salem, NC: John F. Blair, 2004. Shows the difficulties facing the colony in the period just before slaves were introduced to Jamestown.

Secondary Sources

Berlin, Ira. *Generations of Captivity: A History of African American Slaves.* Boston: Belknap Press, 2004. Berlin divides slaves into generations, with the chapter on the "Charter Generation" covering the Jamestown slaves.

Berlin, Ira. *Many Thousands Gone: The First Two Centuries of Slavery in North America*. Boston: Belknap Press, 2000. Examines the different lives led by slaves in the various sections of North America.

Countryman, Edward, ed. *How Did American Slavery Begin?* Boston: Bedford St. Martin's, 1999. A collection of essays in which historians debate how slavery became established in the American colonies.

Gately, Iain. *Tobacco: The Story of How Tobacco Seduced the World*. New York: Grove Press, 2001. A popular history of tobacco.

Goodman, Jordan. *Tobacco in History: The Cultures of Dependence*. New York: Routledge, 1993. Explores the relationships of different groups of people, including slaves, with tobacco.

Hashaw, Tim. *The Birth of Black America: The First African Americans and the Pursuit of Freedom at Jamestown*. New York: Basic Books, 2007. Hashaw traces the first African Americans back to Angola and sketches their lives in British America.

Jewett, Clayton E., and John O. Allen. *Slavery in the South: A State-by-State History*. Westport, CT: Greenwood Press, 2004. A chapter is dedicated to the history of slavery in Virginia.

Kolchin, Peter. *American Slavery, 1619–1877*. Boston: Hill and Wang, 2003. Traces the history of slavery and sets the American version in world context.

Morgan, Edmund S. *American Slavery, American Freedom: The Ordeal of Colonial Virginia*. New York: W.W. Norton, 1995. Explains how Virginians developed the system of slavery at the same time that they developed support for a republican political system.

Tormey, James. *John Rolfe of Virginia*. Silver Spring, MD: Beckham, 2006. A novel of Rolfe's life that focuses on his struggles in Jamestown.

World Wide Web

"Anthony Johnson—First Slave Owner in Virginia." http://www.geocities.com/ irby.geo/slave/fsoiv.html. Reprints a 1654 petition in which John Casor, an African American owned by Anthony Johnson, an African who arrived in Virginia in 1620, argues for his freedom. The document shows disagreement over whether an African should be regarded as a slave or an indentured servant.

The Atlantic Slave Trade and Slave Life in the Americas: A Visual Record. http:// hitchcock.itc.virginia.edu/Slavery/. This collection includes 1,235 images relating to slavery.

"Captive Passage: Arrival in the New World." http://www.mariner.org/captive-passage/arrival/arr015.html. Part of the online Mariner's Museum, this site describes the religion of the slaves arriving from Africa. It contains links to other sites that describe the daily lives of slaves.

"Jamestown Settlement." http://www.historyisfun.org/Jamestown-Settlement. htm. The official site for restored Jamestown, this site contains instructions for visiting Jamestown and a map of the area.

"Profile: Anthony Johnson." http://www.inrich.com/cva/ric/news/black history.apx.-content-articles-RTD-special-0547.html. Johnson is the earliest known African to live in Virginia, coming to the land in 1620.

"Virtual Jamestown." http://virtualjamestown.org. Explores the legacies of the 1607 Jamestown settlement, including slavery.

Multimedia Source

Africans in America. Boston: PBS, 1998. 2 DVDs. This six-part documentary includes a chapter on the establishment of slavery in Virginia.

3. Slave Codes Are Established (1660s)

Africans who came to the British colonies in the first decades of settlement were treated like most Virginia colonists. They were viewed as indentured servants and, after a period of laboring for a master, received their freedom. Slavery gradually became established in the latter half of the seventeenth century. By 1700, African servants in bondage could expect to be slaves all of their lives.

Africans may never have been treated as full equals. Most white servants came to the colonies voluntarily and worked under a written contract of indenture for a specified period of time, usually four to seven years. The master of a white indentured servant could not, at his sole desire and discretion, prolong the period of servitude. To extend the original indenture for any reason, masters and servants had to receive permission from the court. In contrast, the Africans who stepped onto American shores did not come voluntarily and apparently were sold into service without benefit of a written contract of indenture for a specific period. Yet there was apparently no sharp distinction made by the colonists between African and white servants in the early years of British America. In the 1640s, the legal system did not yet regard slavery as hereditary.

It is a bit puzzling why the English colonists chose to acquire slaves. Unlike the Spanish and Portuguese, who had a history of enslaving West Africans, the English did not have any slaves in England. They did, however, have a clear understanding of the circumstances under which individuals might lose their freedom and be designated as slaves. This understanding came from the history of slavery in the ancient world and in biblical sources, especially the Old Testament.

The British colonies would often follow the Spanish and English practice that blacks who had been baptized into the Christian religion were to be accorded the privileges of a free person. However, blacks in court cases were typically identified as "Negro" while whites were not identified by race. The descriptor indicates that African Americans were marked as inferior and whites as superior in a subtle way. By 1662, the legal system would begin to place blacks in lifetime and hereditary slavery. The reasons appear to be economic and social. Blacks were perceived as inferior, and workers were desperately needed for such labor-intensive crops as tobacco and rice. By 1680, clergyman Morgan Godwyn could declare, "These two words, *Negro* and *Slave* [are] by custom grown Homogeneous and Convertible; even as *Negro* and *Christian, Englishman and Heathen,* are by the like Custom and Partiality made Opposites."

TERM PAPER SUGGESTIONS

1. Explain why the status of slave became reserved for people of West African ancestry rather than those of Native American or English ancestry.
2. Discuss why racial lines hardened and the distinction between whites and blacks became so sharp.
3. Discuss "what if" racial lines had never hardened and blacks were treated as indentured servants.

ALTERNATIVE TERM PAPER SUGGESTIONS

1. Design a YouTube video that shows the effects upon colonial people of the establishment of slavery in North America.
2. Create a Web site that urges colonial Americans to challenge the establishment of sharp racial divisions between white and blacks.
3. Assume that you are a black person who is attempting to go to court in 1665 Virginia to argue for your freedom. Write a letter to the judge in which you defend your right to be freed.

SUGGESTED SOURCES

Primary Source

Holt, Thomas C., and Elsa Barkely Brown, eds. *Major Problems in African-American History: From Slavery to Freedom, 1619–1877.* Boston: Houghton Mifflin, 2000. Includes a 1664 document, "An Act to Discriminate Between Africans and Others in Maryland," and a 1705 guide to distinguishing slaves from indentured servants in Virginia.

Secondary Sources

Berlin, Ira. *Many Thousands Gone: The First Two Centuries of Slavery in North America.* Boston: Belknap Press, 2000. Examines the different lives led by slaves in the various sections of North America.

Countryman, Edward, ed. *How Did American Slavery Begin?* Boston: Bedford St. Martin's, 1999. A collection of essays in which historians debate how slavery became established in the American colonies.

Davis, David Brion. *Inhuman Bondage: The Rise and Fall of Slavery in the New World.* New York: Oxford University Press, 2006. Discusses the ancient and biblical justifications for slavery, with additional chapters on the history of antiblack racism in the New World and slavery in colonial America.

Kolchin, Peter. *American Slavery, 1619–1877.* Boston: Hill and Wang, 2003. Traces the history of slavery and sets the American version in world context.

Morgan, Edmund S. *American Slavery, American Freedom: The Ordeal of Colonial Virginia.* New York: W.W. Norton, 1995. Explains how Virginians developed the system of slavery at the same time that they developed support for a republican political system.

Smedley, Audrey. *Race in North America: Origin and Evolution of a Worldview.* Boulder, CO: Westview, 2007. Explains why the British colonists defined race as a new form of social stratification and a justification for inequality among the people of North America.

Wood, Betty. *The Origins of American Slavery: Freedom and Bondage in the English Colonies.* New York: Hill and Wang, 1997. Shows that a mix of greed and prejudice fueled the development of slavery throughout the Caribbean and along the East Coast.

World Wide Web

The Atlantic Slave Trade and Slave Life in the Americas: A Visual Record. http://hitchcock.itc.virginia.edu/Slavery/. This collection includes 1,235 images relating to slavery.

"Common Place." http://www.common-place.org/vol-01/no-04/. Produced for scholars by the American Antiquarian Society and the Gilder Lehrman Institute of American History, this site includes a discussion on the portrayal of slavery in the media.

"Digital History: Virginia Slave Laws." http://www.digitalhistory.uh.edu. Discusses the hardening of racial lines in Virginia and reprints several documents from 1662 to 1669 that show this hardening.

Multimedia Source

Africans in America. Boston: PBS, 1998. 2 DVDs. Includes a segment on the differing legal treatment of blacks and whites in early America.

4. Bacon's Rebellion (1675)

Bacon's Rebellion is viewed as a critical step in the establishment of slavery in North America. It proved the most serious challenge to royal authority in the English colonies prior to the American Revolution. The turmoil ultimately led to the replacement of indentured servants with slaves, who were perceived as less troublesome. At the start of the rebellion, there were no more than 7,000 slaves in all of England's North American colonies. The number of slaves after 1680 increased dramatically as poor white settlers unwittingly drew the region more deeply into slavery.

Bacon's Rebellion erupted in Virginia in 1676 after Governor William Berkeley and Nathaniel Bacon could not agree on how to best address conflict with the Susquehannock Indians. Bacon led poor whites and indentured servants. Berkeley tried to avoid war with the Susquehannocks. Metacom's War, also known as King Philip's War, had just begun in 1675 in New England. It would end in spring 1676 after about 800 English settlers had been killed and many towns left in ashes. The war began over the settlers' desire for Native American land, the ever-increasing encroachment of American livestock onto Indian fields, the decline of the fur trade, resistance to Christian missionaries, and the fear of young warriors that the Native American way of life was in danger of disappearing. Virginia Indians had the same concerns as the New England Native Americans. Berkeley wanted to avoid similar instability, death, and destruction in Virginia.

However, many colonists wanted to attack. The opportunities available to indentured servants in the Chesapeake to achieve the upward social, economic, and political mobility that had lured so many of them across the Atlantic had diminished substantially in the second half of the century. Most found work after their terms of service as hired hands. Land, the one sure way to freedom and to wealth, remained beyond their reach as long as the Indian lands were off limits. As a member of the elite, Berkeley valued stability and security more than the wishes of the poor to acquire land.

The revolt collapsed fairly quickly. Berkeley assembled a fleet and retook Jamestown in August. Bacon laid siege to the city. However, Bacon died in October 1676, and the revolt ended shortly thereafter.

TERM PAPER SUGGESTIONS

1. Using the advertisements found on the Virginia runaways Web site, compare and contrast the ways in which owners perceived slaves and indentured servants. Why did owners hold these different perceptions? What were the ramifications of these perceptions upon slaves and indentured servants?

2. Discuss why African slavery became established in North America. What were the advantages of owning slaves compared to the benefits of possessing indentured servants? What were the disadvantages?

3. The inventory of Captain Anthony Beck has been used by archeologists to draw conclusions about the lives of slaves. In an essay, use the inventory to hypothesize about what life was like for Beck's slaves.

4. Write an essay exploring "what if" Bacon's Rebellion had never occurred. Do you believe that slavery would have become firmly established in the British colonies? Explain.

ALTERNATIVE TERM PAPER SUGGESTIONS

1. Write a short story that describes an indentured servant's plan to run away. What would this man or woman need to be successful?

2. Create runaway advertisements for an escaped indentured servant and an escaped slave. What information will you include to get the best chance of recovering your property?

SUGGESTED SOURCES

Primary Source

Holt, Thomas C., and Elsa Barkley Brown, eds. *Major Problems in African American History: From Slavery to Freedom, 1619–1877.* Boston: Houghton Mifflin, 2000. This collection of primary and secondary sources includes a 1705 document on distinguishing slaves from indentured servants in Virginia.

Secondary Sources

Jordan, Winthrop D. *The White Man's Burden: Historical Origins of Racism in the United States.* New York: Oxford University Press, 1984. Still readily available, this classic work explains why blacks were chosen as a slave labor force in the Americas.

Kulikoff, Allan. *Tobacco and Slaves: Population, Economy and Society in Eighteenth-Century Prince George's County, Maryland.* Chapel Hill: University of North Carolina Press, 1986. Examines the changing relations between blacks and whites from 1680 to 1800 in the Chesapeake region.

Morgan, Edmund S. *American Slavery, American Freedom: The Ordeal of Colonial Virginia.* New York: Norton, 1975. Written by one of the most renowned historians, this book shows why the Virginia planters required coerced labor that came initially in the form of poor whites and subsequently in the form of African slaves.

Smedley, Audrey. *Race in North America: Origin and Evolution of a Worldview.* Boulder, CO: Westview Press, 2007. Explains why the English picked Africans to enslave rather than any other ethnic group and how slavery became established in the wake of Bacon's Rebellion.

Webb, Stephen. *1676: The End of American Independence.* New York: Knopf, 1984. One of the best available histories of Bacon's Rebellion.

Wood, Peter. *Strange New Land: African Americans, 1617–1776.* New York: Oxford University Press, 1996. A very readable and well-researched general history of blacks in the colonial era.

Yentsch, Anne E. *A Chesapeake Family and Their Slaves: A Study in Historical Archaeology.* New York: Cambridge University Press, 1994. Explores everyday life for African Americans and whites at the time of Bacon's Rebellion.

World Wide Web

"Estate Inventory of Captain Anthony Beck." http://www.keyschool.org/londontown/Pages/Pages/inventry.html. Beck, of London Town, Maryland in the Chesapeake region, died in 1749 and left several slaves as part of his estate.

"Virginia Runaways." http://people.uvawise.edu/runaways/. Eighteenth-century Virginia newspaper advertisements for runaway white indentured servants and slaves of African ancestry are reprinted.

"Virtual Jamestown." http://virtualjamestown.org. Explores the legacies of the 1607 Jamestown settlement, including slavery.

Multimedia Sources

Africans in America. Boston: PBS, 1998. 2 DVDs. This six-part documentary includes a chapter on the effect of Bacon's Rebellion upon the establishment of slavery in British America.

Slavery and Freedom: United States History, Origins to 2000. Wynnewood, PA: Schlessinger Media, 2003. DVD. Shows the impact of indentured servitude and chattel slavery upon American life and values.

5. The Great Awakening (1720s–1760s)

The Great Awakening, strongest in the North, focused on reaching out to people and converting them to Christianity. It challenged the old sources of cultural and religious authority by deeming them too weak and too bound by tradition to meet the challenges of the day. The revival proved a profound challenge to early America and shaped the country in numerous ways.

The proponents of the Great Awakening saw a "new light" that dwelled in every individual. This light, within the awakened, would enable them to achieve grace through conversion. When enough people were "born again," a new sense of community would be created, a new brotherhood of man established, and America would serve as a model to people throughout the world. The Awakening started to stir in the 1720s in Massachusetts. It did not strike with full force until the 1739 arrival in North America of English itinerant preacher George Whitefield. An especially dramatic performer, he would attract thousands to fields to hear him speak. While Whitefield only touched on a critique of the wealthy, other preachers were more radical. They encouraged people to abandon their ministers, condemned those who exploited the poor, and encouraged ordinary people to resist those who took advantage of them and deceived them. Not surprisingly, this message struck a particular chord with African Americans.

The emphasis of the revival upon the spoken word rather than the written word helped it advance among blacks, a people with a long oral tradition in contrast to the Europeans' written tradition. Blacks frequently attended revival meetings in the North. Whitefield commented that African Americans could be "effectually wrought upon, and in an uncommon manner" and that he had developed "a most winning way of addressing them." Blacks in New England who converted to Christianity were encouraged to invite other African Americans to join their churches.

Enslaved Africans arriving in the South prior to the nineteenth century were not likely to be converted to Christianity. Many planters erroneously believed that conversion required emancipation, an acknowledgement of the old Spanish and English practices that a heathen who became a Christian would also become a free person. Others feared that Christianity would result in slaves who could read the Bible and other documents. Such education would presumably make slaves less easy to control and more likely to plot rebellion. Last, language barriers and African resistance to the faith of their oppressors ensured that Christianity would not yet take firm root.

However, the Great Awakening did make some inroads in parts of the South, typically Virginia. Presbyterians in the 1740s were the first to invite people to come to Christ. The Baptists and Methodists held revivals in the South in the 1760s and 1770s. All the evangelical denominations reported growing numbers of blacks among their followers.

The Great Awakening may have had a more significant and long-range impact upon blacks than on any other northern group, including whites and Indians. While only a tiny proportion of blacks were active Christians before the Revolution, great changes were underway as a result of the revival. Christianity promised some small measure of fulfillment in a life that otherwise had little of it. The Great Awakening set the foundation upon which future generations of African Americans would construct the central institution of African American life.

TERM PAPER SUGGESTIONS

1. What effects did the Great Awakening have upon African Americans in the Baptist church?
2. What was the impact of the Great Awakening upon blacks in the Methodist tradition?
3. How did religion help slaves cope with the effects of being in bondage?
4. What effect did the Great Awakening have upon the abolition movement?

ALTERNATIVE TERM PAPER SUGGESTIONS

1. African Americans have a long tradition of expressing their religious faith through song. Research these songs.

2. Black pioneer poet Phyllis Wheatley wrote about the effects of the Great Awakening upon her life. Write a poem that shows the effects of the revival upon another slave.

3. Write a sermon from the perspective of a white preacher during the Great Awakening arguing for or against religion as a cure for the social ill of slavery.

SUGGESTED SOURCES

Primary Source

Holt, Thomas C., and Elsa Barkley Brown, eds. *Major Problems in African-American History: From Slavery to Freedom, 1619–1877.* Boston: Houghton Mifflin, 2000. Includes a 1740 effort by George Whitefield to promote the conversion of blacks and a 1770 homage by the first African American poet, Phyllis Wheatley, to Whitefield.

Secondary Sources

Bonomi, Patricia U. *Under the Cope of Heaven: Religion, Society, and Politics in Colonial America.* New York: Oxford University Press, 2003. One of the most readable accounts of the Great Awakening, with a small number of pages devoted to the effects of the revival upon African Americans.

Bumsted, J. M., and John E. Van de Wetering. *What Must I Do To Be Saved: The Great Awakening in Colonial America.* Hinsdale, IL: Dryden Press, 1976. A good general history of the revival.

Nash, Gary B. *Red, White, and Black: The Peoples of Early North America.* Englewood Cliffs, NJ: Prentice Hall, 1992. Discusses the Great Awakening in a chapter devoted to the transformation of European society.

Raboteau, Albert J. *Slave Religion: The "Invisible Institution" in the Antebellum South.* New York: Oxford University Press, 2004. Despite the title, this book does include limited coverage of the Great Awakening among African Americans in the North as well as the South.

World Wide Web

"The Great Awakening Lesson Plan: African-American Churches and Abolition." http://www.slaveryinamerica.org/history/hs_lp_greatawakening.htm. Created by Donna Hendry, this part of Slavery in America meets National Curriculum Standard for the teaching of American history. It includes material about individuals who were involved in the Great Awakening or affected by the Great Awakening.

"History of Negro Baptist Churches in America." http://www.reformedreader
.org/history/negrobaptistchurches.htm. The Walter H. Brooks article
reprinted includes primary document quotes about the involvement of
blacks with religion in the colonial era.

Multimedia Sources

Africans in America. Boston: PBS, 1998. 2 DVDs. Includes discussion of the
impact of religion upon African Americans.
Slavery and Freedom: United States History, Origins to 2000. Wynnewood, PA:
Schlessinger Media, 2003. DVD. Includes a segment on the social
impact of the Great Awakening.

6. Stono Rebellion (1739)

The Stono Rebellion in September 1739 became the largest slave uprising
in North America prior to the American Revolution. It was just one of
many ways in which slaves actively opposed bondage. The rebellion led
whites to adopt several strategies to better control slaves, including a
short-lived ban on the importation of new slaves and longer-lived interest
in stopping the importation of slaves directly from Africa.

The rebellion began before dawn on Sunday, September 9 as an effort
by about 60 to 100 slaves to reach St. Augustine to claim freedom in
Spanish-controlled Florida. It started on a branch of the Stono River, near
Charleston, South Carolina. The revolt may have been timed to take
place before September 29, when a law requiring all white men to carry
firearms to Sunday church services would have gone into effect. The law
was an effort to reduce the likelihood of slave revolts.

The slaves broke into a store near the Stono Bridge to equip themselves
with guns and ammunition. They killed two white men before burning a
house and killing three more people. The rebels then turned southward
and reached a tavern, where they spared the innkeeper because he had a
reputation for being kind to his slaves. The innkeeper's neighbors were
not as well regarded. The rebels burned four of their houses, ransacked
another, and killed every white that they found. Other slaves joined the
rebellion. Reports indicate that the rebels used drums, raised a large flag
or banner, and shouted, "Liberty!" as they continued to march toward
St. Augustine.

Lieutenant Governor William Bull, traveling with four companions to Charleston, met the rebels. He escaped and raised the alarm. By this time, the rebels had walked for about 10 miles and may have been tiring. They stopped in a field to rest and to give more slaves time to join them before crossing the Edisto River. However, between 20 and 100 armed planters and militiamen were rushing to meet them. The subsequent battle near Jacksonborough resulted in a white victory. The rebels fought courageously but could not defeat superior firepower. Some slaves who had been forced to join the rebellion were spared, while others were shot. Some rebels were decapitated, with their heads placed upon posts as a warning to others. Thirty slaves escaped, but most were hunted down and killed within the week in a second battle.

In the immediate wake of the uprising, militia companies remained on guard. Some whites fled the Stono region for fear that not all of the slaves involved in the rebellion had been caught. These fears were not without merit. Some of the rebels were rounded up in the spring of 1740, and one leader remained on the loose until 1742. Forty whites and 60 African Americans at least died in the rebellion.

The rebellion, like subsequent ones, resulted in efforts to limit the activities of slaves and free blacks. The 1740 Negro Act required masters to seek the approval of the legislature before granting freedom to slaves. It also mandated military service for every man. The colony banned the importation of new slaves in 1741 in an effort to stop the growth of South Carolina's black population, already a majority of the people. Undoubtedly, some whites looked with fear at the slaves in their midst for many years to come.

TERM PAPER SUGGESTIONS

1. What was the impact of the Stono Rebellion upon slavery?
2. The claim that slaves did not join together to actively resist slavery is often heard. Refute this argument using the Stono Rebellion.
3. A 1739 document, found at http://www.pbs.org/wgbh/aia/part1/1h312t.html, indicates that both slaves and Native Americans fought the slaves who participated in the Stono Rebellion. Explore why some slaves chose to rebel and some did not.
4. Research the life of a typical slave in South Carolina prior to the Stono Rebellion.
5. In 1822, Denmark Vesey led a slave uprising in South Carolina. Compare and contrast Vesey's Rebellion with the Stono Rebellion. Can you see any differences in the white response to each revolt?

6. Explore different types of slave resistance. Are some more successful than others? How do you define success?

ALTERNATIVE TERM PAPER SUGGESTIONS

1. Assume that you are a newspaper reporter for a newspaper that opposes slavery. Write a front-page story, complete with pictures, that tells the story of Stono.
2. Slaves had a tradition of using the arts, especially music, to express feelings that could not be safely stated in other ways. Create a song or a piece of art to illuminate the Stono Rebellion.

SUGGESTED SOURCES

Primary Source

Smith, Mark M., ed. *Stono: Documenting and Interpreting a Southern Slave Revolt.* Columbia: University of South Carolina Press, 2005. A collection of mostly primary documents that offer accounts of the violence, discussions of Stono's impact upon whites, and public records relating to the uprising. Several essays by historians who interpret Stono are included.

Secondary Sources

Kly, Y. N. *The Invisible War: African American Anti-Slavery Resistance from the Stono Rebellion through the Seminole Wars.* Atlanta, GA: Clarity Press, 2008. Challenges the popular idea, frequently repeated in history books, that slaves did not collectively resist slavery.

Morgan, Philip D. *Slave Counterpoint: Black Culture in the Eighteenth-Century Chesapeake and Lowcountry.* Chapel Hill: University of North Carolina, 1998. Covers the lowcountry of South Carolina and describes the daily lives of slaves.

Wood, Peter H. *Black Majority: Negroes in Colonial South Carolina from 1670 through the Stono Rebellion.* New York: Knopf, 1975. A classic work of history and still one of the best sources on slavery in the antebellum South.

World Wide Web

"Africans in America: The Terrible Transformation—Stono Rebellion." http://www.pbs.org/wgbh/aia/part1/1p284.html. Includes contemporary documents relating to the rebellion as well as reports by historians about Stono.

"Black Resistance: Slavery in the U.S." http://www.afroam.org/history/slavery/
main.html. Discusses the different ways in which slaves resisted and
includes a Lerone Bennett poem about slavery.

"The Stono Rebellion." http://www.bedfordstmartins.com/history/modules/
mod04/main.htm. Provides an account of Stono, a quiz on Stono, suggestions for short essays, a reading guide, and links to sites about Stono.

"Stono Rebellion: The Black Past Remembered." http://www.blackpast.org/
?q=aah/stono-rebellion-1739. An illustrated encyclopedia article about
Stono.

Multimedia Source

Africans in America. Boston: PBS, 1998. 2 DVDs. Includes a segment on the
Stono Rebellion.

7. New York Conspiracy Trials (1741)

In 1741, the largest slave rebellion in the North took place when slaves
rose against their masters in New York City. Many of the details of the
revolt are in dispute, including whether a rebellion actually occurred.
New York Supreme Court trials implicated nearly 200 New Yorkers,
white and black, young and old, slave and free. Thirty slaves and 4 whites
were executed, with more than 70 others banished from the city. The episode sheds light on slavery in the North in the mid-eighteenth century.

Slave labor in New York City would not become common until the
eighteenth century. When the Dutch surrendered New Amsterdam to
England in 1664, only about 400 slaves lived in the city, and they had
been used chiefly for construction projects. At the start of the eighteenth
century, New York City merchants began to take an increasing interest
in the slave trade, selling Africans to work on the shipping docks, to till
fields, to tend herds, and to work for artisans in shops. Between 1700
and 1750, about 7,400 slaves arrived in New York City. By mid-century,
people of African ancestry made up roughly 20 percent of the population.
Roughly half of the households in the city owned one or more slaves. The
young metropolis had the greatest concentration of slaves north of
Virginia.

The number of slaves, many of whom were defiant, frightened many
white New Yorkers. The threat of a slave revolt hung over the city. The
first outbreak of violent collective slave resistance occurred in 1712.

A group of slaves set fire to buildings and ambushed the whites who rushed to put out the flames. (In this era of wooden buildings and little fire-fighting equipment besides buckets of water, fires did burn down entire towns and cities.) Two dozen slaves were eventually hanged, burned at the stake, or broken on the wheel.

In 1741, rumors spread of another attempt by slaves to burn down the city, murder most of the white inhabitants, and turn New York over to Britain's Catholic enemies. The fears may have been fueled by a 1736 slave uprising on the Caribbean island of Antigua, in which slaves threatened to burn, kill, and turn the island over to Spain. By 1741, Britain and Spain were at war, and New York had just sent 500 volunteers to help Britain recover one of its Caribbean possessions from the Spanish. There was also a rash of fires throughout the city, including the destruction of Fort George on the tip of Manhattan, and there was a report that a slave had been seen sprinting away from one of the burning buildings. The New York Supreme Court immediately established a grand jury, consisting of 17 of the wealthiest and most prominent white men in the city, to investigate on April 21, 1741. The first executions occurred on May 11. The governor offered a pardon to anyone who confessed or informed. Under New York's revised slave code of 1730, one slave's testimony was sufficient to convict another slave of conspiracy.

TERM PAPER SUGGESTIONS

1. The New York Conspiracy Trials of 1741 were influenced by other slave rebellions, including the Stono Rebellion. Compare and contrast slave rebellions.

2. A historian argues that to believe that there was a conspiracy in 1741 is to support the racism of a court that executed so many black men on so little evidence. Do you agree or disagree? Support your argument with evidence from the trials.

3. Slavery in the North receives little attention when compared with slavery in the South. Compare and contrast slavery in New York with that of slavery in a southern colony.

4. Trace the history of slavery in New York.

ALTERNATIVE TERM PAPER SUGGESTIONS

1. Prepare a podcast for the people of Virginia about the purported New York slave revolt of 1741. Make sure that you include lists of reasons why the slaves are rebelling and a description of how they are rebelling.

2. Assume that you are a newspaper reporter for an antislavery newspaper. Prepare an op-ed piece that tears apart the New York City legal system. Is it possible to ever determine the truth behind charges of slave plots, when the evidence has been gathered by powerful whites who set the terms by which the enslaved are allowed to speak, at risk of their lives? Analyze the usefulness of such evidence.

SUGGESTED SOURCES

Primary Source

Zabin, Serena R., ed. *The New York Conspiracy Trials of 1741: Daniel Horsmanden's Journal of the Proceedings*. Boston: Bedford St. Martin's, 2004. The best collection of primary sources on the conspiracy trials, this book includes a history of slavery in British New York, the journal of a judge, the confession of a conspirator, and several other documents.

Secondary Sources

Davis, Thomas J. *A Rumor of Revolt: The "Great Negro Plot" in Colonial New York*. Boston: University of Massachusetts Press, 1990. A narrative history of the conspiracy.

Higginbotham, A. Leon. *In the Matter of Color: Race and the American Legal Process, The Colonial Period*. New York: Oxford University Press, 1978. Traces the legal workings of the colonial era with respect to slaves and free people of color.

Hodges, Graham Russell. *Root and Branch: African Americans in New York and East Jersey, 1613–1863*. Chapel Hill: University of North Carolina Press, 1999. A good general history of people of African ancestry in colonial New York.

Hoffer, Peter Charles. *The Great New York Conspiracy of 1741: Slavery, Crime, and Colonial Law*. Lawrence: University Press of Kansas, 2003. Part of a legal history series, this book shows how slave conspiracies were a central feature of the law of slavery, since such purported revolts reflected the white belief that slaves were always conspiring against their masters.

Kammen, Micahel. *Colonial New York: A History*. New York: Oxford University Press, 1975. The best general history of colonial New York.

Linebaugh, Peter, and Marcus Rediker. *The Many-Headed Hydra: Sailors, Slaves, Commoners, and the Hidden History of the Revolutionary Atlantic*. Boston: Beacon Press, 2000. Sets the slave conspiracy in the context of Atlantic history.

World Wide Web

"Daniel Horsmanden, The New York Conspiracy." http://www.yale.edu/glc/archive/895.htm. Part of the Gilder Lehrman Center for the Study of Slavery, Abolition, and Resistance, this page includes an excerpt from the journal of the chief justice and recorder of the city of New York in 1741.

"H 101—Lab Exercise: The New York Conspiracy (1741)." http://users.erols.com/bcccsbs/nyconsp.htm. A lesson in the Social and Behavioral Sciences E-Lab, this site includes links to excerpts from *A Journal of the Proceedings in the Detection of the Conspiracy formed by Some White People, in Conjunction with* Negro *and other* Slaves, *for the Burning of the City of New York in America, and Murdering the Inhabitants* (1744).

"The New York Conspiracy—1741." http://www.thehistorybox.com/ny_city/riots/printerfriendly/nycity_riots_article4a.htm. This site is a summary of the incident.

8. George Washington Bans Black Men from Revolutionary Forces (1775)

From the first days of the American Revolution, blacks participated in the movement to gain freedom from Great Britain. Perhaps most famously, Crispus Attucks, a black man, became the first person to fall during the Boston Massacre of 1770 and thus the first American to lose his life in the war for independence. Blacks fought alongside whites at some of the early battles of the war, including Lexington, Concord, and Bunker Hill. Yet most patriot leaders refused to permit African Americans to fight on the American side at all.

When George Washington, a Virginia planter who owned slaves, took command of the Continental Army in 1775, he barred the further recruitment of black soldiers. State militias followed Washington's lead and banned both free blacks and slaves from military service. The idea of putting weapons in the hands of blacks raised white fears of a violent slave uprising, especially in the Deep South where blacks far outnumbered whites. There were also concerns that treating blacks as equals in the military might give African Americans the notion that they were equal with whites in other areas as well.

Yet, two years into the war, white patriots decided to recruit African American soldiers. On January 12, 1777, Washington issued general orders that recruiters "enlist none but Freemen," with the understood implication that the recruit could be black just as long as he was not property. The motivation was practical. As the war dragged on and the initial fervor vanished, not enough white men were volunteering to fill the military ranks. To address this shortage of manpower, the states began to accept free black men into military units in 1777. Some masters sent slaves to take their places in units, with the tacit understanding that military service would lead to freedom at the war's end. Most African Americans serving in state militias fought alongside white soldiers, although Rhode Island and Connecticut had all-black regiments led by white officers. Massachusetts' all-black unit, the Bucks of America, was led by Samuel Middleton, the only black commissioned officer in the Continental Army. Militia service was generally short term and within state boundaries. The Continental Army wanted long-term soldiers who served wherever needed.

Most slaves resided in the South, and most southerners refused to surrender their slaves for any reason, including military service. Washington, like many of his revolutionary peers, professed a hatred for slavery yet refused to free his own slaves. Maryland permitted slaves to serve with the consent of their masters, but few slaveowners gave such consent. Virginia enforced a draft in 1777, with free blacks as the first to be called up, because white patriot leaders believed that they were expendable. Legislatures in South Carolina and Georgia banned any form of black enlistment.

Blacks wanted to serve in the military for a range of reasons. Some, including James Forten of South Carolina, fought to gain liberty for the United States. Many others fought to prove that they were men, as deserving of rights and privileges as other men. African Americans believed revolutionary rhetoric about the natural rights of man and personal freedom. They wanted "life, liberty, and the pursuit of happiness." They expected that independence for America would be the start of racial equality.

With the end of the war, most blacks went home. Some received freedom, but some were betrayed by slaveowners who kept their soldier-slaves as slaves. In 1783, Virginia passed legislation freeing African Americans still held as slaves despite their wartime enlistment. The number of blacks freed as the result of military service is unknown, but it is not thought to be a large group.

TERM PAPER SUGGESTIONS

1. The Revolutionary War was fought to free Americans. Consider who was defined as an "American" before the Revolutionary War. Discuss how an American identity began to be formed during the Revolution.

2. Compare and contrast the opportunities that were available to a free black man and to George Washington. How were they similar? How were they different?

3. Discuss African Americans in the American Revolution. Consider why whites hesitated to enlist black servicemen and why blacks participated in the war.

4. Consider the opportunities for freedom offered by the American Revolution. Discuss who could take advantage of those opportunities, who could not, and why these differences existed.

5. Black men could theoretically gain freedom by fighting, but black women could not. Analyze how race and gender influenced individual rights and freedoms during the revolutionary era.

6. Use the World Wide Web materials on James Armistead and Jeffrey Brace to discuss the life of a black soldier in the Revolutionary War.

ALTERNATIVE TERM PAPER SUGGESTIONS

1. Assume that you a free black man in New York. In a letter to a newspaper, explain why you have chosen to enlist in the state militia or why you are declining military service.

2. Assume that you are a white patriot leader. In a letter to George Washington, try to persuade him to remove his ban on African Americans in the Continental Army.

3. Assume that you are a black slave who fought in the Revolutionary War but did not get your freedom as promised. Write a letter to the General Assembly in which you argue for your freedom to be granted.

SUGGESTED SOURCES

Primary Sources

Holt, Thomas C., and Elsa Barkley Brown, eds. *Major Problems in African American History: From Slavery to Freedom, 1619–1877*. Boston: Houghton Mifflin, 2000. This collection of primary and secondary sources includes a petition from Saul, a slave and veteran of the Revolutionary War, who sought his freedom.

Sterling, Dorothy, ed. *Speak Out in Thunder Tones: Letters and Other Writings by Black Northerners, 1787–1865*. New York: Da Capo Press, 1998.

Originally published in 1973, this is a superb collection of writings by blacks.

Secondary Sources

Axelrod, Alan. *The Real History of the American Revolution: A New Look at the Past.* New York: Sterling, 2007. This is a good general history of the Revolution.

Buckley, Gail Lumet. *American Patriots: The Story of Blacks in the Military from the Revolution to Desert Storm.* New York: Random House, 2002. This is a general history of the military involvement of African Americans.

Foner, Philip S. *Blacks in the American Revolution.* Westport, CT: Greenwood Press, 1975. This general history covers the role of black regiments on both sides of the fighting.

Frey, Sylvia R. *Water From the Rock: Black Resistance in a Revolutionary Age.* Princeton, NJ: Princeton University Press, 1993. Examines the thoughts of black Americans during the American Revolution.

Kaplan, Sidney, and Emma Nogrady Kaplan. *The Black Presence in the Era of the American Revolution, 1770–1800.* Boston: University of Massachusetts, 1989. Created to accompany a 1973 exhibition in the National Portrait Gallery, this heavily-illustrated book shows that blacks were involved in almost every military campaign in the Revolution.

Quarles, Benjamin, and Thad W. Tate. *The Negro in the American Revolution.* Chapel Hill: University of North Carolina Press, 1996. This classic book, first published in 1961, remains the best history of African Americans in the American Revolution.

Raphael, Ray. *A People's History of the American Revolution: How Common People Shaped the Fight for Independence.* New York: Harper, 2002. Examines the responses of free and enslaved African Americans, as well as other individuals, to the American Revolution.

World Wide Web

"Age of Revolution: The Black American." http://forum.wgbh.org/wgbh/forum.php?lecture_id=1774. In an online lecture, Professor Gary Nash discusses African American involvement in the Revolutionary War as well as what has been taught about blacks in the war.

"The Blind African Slave or Memoirs of Bovrereau Brinch, Nick-Named Jeffrey Brace . . . " http://docsouth.unc.edu/neh/brinch/brinch.html. Brace was a black veteran of the American Revolution. He applied for a veteran's pension but ran into trouble because his name did not appear on company muster rolls or pay rolls. In his application, found at http://www.americanrevolution.org/rees.html, Brace attached depositions that illuminate the experiences of black veterans.

"The Colored Patriots of the American Revolution, with Sketches of Several Distinguished Colored Persons to Which Is Added a Brief Survey of the Condition and Prospects of Colored Americans." http://docsouth.unc.edu/neh/nell/nell.html. This is an electronic edition of an 1855 book by William Cooper Nell, the first black historian.

"James Armistead Biography." http://americanrevwar.homestead.com/files/JAMES.HTM. Armistead, a slave, served as a spy for the Marquis de Lafayette during the American Revolution and provided critical intelligence about British forces.

"John Laurens's Black Regiment Proposal." http://www.earlyamerica.com/review/2003_winter_spring/slavery_liberty.htm. John Laurens, a South Carolina patriot, argued that it was hypocritical for whites to seek freedom while they held blacks in bondage.

"Master/Slave Enlistment Agreement, 1777." http://www.freemaninstitute.com/BCF%20Continental%20Army.htm. This contract permits Connecticut slave Juba Negro to join the Continental Army.

Multimedia Source

Africans in America. Boston: PBS, 1998. 2 DVDs. This six-part documentary includes chapters on blacks in the Revolutionary War.

9. Lord Dunmore Offers Freedom to Blacks Who Join the British (1775)

John Murray, Fourth Earl of Dunmore, offered freedom to slaves willing to serve in the British forces during the American Revolution. The Scotland-born noble moved to Virginia in 1771 to pursue greater economic opportunities. Dunmore's charm and his skill at claiming western lands for Virginians made him personally popular with the colonists and blinded him to the rising political tensions. He firmly believed that most Virginians were loyal to the Crown and that the troublemakers could be easily contained. In April 1775, Dunmore seized powder in the public magazine at Williamsburg and threatened to raise slaves against anyone who challenged his right to do so. The governor then began to be reviled. He soon became one of the most hated men in America.

After defeating the colonial militia at Kemp's Landing on November 14, 1775, Dunmore used the victory to announce a plan long contemplated by the British. Without official permission, he declared Virginia to be in rebellion and called upon all Virginians, including slaves, to rally to the king's aid. He promised freedom to any slave who joined him. The proclamation was designed to encourage the defection of useful slaves without instigating a general slave insurrection. Rebellious planters, deprived of their workers, would be forced to return to their homes to protect their families and property.

About 500 blacks joined Dunmore within two weeks of his call. Most of the slaves who deserted to the British came as individuals or in small groups. Only on a few occasions did the entire workforce of a plantation escape together. The men, used chiefly in a military force known as Lord Dunmore's Ethiopian Regiment, wore uniforms with "Liberty to Slaves" emblazoned across the chest. However, most of the slaves who joined Dunmore's camp fell to such diseases as smallpox, and Dunmore's regiment remained small.

The threat of punishment and the difficulty of reaching the British ships from land discouraged many blacks from joining Dunmore. It is estimated that not more than 800 slaves succeeded in reaching the British lines, with perhaps 100 men accompanying their loyalist masters. Additionally, fear of united action by slaves so badly frightened uncommitted slaveowners that they joined the revolution. In 1776, a series of military defeats prompted the British to abandon Virginia. In early August, they set sail with about 300 of the healthiest ex-slaves for New York.

Other British commanders would copy Dunmore and offer freedom to slaves deserting their rebel masters. It is estimated that this policy brought thousands of slaves to the British lines. But the British never permitted black regular troops. Many of the surviving men of the Ethiopian Regiment immigrated as free persons with their family members to Nova Scotia and England.

TERM PAPER SUGGESTIONS

1. Discuss the reasons why blacks joined the British and the implications of their decision to fight.
2. Assume that the American Revolution failed. Examine why blacks fought for the British and analyze how life would have changed for the better or the worse for African Americans because of this support.

3. Many white Americans were frightened by the existence of black soldiers. This fear helped create anti-British sentiment among the slaveholders of the South. Comment on why many whites did not support blacks in uniform.

4. One of the saddest aspects of the American Revolution is the fate of the Loyalists. Discuss what happened to black Loyalists upon the end of the war.

5. Did anything change for blacks in the United States because of the involvement of African Americans with the American Revolution? Discuss black life in the aftermath of the war.

ALTERNATIVE TERM PAPER SUGGESTIONS

1. Look at the wanted poster for Colonel Tye at http://www.pbs.org/wgbh/aia/part2/2p52.html. Assume that you are a black slave who joined Dunmore's Ethiopian Regiment alongside Colonel Tye. Design a wanted poster for your capture.

2. Assume that you are a slave in Virginia with the ability to write and send letters. Write a letter to a black newspaper in the North explaining why you decided to join Dunmore's Ethiopian Regiment or why you refused to do.

3. Assume that you are a black Loyalist who has been evacuated to Nova Scotia. Write a letter to a friend explaining your thoughts about leaving America and beginning a new life in Canada.

SUGGESTED SOURCES

Primary Sources

Carpenter, S. D. *Logic of History: Five Hundred Political Texts.* Ann Arbor: University of Michigan Library, 2005. This collection of reprints includes Dunmore's Proclamation.

Holt, Thomas C., and Elsa Barkley Brown, eds. *Major Problems in African American History: From Slavery to Freedom, 1619–1877.* Boston: Houghton Mifflin, 2000. This is a collection of primary and secondary sources that includes Dunmore's Proclamation.

"Proclamation of the Earl of Dunmore, 1775." http://www.pbs.org/wgbh/aia/part2/2h42.html. A reproduction of the original proclamation.

Sterling, Dorothy, ed. *Speak Out in Thunder Tones: Letters and Other Writings by Black Northerners, 1787–1865.* Da Capo Press, 1998. Originally published in 1973, this is a superb collection of writings by blacks.

Secondary Sources

Berkeley, Francis L. *Dunmore's Proclamation of Emancipation.* Charlottesville: University of Virginia Press, 1941. This work, still readily available at the millennium, is the only book focused entirely on Dunmore's Proclamation.

Foner, Philip S. *Blacks in the American Revolution.* Westport, CT: Greenwood Press, 1975. This general history covers the role of black regiments on both sides of the fighting.

Frey, Sylvia R. *Water From the Rock: Black Resistance in a Revolutionary Age.* Princeton, NJ: Princeton University Press, 1993. Examines the thoughts of black Americans during the American Revolution.

Kaplan, Sidney, and Emma Nogrady Kaplan. *The Black Presence in the Era of the American Revolution, 1770–1800.* Boston: University of Massachusetts, 1989. Created to accompany a 1973 exhibition in the National Portrait Gallery, this heavily-illustrated book shows that blacks were involved in almost every military campaign in the Revolution.

Quarles, Benjamin, and Thad W. Tate. *The Negro in the American Revolution.* Chapel Hill: University of North Carolina Press, 1996. This classic book, first published in 1961, remains the best history of African Americans in the American Revolution.

Raphael, Ray. *A People's History of the American Revolution: How Common People Shaped the Fight for Independence.* New York: Harper, 2002. Examines the responses of free and enslaved African Americans, as well as other individuals, to the American Revolution.

Selby, John E. *Dunmore.* Williamsburg: Virginia Independence Bicentennial Commission, 1977. The best biography of the British leader.

World Wide Web

"Black Loyalist Communities in Nova Scotia." http://museum.gov.ns.ca/black-loyalists/. The Nova Scotia Museum has an online exhibit on why the black Loyalists crossed to British side in order to gain their freedom. It focuses on the black Loyalist communities, Birchtown and Tracadie, as well as the difficulties that blacks experienced in settling in Nova Scotia.

"Boston King's Memories of the Evacuation from New York, 1798." http://www.pbs.org/wgbh/aia/part2/2h1584.html. Boston King, a black Loyalist, fled with his wife from New York City to live in Great Britain with the aid of the British government.

"British Pass Issued to Black Loyalist, 1783." http://www.pbs.org/wgbh/aia/part2/2h1584.html. African Americans who could establish their service to the British, along with their family members, were issued certificates of freedom, like the one reprinted here, and granted passage out of New York.

"Colonel Tye (1753–1780)." http://www.pbs.org/wgbh/aia/part2/2p52.html. Colonel Tye, also known as Titus, fought for the British with Dunmore's Ethiopian Regiment. He had escaped from slavery in New Jersey 1775, a day after Dunmore issued his proclamation, to join the British. Never formally commissioned by the British, he earned his title for his heroism and skills in combat. The site includes a wanted poster for Colonel Tye as well as a runaway slave notice about Titus.

"Forgotten Fifth: African Americans in the Age of Revolution." http://forum.wgbh.org/wgbh/forum.php?lecture_id=3185. Gary Nash, one of the foremost historians of the American Revolution, discusses African Americans during the Revolutionary War in an online history lecture.

"Rough Crossings: Blacks and the Revolutionary War." http://forum.wgbh.org/wgbh/forum.php?lecture_id=3112. In an online lecture, Professor Simon Schama discusses the escape of many slaves to join the British during the Revolutionary War, as well as what happened to these men and women after Britain's defeat.

Multimedia Source

Africans in America. Boston: PBS, 1998. 2 DVDs. This six-part documentary includes chapters on blacks in the Revolutionary War.

10. Declaration of Independence (1776)

African Americans took advantage of the American Revolution to seek liberty in a range of ways. While some physically fought to gain freedom, others petitioned for it using some of the same language with which whites argued for liberty from Great Britain. With heavy opposition in the South to such "thoughtless imitation," as planter Henry Laurens of South Carolina phrased it, blacks in the North were more active in presenting their case for freedom. The creation of the Declaration of Independence in 1776, with its statement that "all men are created equal; that they are endowed by their Creator with certain unalienable rights; that among these are life, liberty, and the pursuit of happiness," gave them a strong argument for emancipation.

On July 2, 1776, the Continental Congress adopted Richard Henry Lee's Resolution of Independence, but the delegates also wanted to set forth their principles with a formal declaration and appointed a committee. Thomas Jefferson, an owner of more than 175 slaves, was chosen by the committee to draft the declaration. He produced a document that was debated and changed by Congress. One of the most elegant essays ever written, the Declaration of Independence was approved on July 4 though not signed by all members of Congress until November. The famous words of the preamble remain far better known than the list of accusations aimed at the king that Jefferson also added.

With the Declaration, Americans broke their last remaining ties to England and created a document that would be cited, debated, and copied by generations throughout the world.

By declaring that the power of government derived from the consent of the governed, the framers of the Declaration challenged the very concept of monarchy. The idea that "all men are created equal" meant that free citizens were politically equal and did nothing for the status of slaves or women, at least initially. To found a country upon liberty and then deny liberty to many people within the country created an uncomfortable contradiction. The increasing attacks upon slavery in the next decades owed much to the language and ideas of the Declaration of Independence. It is a founding document of American democracy for both whites and blacks.

TERM PAPER SUGGESTIONS

1. How revolutionary was the American Revolution? How did the revolutionary rhetoric apply to the lives of enslaved Africans and free blacks?
2. Rewrite the Declaration of Independence to make it explicitly apply to people of African ancestry.
3. Compare and contrast how blacks and whites defined the terms "freedom" and "liberty" in the era of the American Revolution.

ALTERNATIVE TERM PAPER SUGGESTIONS

1. Create a YouTube video that explores the meaning of the Declaration of Independence.
2. Compose a song or a poem that shows how the Declaration of Independence affected the lives of blacks.

SUGGESTED SOURCES

Primary Sources

Ali-Ber, Hakeem W. *The Declaration of Black Independence.* Philadelphia: Xlibris, 2006. This is a black nationalist version of the Declaration that states the nature of the injustices that African Americans have suffered at the hands of their oppressors and calls for greater political participation by blacks.

Holt, Thomas C., and Elsa Barkley Brown, eds. *Major Problems in African-American History: From Slavery to Freedom, 1619–1877.* Boston: Houghton Mifflin, 2000. Contains a 1791 petition in which free blacks in South Carolina request equal rights using language from the Declaration of Independence.

Katz, Daniel R., ed. *Why Freedom Matters: The Spirit of the Declaration of Independence in Prose, Poetry, and Song from 1776 to the Present.* New York: Workman, 2003. Celebrates freedom in over 100 speeches, letters, essays, poems, and songs from people such as slaves, abolitionists, and civil rights workers, among others.

"Revolution—Africans in America." http://www.pbs.org/wgbh/aia/part2/title.html Contains primary sources relating to the Revolution and the Declaration of Independence.

Secondary Sources

Armitage, David. *The Declaration of Independence: A Global History.* Boston: Harvard University Press, 2007. Examines how the Declaration of Independence influenced the revolutionary struggles of people around the world.

Lossing, Benson J. *Lives of the Signers of the Declaration of Independence.* Aledo, TX: Wallbuilder Press, 1995. Brief biographies of the 56 signers of the Declaration.

Wills, Garry. *Inventing America: Jefferson's Declaration of Independence.* New York: Mariner Books, 2002. One of the best and, at 432 pages, one of the most thorough analyses of the Declaration.

World Wide Web

"The African American Registry." http://www.aaregistry.com/detail.php?id=613. Includes a rough draft of Jefferson's Declaration as well as a discussion of the impact of the document upon slaves.

Multimedia Sources

Africans in America. Boston: PBS, 1998. 2 DVDs. Includes a segment on the application of revolutionary rhetoric to the lives of African Americans, both enslaved and free.

The Declaration of Independence. New York: Full Circle Entertainment, 2004. DVD. An introduction to the Declaration.

11. Northwest Ordinance Bars Slavery from Western Territories (1787)

The Northwest Ordinance, covering land above the Ohio River and east of the Mississippi River, began as a means of establishing a formal procedure for transforming territories into states. Once a territory had a population of 60,000 people, a convention could be held to draft a state constitution and apply to Congress for statehood. Once admitted to the union, a state would be fully equal with the older states. The Ordinance included a bill of rights that guaranteed religious freedom, representation in proportion to population, trial by jury, and other protections. It also banned slavery permanently from the Northwest Territory.

The Northwest Ordinance stated that "there shall be neither slavery nor involuntary servitude in the said Territory, otherwise than in the punishment of crimes, whereof the party shall have been duly convicted; *provided,* always, that any person escaping into the same, from whom labor or service is lawfully claimed in any one of the original States, such fugitive may be lawfully reclaimed and conveyed to the person claiming his or her labor or service aforesaid."

The antislavery provision did not aim to protect African Americans. Whites who did not own slaves who moved into the Northwest Territory were very hostile toward slavery. They held this anger because of self-interest, not because of any humanitarian attitudes toward African Americans. The whites of the Northwest believed that the use of enslaved blacks would eventually lead to the creation of a large free black population, which would compete with whites for land and other resources. They also argued that southerners freed their most troublesome and unproductive slaves, thereby creating a problem population. Accordingly, whites in the Northwest did their utmost to keep both slaves and freed blacks out of the region.

In the wake of the Northwest Ordinance, state constitutions of the Northwest Territory contained discriminatory provisions against blacks. However, the Ordinance also helped set up a divide between the North and the South. As the original states of the North gradually freed slaves, the Ohio River boundary of the Old Northwest extended the line between freedom and slavery all the way to the Mississippi River.

TERM PAPER SUGGESTIONS

1. Argue whether the Constitution gave the U.S. government the right to ban slavery in the Old Northwest. A copy of the Constitution can be found at http://www.constitution.org/constit_.htm.

2. Imagine "what if" slavery had been permitted in the Northwest Territory. How would the history of these states and the United States be different?

3. Imagine "what if" slavery had been banned in all new lands acquired by the United States after the founding of the country in 1776. Would the country have remained on the path to the Civil War?

4. The Northwest Ordinance is not a document that reflects any concern for slaves. It is, instead, a reflection of the desire of white pioneers to ban African Americans from the Northwest Territory. Many laws created by the federal government have had consequences that were not intended. What were the unintended consequences of the Northwest Ordinance for African Americans?

ALTERNATIVE TERM PAPER SUGGESTIONS

1. Imagine that you are trying to sell land in the Northwest Territory to whites. Create a Web site that advertises the Northwest Territory.

2. Obtain an online map of the Northwest Territory at the time of the Ordinance of 1787 and after states had been created in the region. Design a series of hyperlinks that outline and explain the political, social, and economic effects of the Ordinance.

SUGGESTED SOURCES

Primary Sources

MacNaul, Willard C. *The Relations of Thomas Jefferson and James Lemen in the Exclusion of Slavery from Illinois and the Northwest Territory with Related Documents, 1781–1818.* Whitefish, MT: Kessinger, 2007. Reprints documents showing efforts by government officials to ban the spread of slavery to the Old Northwest. Lemen, a minister and personal friend of President Thomas Jefferson, founded antislavery churches.

Middleton, Stephen. *The Black Laws in the Old Northwest: A Documentary History.* Westport, CT: Greenwood Press, 1993. All of the states covered by the Northwest Ordinance created laws that limited the rights of African Americans. After a brief preface, Middleton reprints this legislation, thereby challenging the notion that the Northwest Ordinance brought freedom for blacks.

Walsh, Robert. *Free Remarks on the Spirit of the Federal Constitution, the Practice of the Federal Government, and the Obligations of the Union, Respecting the Exclusion . . . Slavery from the Territories and New States.* Ithaca, NY: Cornell University, n.d. This book from 1819 has been reproduced from digital images held in the Cornell University Library Samuel J. May Anti-Slavery Collection. Walsh was a Philadelphia-based essayist who achieved considerable fame as an antislavery activist in the first half of the nineteenth century.

Secondary Sources

Berwanger, Eugene H. *The Frontier Against Slavery: Western Anti-Negro Prejudice and the Slavery Extension Controversy.* Urbana: University of Illinois Press, 2002. In a book first published in 1967, Berwanger argues that the Northwest Ordinance banned slavery because of the whites-only prejudices of the pioneers rather than from any humanitarian concerns for African Americans.

Franklin, John Hope, and Alfred A. Moss Jr. *From Slavery to Freedom: A History of African Americans.* New York: Knopf, 2000. Originally published in 1947 and updated, this is a general history of blacks in America with coverage of the Northwest Ordinance. John Hope Franklin pioneered the field of African American history.

Kolchin, Peter. *American Slavery, 1619–1877.* Boston: Hill and Wang, 2003. Traces the history of slavery and sets the American version in world context.

Litwack, Leon F. *North of Slavery: The Negro in the Free States, 1790–1860.* Chicago: University of Chicago Press, 1965. Despite the dated language, this remains a solid study of the lives of African Americans in the Old Northwest.

Wright, Gavin. *Slavery and American Economic Development.* Baton Rouge: Louisiana State University Press, 2006. Argues that slavery never took root in the Northwest Territory because of the ban embedded in the Northwest Ordinance, thereby setting the North and South on different economic paths.

World Wide Web

"African American Perspectives: Pamphlets from the Daniel A. P. Murray Collection, 1818–1907." http://memory.loc.gov/cgi-bin/query/r?ammem/murraybib:@field(NUMBER+@band(lcrbmrp+t2413)). This Library of Congress site reproduces an essay on the slavery ban in the Northwest Ordinance and the men who drafted the document. It can also be accessed through the "Primary Documents in American History" site listed below.

"Causes of the Civil War: The Northwest Ordinance (1787) and the U.S. Constitution by Michael J. Swogger." http://www.suite101.com/article.cfm/american_civil_war_retired/3568. Makes claims about the causes of the Civil War that many other historians dispute and provides little insight into the Northwest Ordinance or the Constitution.

"Digital History." http://www.digitalhistory.uh.edu/documents/documents_p2.cfm?doc=301. Provides a short history of the debate over western lands, including the expansion of slavery into the Northwest Territory.

"Primary Documents in American History: The Northwest Ordinance." http://www.loc.gov/rr/program/bib/ourdocs/northwest.html. This Library of Congress site includes an image of the original Northwest Ordinance as well as brief introduction to the document.

12. 3/5 Compromise Is Added to the Constitution (1787)

Americans as a whole did not give much thought to slavery until they began to think about demanding liberty for themselves. The U.S. Constitution is the first document from the new federal government to mention slavery, albeit implicitly. Its support of slavery would be cited for years as a justification for maintaining the peculiar institution.

The Constitutional Convention was held in Philadelphia in May 1787. All states except Rhode Island eventually sent representatives. Although the delegates had many disagreements, most shared basic assumptions about the nature of people and of government. They believed that people were driven by self-interest and that ambition could only be checked by ambition. To block attempts to monopolize power, the framers of the Constitution built in checks and balances within the units of government.

The executive, the legislature, and the judiciary would share power. To guarantee that large states did not dominate the government, the lower branch would be elected by the people while the upper house would be chosen by state legislatures.

Many delegates who attended the convention owned slaves and viewed slavery as an evil necessary for economic success. Other delegates, however, believed that slavery should not exist in the new nation. In later years, James Madison, the principal author of the Constitution, told a friend that trying to abolish slavery in 1787 would be akin to setting "a spark to a mass of gunpowder." To keep the South in the Union, northern leaders believed that they had to sacrifice freedom for African Americans.

The Constitution is filled with language that implicitly references slavery. Most famously, the document states that the number of seats each state would have in the House of Representatives (which is based on a state's population) would be based partly on three-fifths of "other persons." As the Constitution includes an earlier reference to "free Persons, including those bound to Service for a Term of Years and excluding Indians," the other persons can only be slaves. The effect of this language was to give the southern states additional political power since there were far more slaves than free persons in the region.

Ratification of the Constitution took place on June 21, 1788 after opponents were won over by supporting the first 10 amendments, which guaranteed popular liberties in the Bill of Rights. The Constitution has remained vital in part because of its amending process, a remedy used to win supporters at its birth and to pass legislation giving full citizenship to blacks in the wake of the Civil War.

TERM PAPER SUGGESTIONS

1. Discuss whether the Constitution strengthened the institution of slavery in the United States.
2. Discuss the pros and cons of the Constitution with respect to slavery.
3. The Constitution never mentions the word "slave" or "slavery." Whenever the subject arises, other words are used. Discuss why the framers avoided these words.
4. Some abolitionists in the nineteenth century regarded the Constitution as a proslavery document. Do you agree? Explain.

ALTERNATIVE TERM PAPER SUGGESTIONS

1. Write a series of letters reporting what you, as a delegate to the convention, have seen and heard. Give your opinion about whether African Americans are better off living under the Constitution.

2. Prepare a podcast for the people of New York about the Constitutional Convention being held in Philadelphia. Make sure that you include lists of reasons why some delegates are opposing the inclusion of slavery in the document and why others are insisting that slavery be supported.

SUGGESTED SOURCES

Primary Sources

Bowditch, William I. *Slavery and the Constitution.* Ithaca, NY: Cornell University Library, n.d. This is a work from 1849 that has been reproduced from digital images in the Cornell University Library Samuel J. May Anti-Slavery Collection.

Brewster, Francis E. *Slavery and the Constitution: Both Sides of the Question.* Ithaca, NY: Cornell University Library, n.d. This is a work from 1850 that has been reproduced from digital images in the Cornell University Library Samuel J. May Anti-Slavery Collection.

Clark, Rufus W. *A Review of the Rev. Moses Stuart's Pamphlet on Slavery, Entitled Conscience and the Constitution.* Ann Arbor: Scholarly Publishing Office, University of Michigan Library, 2006. This is a reprint of a publication held in the University of Michigan Library.

"Constitution of the United States." http://www.constitution.org/constit_.htm. Reprints the Constitution.

Holt, Thomas C., and Elsa Barkley Brown, eds. *Major Problems in African-American History: From Slavery to Freedom, 1619–1877.* Boston: Houghton Mifflin, 2000. Includes an 1829 document in which an antebellum legal scholar struggles with the concept of slaves as persons and as property.

Jefferson, Thomas, et al. *The Constitution of the United States, the Declaration of Independence, and the Articles of Confederation.* N.P.: Wilder, 2008. Reprints the major documents of the founding of the United States.

Kaminski, John, ed. *A Necessary Evil?: Slavery and the Debate Over the Constitution.* New York: Madison House, 1995. This set of primary sources includes coverage of slavery and the Constitution's ratification as well as descriptions of how white attitudes toward slavery changed between the Revolutionary War era and the National era.

Richardson, N. S. *The Union, the Constitution, and Slavery.* Ithaca, NY: Cornell University Library, n.d. This is a work from 1864 that has been reproduced from digital images in the Cornell University Library Samuel J. May Anti-Slavery Collection.

Secondary Sources

Goldstone, Lawrence. *Dark Bargain: Slavery, Profits, and the Struggle for the Constitution.* New York: Walker, 2005. Chronicles the process of creating the Constitution to argue that the document was molded and shaped by slavery.

Young, Randall C. *The Most Dangerous Branch: Slavery, the Courts, and the Constitution.* Westminster, MD: Heritage, 2006. Examines federal court decisions relating to slavery, with a chapter dedicated to the struggles about slavery in the Constitution.

World Wide Web

"The Slavery Compromises." http://www.ucs.louisiana.edu/~ras2777/amgov/slavery2.html. This page discusses the differences over slavery between northern and southern delegates to the Constitutional Convention.

"The Three-Fifths Compromise." http://www.digitalhistory.uh.edu/documents/documents_p2.cfm?doc=306. This Digital History page provides an introduction to the compromise and reprints this passage of the Constitution.

13. Cotton Gin Is Invented (1793)

Eli Whitney ranks alongside Thomas Edison as the inventor who had the greatest impact upon the United States. Along with creating the American system of mass production, Whitney gave birth to the cotton gin that transformed the economy of the United States in the antebellum years.

Born in Massachusetts in 1765, Whitney realized that the South exported only a small amount of its cotton despite a demand from textile mills that far exceeded the available supply. The problem lay in the small seeds that were tightly bound within cotton bolls. The cotton grown on plantations required a labor-intensive process to remove these seeds that took more time that it did to pick the cotton.

Whitney's cotton gin (a shortened version of "engine," which designated a machine) mechanically removed cotton seeds. Slaves fed raw cotton into a hopper, from which a revolving cylinder with wire hooks pulled the cotton through an iron barrier with narrow slots smaller than the seeds. The seeds were blocked by the barrier, allowing only the cotton fibers to pass through. A bristled cylinder, revolving in the opposite direction, then brushed the seedless cotton from the teeth of the first cylinder. The centrifugal force of the second cylinder pushed the cleaned cotton out of the gin.

Whitney's cotton gin allowed one worker to separate seeds from up to 50 pounds of cotton per day. American cotton output increased from only 3,000 bales in 1790, just before the invention of the gin, to 4.5 million bales in 1860, on the eve of the Civil War. In the first half of the nineteenth century, cotton alone accounted for the bulk of exports from the United States, and American cotton primarily fed the textile mills of England. The profits associated with cotton prompted planters to move away from the coast and over to Texas, spreading slavery along the way. Manufactured cotton cloth, once a luxury item that only the wealthy could afford, now came within the financial reach of ordinary people.

TERM PAPER SUGGESTIONS

1. Explore this statement: "Without the invention of the cotton gin, slavery would slowly have died out in America."
2. How did Eli Whitney's invention shape the American South in the antebellum years?
3. What impact did the cotton gin have upon the lives of slaves?

ALTERNATIVE TERM PAPER SUGGESTIONS

1. The National Archives can be searched through the Archival Research Catalog (ARC) at http://www.archives.gov/research/arc/index.html. Using the ARC, research the impact of the cotton gin.
2. Create one chapter of an online graphic novel that features panels showing the impact of the cotton gin upon enslaved African Americans. (You may want to use "Comic Life" software available from the Plasq.com Company.)
3. Create a podcast that includes interviews with actors portraying cotton workers. What was life like on a cotton plantation?

SUGGESTED SOURCES

Primary Source

Olmsted, Frederick Law. *The Cotton Kingdom.* New York: Random House, 1984. First printed in 1861, this book journals Olmsted's travels through the South. It shows the social effects of Whitney's invention.

Secondary Sources

Burton, Anthony. *The Rise and Fall of King Cotton.* London: BBC and Andre Deutsch, 1984. A good summary of the impact of cotton.

Dodge, Bertha. *Cotton: The Plant That Would Be King.* Austin: University of Texas Press, 1984. A history of one of the most famous crops in world history.

Green, Constance M. *Eli Whitney and the Birth of American Technology.* Upper Saddle River, NJ: Pearson Education, 1997. First published in 1965, this remains the standard biography of the inventor.

Mirsky, Jeannette, and Allan Nevins. *The World of Eli Whitney.* New York: Macmillan, 1952. Sets Whitney in context and explains his significance. Nevins has a reputation as one of the best historians of his generation.

Whitten, David O. *Eli Whitney's Cotton Gin, 1793–1993.* Washington, DC: Agricultural History Society, 1994. Focuses on the agricultural impact of Whitney's invention.

Yafa, Stephen. *Cotton: The Biography of a Revolutionary Fiber.* New York: Penguin, 2005. An engaging history of cotton that shows its significance to the United States and the world.

World Wide Web

"The Cotton Gin and Eli Whitney by Mary Bellis." http://inventors.about.com/od/cstartinventions/a/cotton_gin.htm. This site provides a good history of Whitney as well as links to pages within About.com about the history of cotton and Whitney's efforts to produce firearms.

"The Eli Whitney Museum and Workshop." http://www.eliwhitney.org/. This Connecticut museum provides a wonderful history of Whitney and his gin, including an animated patent drawing.

"Eli Whitney's Cotton Gin." http://www.pbs.org/wgbh/aia/part3/3h1522.html. A brief introduction to Whitney with links to primary and secondary sources about the cotton gin, slaves on cotton plantations, and the impact of Whitney's invention.

"Teaching With Documents: Eli Whitney's Patent for the Cotton Gin." http://www.archives.gov/education/lessons/cotton-gin-patent/. Includes a very good history of the gin and its impact as well as images of Whitney's original patent application.

Multimedia Sources

Eli Whitney. Schlessinger Media, 2001. DVD. A biography of the inventor.

Fat Baby Leg. *Theology and Geometry.* Catpault, 2007. MP3 songs. Includes the song "Eli Whitney vs. George Washington Carver," about the white inventor who helped spread slavery and the black inventor who helped African American farmers market their products.

Inventors of the World: Eli Whitney. Schlessinger Media, 2001. VHS. A fictional recreation of Whitney's life that is aimed at secondary school students.

Pere, Bill. *Profiles of Connecticut: Songs About Important People and Events in Connecticut History.* Kidthink Music, 2008. MP3 songs. The song "We All Rely Upon Eli" shows Whitney's impact on the manufacturers of the North.

14. Gabriel's Rebellion (1800)

Gabriel's Rebellion took place in Richmond, Virginia in 1800. Gabriel Prosser, a 24-year-old enslaved blacksmith, led the largest slave plot in the early years of the new nation. The conspiracy reputedly involved most of the slaves in the Richmond area and many throughout the rest of Virginia. It taught slaveowners that they could never count on the submission of the slaves around them.

Born in 1776, Gabriel grew up on the plantation of Thomas Prosser, a tobacco planter with 50 slaves. When Prosser hired him out to work in Richmond, Gabriel read newspaper accounts about the Haitian Revolution. Inspired by the success of the Haitians, Gabriel developed a plan to end slavery in the American South. He had little trouble gaining supporters. As Gabriel and his lieutenants approached slaves, slave after slave expressed a willingness to fight for freedom and to kill whites to achieve liberty.

Gabriel planned to seize Richmond on August 30, 1800, when 1,000 followers would meet, divide into three columns, and enter the state capital under a banner inscribed "Death or Liberty." The first column would burn down the wooden warehouses of the city while the second would seize 4,000 rifles; the third would take Governor James Monroe hostage. The conspirators would kill all of the whites except poor women without slaves, Quakers, Methodists, and known opponents of slavery. Once in control of Richmond, the rebels would call for the abolition of slavery.

A few slaves who declined to join Gabriel reported the plot to their masters. Twenty slaves were arrested, but Gabriel managed to escape to Norfolk. Two black sailors betrayed him for a $300 reward and their own freedom. Charged with conspiracy and insurrection, Gabriel was hung in October 1800. Twenty-six conspirators were ultimately executed with dozens of others transported to slavery in French New Orleans and the West Indies.

TERM PAPER SUGGESTIONS

1. Compare and contrast Gabriel's Rebellion with another slave conspiracy, perhaps the Stono Rebellion or Nat Turner's Rebellion.

2. The Haitian Revolution served for decades as an inspiration to freedom-seeking African Americans and continues to be a landmark event in the history of Africans in the Americas. Trace the history of the Haitian Revolution.

3. Explore why some slaves joined Gabriel's Rebellion while other slaves reported the planned uprising to white authorities.

4. Explore the effect of the slave revolt upon the whites in Virginia. What measures did they take to maintain control over African Americans and to protect their security?

5. The argument that slaves did not actively resist slavery has existed since the end of slavery and has often been used to suggest that slaves did not object to being in bondage. Using Gabriel's Rebellion, challenge this assumption.

ALTERNATIVE TERM PAPER SUGGESTIONS

1. Imagine that you are Gabriel and you are giving an interview just prior to your execution. What issues would you want to cover to make sure that you were heard before your death?

2. Assume that you are a reporter covering the trial of Gabriel Prosser for a British newspaper. Write an editorial describing the revolt and arguing for Gabriel to be regarded as a freedom fighter.

SUGGESTED SOURCES

Primary Source

State of Virginia, Auditor of Public Accounts. *Insurrection Records*. 1800.

Secondary Sources

Aptheker, Herbert. *American Negro Slave Revolts.* New York: International, 1983. A classic book, first printed in 1943, that was the first to challenge the notion that slaves responded docilely to enslavement.

Egerton, Douglas R. *Gabriel's Rebellion: The Virginia Slave Conspiracies of 1800 and 1802.* Chapel Hill: University of North Carolina Press, 1993. Argues that Gabriel's Rebellion and a subsequent slave revolt had more to do with economics and class than slavery and racism.

Hadden, Sally E. "Ploughshares into Swords: Race, Rebellion, and Identity in Gabriel's Virginia, 1730–1810." *Journal of Southern History* 67, no. 1 (February 1, 2001): 153–74. An academic discussion of the rebellion. Ploughshares are farm tools. The article title twists the old idea of beating swords into ploughshares to ensure peace by referencing Gabriel's turning of ploughshares into swords to gain freedom.

World Wide Web

"The Gabriel Prosser Slave Revolt." http://chss.montclair.edu/english/furr/spl/gabrielrevolt.html. Consists entirely of reprinted passages from Herbert Aptheker's book.

"Gabriel's Conspiracy." http://www.pbs.org/wgbh/aia/part3/3p1576.html. Part of the Africans in America series, this site includes the confession of one of the conspirators and a Thomas Jefferson letter that shows the response of a white slaveholder to the revolt. Jefferson famously hated slavery but did not think that African Americans possessed the intellect to survive on their own.

"Gabriel's Rebellion by John Grunewald." http://niahd.wm.edu/index.php?browse=entry&id=3076. Created as a classroom lesson, this is a good short history of the slave revolt.

Multimedia Source

Africans in America. Boston: PBS, 1998. 2 DVDs. This six-part documentary includes a segment on Gabriel's Conspiracy.

15. New Jersey Becomes the Last Northern State to Abolish Slavery (1804)

African Americans in the South during the years of slavery often viewed the North as the land of freedom. This perception has existed into the modern era, yet it is inaccurate. The North may have abolished slavery before the South, with New Jersey as the last state to end the peculiar institution, but it remained a region unfriendly toward African Americans.

The American Revolution galvanized abolitionists in the North. The republican ideals of the Revolution led some people to question the suitability of fighting for freedom while denying freedom to people of African ancestry. Rhode Island became the first state to abolish slavery in 1774 because of this conflict between slavery and republicanism. Vermont followed in 1777. As New Jersey's Governor William Livingston argued in a 1786 letter, slavery could not be reconciled with Christianity, humanity, and liberty.

Quakers led much of the fight against slavery. They argued that this peculiar institution brought God's divine retribution. Accordingly, Quaker legislators introduced bills in state legislatures to regulate the slave trade, improve the treatment of slaves, and ease the rules for emancipating slaves. They also led the fight to legally abolish slavery. Pennsylvania, a state founded by Quakers, became the third state to abolish slavery in 1780. The rest of the original colonies in the North followed with New Jersey in 1804 becoming the last state to end slavery.

New Jersey's law proved typical in that it provided for gradual emancipation rather than immediate freedom. Parts of the legislation copied New York's emancipation law in that any child born to a slave would serve a 28-year indenture for men or a 25-year term for women. Slaveowners would receive restitution from the state for the loss of their property. Unlike New York, New Jersey never completely ended slavery. Slaves were recorded in the state in 1865 when the Thirteenth Amendment finally outlawed slavery throughout the United States.

TERM PAPER SUGGESTIONS

1. Did the abolition of slavery make the North into a land of freedom, as many slaves thought? Discuss.
2. When did your state vote to abolish slavery? Discuss the history of slavery in your state.
3. Compare and contrast the lives of enslaved African Americans and free African Americans in the North.
4. Discuss the involvement of the Quakers in the fight against slavery.

ALTERNATIVE TERM PAPER SUGGESTIONS

1. Imagine that you are a slave in the North. In journal entries, portray your life.
2. Assume that you have been asked to participate in a panel about slave reparations. Create a Microsoft PowerPoint presentation showing how slavery and racism affected blacks in the North in the late eighteenth and first half of the nineteenth century.
3. Design a Web-based annotated chronology of the abolition of slavery in the United States.

SUGGESTED SOURCES

Primary Source

Truth, Sojourner. *Narrative of Sojourner Truth.* New York: Penguin Classics, 1998. Truth began her life as a slave in New York City. Her narrative about life as a slave and as a mother of slave children in the North is quite poignant.

Secondary Sources

Davis, David Brion. *Inhuman Bondage: The Rise and Fall of Slavery in the New World.* New York: Oxford University Press, 2006. Part of the new trend to place the United States in the context of world history, this book gives a fascinating broad perspective on the slave trade.

Hodges, Graham. *Root and Branch: African Americans in New York and East Jersey, 1613–1863.* Chapel Hill: University of North Carolina Press, 1999. Good, descriptive study of black life in the middle states.

Litwack, Leon F. *North of Slavery: The Negro in the Free States, 1790–1860.* Chicago: University of Chicago Press, 1967. The vast majority of books devoted to slavery focus on the South. Litwack's book pioneered by focusing on the lives of blacks, both free and enslaved, in the North. His work, which shows that northern blacks had little freedom even after emancipation, remains a useful study today.

McManus, Edgar. *Black Bondage in the North.* Syracuse, NY: Syracuse University Press, 1973. One of the best descriptions of what it was like to be a slave in the North.

Rael, Patrick. *Black Identity and Black Protest in the Antebellum North.* Chapel Hill: University of North Carolina Press, 2002. Shows the myriad ways in which blacks resisted slavery and racism in the North in the years before the Civil War. African Americans drew on Enlightenment and Revolutionary ideals to form a racial identity and protest white supremacy.

Sweet, John Wood. *Bodies Politic: Negotiating Race in the American North, 1730–1830.* Philadelphia: University of Pennsylvania Press, 2006. Massive study of the meaning of citizenship in the colonial and early national North.

Zilversmit, Arthur. *The First Emancipation: The Abolition of Slavery in the North.* Chicago: University of Chicago Press, 1967. Still one of the few studies of the abolition of slavery in the North.

World Wide Web

"Abolishing Slavery in America." http://www.buzzle.com/articles/abolishing-slavery-in-america.html. Lists the year in which each northern state abolished slavery and lists the states that never allowed slavery within their borders.

"One People's Project: Last Northern State to Abolish Slavery Becomes First Northern State to Apologize for It." http://onepeoplesproject.com/index.php?option=com_content&task=view&id=1299&Itemid=2. Discusses the New Jersey legislature's 2008 decision to apologize for slavery.

"Race-Based Legislation in the North." http://www.pbs.org/wgbh/aia/part4/4p2957.html. Part of the Africans in America site, this page shows that the North was not the land of freedom. The page includes links to discussions of northern racism by noted historians.

"Slavery in New Jersey." http://www.slavenorth.com/newjersey.htm. One of the best sites devoted to the abolition of slavery, this page has links to essays on the end of slavery in all of the northern states as well as a page that explains how northerners profited from the slave trade.

Multimedia Source

Africans in America. Boston: PBS, 1998. 2 DVDs. This six-part documentary includes segments on blacks in the North, including a long piece on African Americans in Philadelphia, purportedly the "City of Brotherly Love."

16. Congress Ends U.S. Participation in the Atlantic Slave Trade (1808)

The Atlantic slave trade came under heavy attack during the American Revolution when the principles of freedom contrasted sharply with the practice of slavery. However, the economic dependence of southern states upon slavery kept the founders of the new nation from abolishing the peculiar institution. Abolition only came when the South no longer needed imported West African slaves.

A certain amount of disgust had long surrounded the transatlantic slave trade. The sailors who transported slaves out of Africa were on board slave ships because no other captains would take them. The business of carrying humans into slavery in another hemisphere simply did not seem like an honorable way to make a living. The slave trade had developed such a notorious reputation for cruelty by 1776 that Thomas Jefferson, a Virginia slaveowner, sought to include a reference to the practice in his original draft of the Declaration of Independence. Jefferson's reference was struck out of the final draft at the insistence of other southern slave-owners. A sense of propriety also played a role in the deletion. For delegates who felt slavery was an embarrassment to the young nation, it seemed hypocritical to blame King George III for a trade in which colonists had eagerly participated. Rather than highlight such an egregious contradiction, many felt it was better to ignore it.

At the Constitutional Convention of 1787, this issue of abolishing the transatlantic slave trade again arose. Delegates from Georgia and South Carolina believed slavery to be necessary to the economies of their regions and blocked a ban. The South had suffered the loss of slaves during the Revolution to disease, kidnapping, relocation, and war. The region did not believe that it could rebuild without repopulating the slave community as quickly as possible—via imported slaves.

In the next years, abolitionists in Great Britain greatly increased their efforts to end the African trade. In 1807, Great Britain banned the traffic of slaves. A year later, the United States officially ended its participation in the trade, influenced by the British ban. By this time, the South had reestablished its slave population through importation of slaves and natural increase. It no longer needed the Atlantic slave trade. The abolition of slavery in the North ended the demand for slaves in that region. The ban created little controversy when it finally passed Congress on March 2, 1807. It took effect on January 1, 1808.

TERM PAPER SUGGESTIONS

1. What effect did the abolition of the slave trade by Great Britain have upon the United States?

2. Why did the United States choose to end the transatlantic slave trade but allow slavery to continue to exist within its borders?

3. The transatlantic slave trade ban passed during the administration of President Thomas Jefferson, a slaveowner, with Jefferson's support. Explore Jefferson's views on slavery.

4. Trace the impact of the abolition of the transatlantic slave trade.

5. Go to http://www.american.edu/TED/slave.htm and look under "Related Cases" for examples of other abuses of workers. Compare and contrast the Atlantic slave trade with one of the cases listed.

ALTERNATIVE TERM PAPER SUGGESTIONS

1. Does the Atlantic slave trade still exist, albeit in a different form? Use the Web to research the history of modern slave trafficking into the United States. To evaluate Web sites, use the CRAAP test available at http://www.csuchico.edu/lins/handouts/evalsites.html.

2. The image at http://www.unmultimedia.org/photo/detail/166/0166126.html shows a dancer's commemoration of the anniversary of the abolition of the transatlantic slave trade. Create a song or other artwork to commemorate the end of the trade.

SUGGESTED SOURCES

Primary Sources

Basker, James G. *Early American Abolitionists: A Collection of Antislavery Writings.* New York: Gilder Lehrman Institute of American History, 2005. Shows resistance to the Atlantic slave trade.

Ross, William T. *Documents Illustrative of the History of the Slave Trade to America.* Buffalo, NY: William S. Hein, 2002. Contains a wealth of primary sources that illustrate the Atlantic slave trade.

Secondary Sources

Anstey, Roger. *The Atlantic Slave Trade and British Abolition, 1760–1810.* London: Macmillan, 1975. Still a very good study of the British involvement with the transatlantic slave trade in its waning years.

Bailey, Anne C. *African Voices of the Atlantic Slave Trade: Beyond the Silence and the Shame.* Boston: Beacon Press, 2005. The only book to show the African view of the Atlantic slave trade.

Blackburn, Robin. *The Overthrow of Colonial Slavery, 1776–1848.* New York: Verso, 1988. Massive study of the abolition of slavery in the New World.

Davis, David Brion. *Inhuman Bondage: The Rise and Fall of Slavery in the New World.* New York: Oxford University Press, 2006. Part of the new trend to place the United States in the context of world history, this book gives a fascinating broad perspective on the slave trade.

Mason, Mathew. *Slavery and Politics in the Early American Republic.* Chapel Hill: University of North Carolina Press, 2006. One of the best studies of slavery in the first years of the United States.

Thomas, Hugh. *The Slave Trade: The Story of the Atlantic Slave Trade, 1440–1870.* New York: Simon and Schuster, 1999. A 900-page history that focuses on the economics, social acceptance, and politics of the slave trade.

World Wide Web

"The Abolition of the Slave Trade." http://abolition.nypl.org/. Created by the New York Public Library and the Schomburg Center for Research in Black Culture, this is the most extensive site devoted to the abolition of the transatlantic slave trade. It includes images, superb maps, essays, and a timeline. Many of the primary sources listed are not readily available elsewhere.

"1807 Abolition of Slavery Act." http://www.spartacus.schoolnet.co.uk/Lslavery07.htm. Covers the end of slavery in Great Britain.

"TED Case Studies: Abolition of the Atlantic Slave Trade in the United States." http://www.american.edu/TED/slave.htm. Wonderful essay on the abolition of the slave trade including the legacy of abolition. The site, aimed at legal scholars, includes references to modern legal decisions that touch on the issue of involuntary labor.

"Timeline: The Abolition of the Atlantic Slave Trade." http://www.historynet.com/timeline-the-abolition-of-the-slave-trade.htm. The focus is on British opposition to the slave trade, particularly William Wilberforce's objections.

Multimedia Source

Eltis, David, et al. *The Trans-Atlantic Slave Trade: A Database on CD-ROM.* New York: Cambridge University Press, 2000. Contains the records of 27,233 transatlantic slave ship voyages made between 1595 and 1866 by Europeans. The software allows users to select data according to time period or geographic area. Data can be downloaded into other software.

17. Richard Allen Establishes the African Methodist Church (1816)

The church has played a prominent role in the lives of African Americans in modern America. It served as a source of inspiration during the civil rights struggles of the 1950s and 1960s. It continues to serve today as a center of community life. Much of the credit for the place of the church in African American life can be given to Richard Allen. By founding the African Methodist Church, he created a place where blacks could worship without friction from whites.

Allen, born into slavery in 1760 in Philadelphia, was sold in 1777 to Stokely Sturgis. Through the efforts of an itinerant Methodist preacher, Sturgis came to believe that slavery was wrong, and he allowed Allen to purchase his freedom. Allen spent the next several years serving as a Methodist preacher to blacks and whites alike in Maryland, Delaware, Pennsylvania, and New Jersey. At this time, few blacks attended public worship. When blacks tried to attend services at St. George's Church in Philadelphia in 1787, they were asked by whites to leave. Allen responded by joining with a few associates to establish St. Thomas African Episcopal Church in 1794. The church became the first independent black church in North America. In 1794, Allen founded Bethel Church, which would eventually become the mother church of the African Methodist Episcopal denomination.

Aware of continuing friction between black and white Methodists, Allen invited black congregations to join together. On April 9, 1816, 60 delegates from 5 black congregations agreed to form the African Methodist Episcopal Church. Allen became its bishop on April 11, 1816. Confined to the northern states before the Civil War, the church spread rapidly in the South after the war. It now has over one million members. The African Methodist Episcopal Zion Church, founded in New York City in 1796, is a separate denomination that did not become independent from whites until 1821.

For Allen, the Methodist emphasis on the simplicity of the gospel offered salvation from sin and physical slavery. He spent much of the remainder of life working against the emigration of free blacks to Africa and supporting efforts to help enslaved blacks in America. He died in 1831.

TERM PAPER SUGGESTIONS

1. Trace the history of the African Methodist Episcopal Church.

2. Like many blacks, Richard Allen opposed the voluntary emigration of African Americans as promoted by the American Colonization Society. Investigate Allen's life. Why did he oppose colonization?

3. Many blacks turned to Christianity in the nineteenth century as a way to fight against racism and slavery. Investigate the history of African Americans and Christianity. Why did Christianity prove comforting to many African Americans?

4. Allen joined many other blacks in nursing whites during a 1793 yellow fever epidemic in Philadelphia. The episode became a failed attempt to bridge the racial divide with whites. Investigate the epidemic and the response to it.

ALTERNATIVE TERM PAPER SUGGESTIONS

1. Interview the minister or another prominent member of your local African Methodist Episcopal church to discover the history of the church in your community. Report on your findings in a podcast.

2. Mother Bethel, the church begun by Allen, is featured in a virtual tour of Philadelphia at http://www.ushistory.org/tour/tour_bethel.htm. Create a virtual tour of black historical landmarks in your city or town.

SUGGESTED SOURCES

Primary Source

Heard, William H. *From Slavery to the Bishopric in the A.M.E. Church: An Autobiography.* N.P.: Old Landmark, 2005. Autobiography of an African American preacher who was born a slave in Georgia but rose to become a bishop in the African Methodist Episcopal Church.

Secondary Sources

Anderson, Laurie Halse. *Fever 1793.* New York: Aladdin, 2002. An exceptionally well researched and engaging historical novel about the yellow fever epidemic that struck Philadelphia. Although the novel, aimed at teens, does not focus upon the black community, it does show the interaction of blacks and whites as well as the hysteria surrounding the disease.

Angell, Stephen Ward, and Anthony B. Pinn, eds. *Social Protest Thought in the African Methodist Episcopal Church, 1862–1939.* Knoxville: University of Tennessee Press, 2000. Shows that the church has long been a leader in resisting race-based oppression.

Campbell, James T. *Songs of Zion: The African Methodist Episcopal Church in the United States and South Africa.* Charlotte: University of North Carolina Press, 1998. Argues that the act of becoming Christian prompted African Americans to reconsider their relationship with their ancestral homeland.

The book also charts the development of independent African American churches.

Klots, Steve, and Nathan Irvin Huggins. *Richard Allen: Black Americans of Achievement.* New York: Chelsea House, 1990. Aimed at secondary school students, this is a good introduction to Allen.

Newman, Richard. *Freedom's Prophet: Bishop Richard Allen, the AME Church, and the Black Founding Fathers.* New York: New York University Press, 2008. The definitive biography of one of the most significant African American leaders of postrevolutionary America as well as a good social history of the early republic.

Walls, William Jacob. *The African Methodist Episcopal Zion Church: Reality of the Black Church.* Philadelphia: A.M.E. Zion Publishing House, 1974. A good if somewhat biased history of the rival denomination from its founding to the 1970s by a church insider.

World Wide Web

"A.M.E. Today." http://www.ame-today.com/. The official site of the African Methodist Episcopal Church, the site includes the history of the organization as well as its current activities and links to A.M.E. publications. Richard Allen is buried on the church grounds.

"Archiving Early America: Richard Allen and African-American Identity - A Black Ex-Slave in Early America's White Society Preserves His Cultural Identity by Creating Separate Institutions by James Henretta." http://www.earlyamerica.com/review/spring97/allen.html. Reprints a Spring 1997 essay from the *Early America Review.*

"Mother Bethel A.M.E." http://www.ushistory.org/tour/tour_bethel.htm. Along with an extremely detailed history of the church, this site provides one of the best biographies of Allen on the Web.

Multimedia Source

Africans in America. Boston: PBS, 1998. 2 DVDs. This documentary includes a chapter on the 1793 Philadelphia yellow fever epidemic that raged for 3 months and killed 5,000 people.

18. American Colonization Society Establishes Liberia (1816)

The American Colonization Society (ACS), begun in Washington, D.C. in 1816 by Presbyterian minister Robert Finley, aimed to remove African

Americans from the United States and resettle them in Africa. Many of the most influential Americans supported the society. By the start of the Civil War, it had relocated more than 10,000 blacks to the organization's colony in Liberia.

The idea of sending people of African ancestry "back" to Africa had circulated since the colonial era. The plan gained steam after the Revolution as northern states began to abolish slavery. For many whites, the deportation and relocation of blacks proved preferable to living and working alongside a large population of free African Americans. Others thought that the racial attitudes of white Americans would never change and that the relocation of African Americans would give them freedom from hatred and restrictions on their liberties.

Colonization proposals also enjoyed the backing of white southerners. Seeking to bolster the institution of slavery, many southerners wanted to remove populations of free blacks who might lend support to slave revolts. Other southerners who were opposed to slavery thought that colonization might encourage slaveowners to free their slaves. Presidents Thomas Jefferson and James Madison, both Virginians, advocated gradual emancipation and deportation to end slavery. Jefferson also argued that emigrating African Americans would bring Western civilization to Africa.

The ACS lobbied the federal government for support for relocation. On March 3, 1819, Congress passed the Slave Trade Act, which authorized the federal government to use the navy to transport illegally enslaved people to Africa. Congress designated $100,000 to finance the program. At gunpoint, a U.S. naval officer persuaded King Peter, chief of the Dey people, to sell the land that would become the colony of Liberia.

By this time, the invention of the cotton gin had begun to dramatically change the economic and political climate of the South. As slave labor became enormously popular and profitable, slaveholders lost interest in emancipation. Lack of support from blacks and leading abolitionists in the North weakened the ACS in that region. By 1860, when colonization essentially stopped, more than 10,000 people had relocated to Liberia. They described the colony as a bleak place with a high death rate, and many apparently would have returned to the United States if they had the financial ability to do so.

TERM PAPER SUGGESTIONS

1. Liberia is the first American colony and the only one with a strong connection to African American history. Report on the history of Liberia.

2. Report on what life was like for the African Americans who immigrated to Liberia. Did they find the happiness that they sought?

3. Examine why whites would support or oppose the colonization movement. You might want to look at abolitionist and newspaper editor William Lloyd Garrison, who initially supported the movement before deciding to oppose it.

ALTERNATIVE TERM PAPER SUGGESTIONS

1. Create an online guide to Liberia that focuses on the African Americans who colonized the country and the nation's links to the United States.

2. Create a Web site that introduces the viewer to Liberia, past and present.

SUGGESTED SOURCES

Primary Sources

American Colonization Society. *Condition of the American Colored Population and of the Colony at Liberia.* Boston: Pierce and Parker, 1833. An obviously biased look at the colonization movement.

American Colonization Society. *The First Annual Report of the American Society for Colonizing the Free People of Color of the United States and the Proceedings of the Society at Their Annual Meeting in the City on Washington on the First Day of January, 1818.* Washington, DC: D. Rapine, 1818. Sets out the goals of the ACS.

Brown, Thomas Cilavan. *Examination of Mr. Thomas C. Brown: A Free Colored Citizen of S. Carolina, as to the Actual State of Things in Liberia in the Years 1833 and 1834.* Ithaca, NY: Cornell University Library, 2006. A reprint of a holding in the Cornell University Library, this pamphlet covers a black resident of Charleston, South Carolina who immigrated to Liberia in 1833 to better his condition and escape the oppressive laws of his home state. Within 14 months, Brown returned to the United States after losing 4 family members to disease in Africa.

Secondary Sources

Burin, Eric. *Slavery and the Peculiar Solution: A History of the American Colonization Society.* Gainesville: University Press of Florida, 2006. An engaging and well-researched history of the ACS.

Clegg, Claude A., III. *The Price of Liberty: African Americans and the Making of Liberia.* Chapel Hill: University of North Carolina Press, 2003. Focuses on the 2,000 black North Carolinians who settled in Liberia in the nineteenth century. Clegg covers the challenges that these individuals faced in Liberia as well as their motivations for fleeing the United States.

McPherson, J. H. T. *History of Liberia.* N.P.: Book Jungle, 2008. A brief sketch of Liberia but still the best available source on its history.

Reef, Catherine. *This Our Dark Country: The American Settlers of Liberia.* New York: Clarion Books, 2002. Aimed at secondary school students, this heavily illustrated history of Liberia focuses on the nineteenth century. Many of the photographs are not available elsewhere.

Yarema, Allan. *The American Colonization Society: An Avenue to Freedom?* Lanham, MD: University Press of America, 2006. A solid history of the ACS but it is surpassed by Burin's book.

World Wide Web

"The African American Mosaic: Colonization." http://www.loc.gov/exhibits/african/afam002.html. This wonderful Library of Congress site includes links to primary documents relating to colonization as well as a history of the movement.

"Africans in America: The American Colonization Society." http://www.pbs.org/wgbh/aia/part3/3p1521.html. This history of the ACS includes links to primary sources and secondary accounts about the movement.

"Background Note: Liberia." http://www.state.gov/r/pa/ei/bgn/6618.htm. Created by the U.S. Department of State's Bureau of African Affairs, this is a superb summary of the history of Liberia. Most of the focus is on modern Liberia.

"Liberia Page." http://www.africa.upenn.edu/Country_Specific/Liberia.html. Produced by the African Studies Center at the University of Pennsylvania, this page includes online resources related to modern Liberia.

Multimedia Source

Africans in America. Boston: PBS, 1998. 2 DVDs. Includes a segment on colonization.

19. Denmark Vesey's Rebellion (1822)

Denmark Vesey, leader of one of the most significant slave revolts in the United States, was probably born on the Danish Caribbean sugar island of St. Thomas around 1767. In 1781, he was purchased by Captain Joseph Vesey, a slave trader, who trained him as cabin boy. Vesey renamed the boy "Telemaque," after the mythical son of Odysseus. In time, he became "Denmark" after the island of his birth.

In 1783, Joseph Vesey settled in Charleston, South Carolina. Denmark, literate and multilingual, lived with the Vesey family and worked in the family's imported goods business as an office clerk and trader. He married a slave woman, Beck, who gave birth to at least three of Vesey's children. Since whites did not recognize the marriages of slaves, Denmark and Beck never lived together and were separated when Joseph Vesey moved his household to an Ashley River plantation. When Denmark won $1,500 in a lottery, he purchased his freedom, returned to Charleston, and became a carpenter.

Vesey, now married to a woman named Susan after his relationship with Beck collapsed, became one of the first members of the African Methodist Episcopal Church, commonly known as the African Church, in Charleston. Embittered by the continuing enslavement of Beck and their children, Vesey turned his back on the New Testament and what he regarded as the false promise of universal brotherhood.

Vesey began to plan to lead his children and friends to freedom in Haiti. What made his conspiracy unique was both Vesey's advanced age of 54 and that he planned a mass exodus of black families out of Charleston. The plot called for slaves in the vicinity of the Ashley and Cooper rivers to slay their masters on the morning of Sunday, July 14, 1822, and fight their way toward the city docks. Although Vesey employed several black men to make weapons, the leading conspirators decided that they would not risk stockpiling weapons or recruiting soldiers before July. Vesey believed that once the revolt began, men would flock to his side.

Despite efforts to maintain silence, conspirator William Paul told of the planned revolt to Peter, a slave, on May 22. At about the same time, another slave, George Wilson, gave information about the plan to his master. Exactly one month later, Vesey was arrested. Found guilty and sentenced to hang, he died on July 2, 1822 along with five other conspirators as an immense crowd of blacks and whites watched. Charleston courts eventually arrested 131 slaves and free blacks, executing 35 and transporting 37 to Spanish Cuba. Twenty-three African Americans were acquitted, two died in custody, three were found not guilty but whipped, and one free black was released on condition that he permanently leave the state. The African Church was razed but was rebuilt in 1865 at the end of the Civil War.

TERM PAPER SUGGESTIONS

1. Throughout history people have disagreed about whether resistance to oppression should be violent or peaceful. Discuss what methods should be used to fight for freedom in general and what tactics were acceptable against slavery in particular.

2. In 2001, the City of Charleston, South Carolina faced a dilemma. After a long fight with some citizens who accused Vesey of planning genocide for whites, black activists persuaded the city to approve a monument honoring Denmark Vesey. Then Michael Johnson, professor of history at Johns Hopkins University, presented evidence suggesting that Vesey did not organize the rebellion that bears his name. Johnson argued that Vesey was simply one of scores of black victims of a conspiracy engineered by the white power structure in 1822. The Vesey rebellion may one of scores of historical myths that are now accepted as fact. Do myths have any value in remembrances of the past? Should Vesey be acknowledged although we do not know for certain if he played a significant role in a slave revolt? Discuss.

3. Gene Sharp, who reports on methods of nonviolent contact in his three-volume *The Politics of Nonviolent Action* (New York: Porter Sargent, 1973), warns that violence by oppressed people usually leads only to repression and resentment. Using Vesey's Rebellion, argue in support of Sharp's thesis.

4. The 1739 Stono Rebellion was the largest slave revolt prior to Vesey's Rebellion. Nat Turner's Rebellion was the most successful slave revolt. Compare and contrast the three slave revolts. Can you see any differences in the white response to each revolt?

5. In the wake of Vesey's Rebellion, the African Church came under heavy attack for purportedly aiding the revolt. Trace the history of Christian opposition to slavery.

6. Historian Albert Raboteau has argued that the white citizens of Charleston leveled the African Church in the wake of Vesey's Rebellion as an attack against black independence and autonomy. He makes a link between this 1822 attack and assaults against black churches during the civil rights movement of the 1960s and in the present. Why do you think he makes that comparison? Do you agree? Why or why not?

7. One of the slaves who reportedly participated in the revolt bore the name of Gullah Jack. Who are the Gullah people? Explore the role that they have played in the history of the United States.

ALTERNATIVE TERM PAPER SUGGESTIONS

1. Imagine that you are Denmark Vesey. Create a Microsoft PowerPoint presentation to persuade others to join in the slave rebellion.

2. Create a Web page to memorialize Denmark Vesey and the other slaves who died in the rebellion. See the Denmark Vesey Spirit of Freedom Monument as an example of one site dedicated to slaves seeking freedom.

3. Create a rap song to honor Denmark Vesey and the freedom-seeking slaves who died alongside him.

SUGGESTED SOURCES

Primary Sources

Vesey, Denmark. *The Trial Record of Denmark Vesey.* Boston: Beacon Press, 1970. Reprints the transcript of the trial.

Walker, Lois A., and Susan R. Silverman. *A Documented History of Gullah Jack Pritchard and the Denmark Vesey Slave Insurrection of 1822.* Lewiston, ME: Edwin Mellen, 2000. Reprints documents relating to the life of one of Vesey's co-conspirators.

Secondary Sources

Bellows, Barbara L. "Designs Against Charleston: The Trial Record of the Denmark Vesey Slave Conspiracy of 1822." *Journal of Southern History* 66, no. 4 (November 1, 2000): 862–82. Aimed at historians, this is a scholarly examination of the trial.

Egerton, Douglas R. *He Shall Go Out Free: The Lives of Denmark Vesey.* Lanham, MD: Rowman and Littlefield, 2004. Re-creates Saint Domingue and South Carolina to explore Vesey's life as an emigrant, a slave, and a freeman.

Lofton, John. *Denmark Vesey's Revolt: The Slave Plot That Lit a Fuse to Fort Sumter.* Kent, OH: Kent State University Press, 1983. Explains why the revolt took place and covers its impact on the antislavery movement and the Civil War.

Paquette, Robert L., and Douglas R. Egerton. "Of Facts and Fables: New Light on the Denmark Vesey Affair." *South Carolina Historical Magazine* 105 (January 2004): 8–48. A good account of what is known and what is rumored about Vesey's Rebellion.

Powers, Bernard E. *Black Charlestonians: A Social History, 1822–1885.* Fayetteville: University of Arkansas Press, 1994. A general history of African Americans in Charleston that sets Vesey's Rebellion in context and shows its lasting impact.

Raboteau, Albert J. *Slave Religion: The "Invisible Institution" in the Antebellum South.* New York: Oxford University Press, 2004. One of the foremost historians of African American religion explores the intersection of faith and rebellion.

Robertson, David M. *Denmark Vesey: The Buried Story of America's Largest Slave Rebellion and the Man Who Led It.* New York: Vintage, 2000. Discusses the reality of Vesey's life, the revolt, and his historical image. The book includes an appendix with a list of those who died with Vesey.

Rodriguez, Junius P., ed. *Encyclopedia of Slave Resistance and Rebellion.* Westport, CT: Greenwood Press, 2006. Contains an entry on Vesey and covers many more rebellions.

Starobin, Robert S., ed. *Denmark Vesey: The Slave Conspiracy of 1822.* Englewood Cliffs, NJ: Prentice-Hall, 1970. A solid account of Vesey's life that has been surpassed by more recent scholarship.

World Wide Web

"Africans in America: The Vesey Conspiracy." http://www.pbs.org/wgbh/aia/part3/3p2976.html. A short account of the rebellion with links to primary sources.

"Africa Within: Denmark Vesey." www.africawithin.com/bios/denmark_vesey.htm. Profiles the slave leader.

"Black History: Denmark Vesey." http://www.gale.cengage.com/free_resources/bhm/bio/vesey_d.htm. An excellent biography of Vesey that shows his significance to the antislavery movement.

"Denmark Vesey Spirit of Freedom Monument." http://denmarkvesey.org/. Purposes to promote the creation of a monument to honor the African Americans in the Carolina lowcountry who fought to liberate themselves from slavery.

"NPR: Denmark Vesey." www.npr.org/templates/story/story.php?storyId=1064594. 1999 audio recording of an interview with David Robertson, a biographer of Denmark Vesey.

"Social and Behavioral Sciences E-Campus H 101—Lab Exercise: The Denmark Vesey Insurrection (1822)." http://users.erols.com/bcccsbs/vesey.htm. Aimed at secondary school students, this is a good introduction to Vesey's Rebellion and includes student exercises.

"This Far by Faith: Denmark Vesey." http://www.pbs.org/thisfarbyfaith/people/denmark_vesey.html. Focuses on the effect of Vesey's actions upon the African Church and includes a history of Vesey's involvement with religion.

Multimedia Source

Africans in America. Boston: PBS, 1998. 2 DVDs. In one of the best historical series yet created, one segment is devoted to Denmark Vesey.

20. Nat Turner's Rebellion (1831)

Nat Turner's Rebellion in Southampton County, Virginia on August 21, 1831 proved to be the most significant slave revolt in American history. It precipitated the collapse of the already weakening antislavery movement in the South and prompted harsh restrictions on the lives of blacks in the South.

Born into slavery in October 1800, Turner experienced visions in his childhood that led him to think that he was destined for a great purpose. A deeply religious child, he spent his time fasting, praying, and speaking with a spirit. As a result, other slaves viewed him as someone chosen by God. In 1825, Turner had a vision of white and black spirits engaged in a battle against the backdrop of a darkened sun. The same vision recurred in 1828, when a spirit advised him to wait for a sign from God to slay his enemies with their own weapons.

In February 1831, a solar eclipse signaled to Turner that it was time to take action. Immediately, he revealed his intentions to four other slaves—Henry Porter, Nelson Edwards, Sam Francis, and Hark Travis. On August 13, the sun had a bluish-green tint from an atmospheric disturbance. Turner took this event as a further sign to act.

On the night of August 21, a group of slaves attacked the family of Joseph Travis, Turner's master. Turner later described Travis as a kind man, against whom he had no complaints. The Travis family died, with one slave even returning to the home to dispatch a sleeping infant that they had initially overlooked. The rebels wanted to leave no survivors. With guns, axes, and other weapons, Turner and his men moved from plantation to plantation in Southampton County killing a total of 57 whites. Turner's band numbered about 60 slaves and free blacks when local authorities managed to rout the group in a battle.

Starting on August 23, the whites of Southampton rose up against the blacks. While Turner evaded capture, white militia murdered over 100 African Americans, making no distinction between those who were rebels and those who were innocent bystanders. More than 60 slaves were arrested, with about 20 more subsequently captured over the next several weeks. Other blacks were beaten or forced to flee from Virginia. Turner, finally caught on October 30, died on November 11, 1831.

TERM PAPER SUGGESTIONS

1. Discuss whether mistreatment alone accounted for Nat Turner's actions or whether his revolt resulted from aspects of slavery. This is a discussion begun by Turner's contemporaries who wondered if other African Americans might be tempted to follow the same destructive path as Turner.

2. Investigate how Virginia responded to Turner's Rebellion.

3. Were resistance and revolt inevitable in a slaveholding society? Was there any way to avoid such outbreaks? Discuss.

4. Compare and contrast Turner's revolt with other slave revolts such as the Stono Rebellion and Gabriel's Rebellion.

5. Discuss what effect the presence of a hostile and potentially dangerous element in southern society had on southern life and culture.

6. Religion is often assumed to be a conservative force. In the case of Nat Turner's Rebellion, religion appears to have been a major motivating factor. How do you account for this discrepancy? Discuss ways in which religion has been employed in support of radical causes.

ALTERNATIVE TERM PAPER SUGGESTIONS

1. Assume that you are a reporter for a northern newspaper that is opposed to slavery. Create a podcast that covers the rebellion.

2. Using a Microsoft PowerPoint presentation, advise your fellow students on how to organize a successful slave revolt. How do you define success?

3. Assume that you are Nat Turner. Using a video camera, give your side of the rebellion.

SUGGESTED SOURCES

Primary Sources

Aptheker, Herbert. *Nat Turner's Slave Rebellion: Together with the Full Text of the So-Called: "Confessions" of Nat Turner Made in Prison in 1831.* Mineola, NY: Dover, 2006. Contains the sources that Aptheker, one of the first to consider the past of African Americans as a field worthy of study, used to construct his books.

Baker, James T. *Nat Turner: Cry Freedom in America.* Fort Worth, TX: Harcourt Brace, 1998. Includes both primary and secondary sources that explain the slave revolt.

Tragle, Henry Irving, ed. *The Southampton Slave Revolt of 1831: A Compilation of Source Material Including the Full Text of the Confessions of Nat Turner.* Amherst: University of Massachusetts Press, 1971. Contains nearly all the surviving primary sources about the revolt.

Turner, Nat. *The Confessions of Nat Turner and Other Related Documents.* New York: St. Martin's Press, 1996. A very good introduction to the revolt combined with the full text of Turner's supposed confession to attorney Thomas Gray.

Secondary Sources

Aptheker, Herbert. *American Negro Slave Revolts.* New York: International Publishers, 1943. Despite its age, this book remains a good account of the various forms of African American resistance to slavery.

Aptheker, Herbert. *Nat Turner's Slave Rebellion.* New York: International Publishers, 1966. A bit dated in its language but still a good history.

Bisson, Terry, and John Davenport. *Nat Turner: Slave Revolt Leader.* Philadelphia, PA: Chelsea House, 2004. Aimed at secondary school students, this is a good overview of the rebellion.

DeLombard, Jeannine Marie. *Slavery on Trial: Law, Abolitionism, and Print Culture.* Chapel Hill: University of North Carolina Press, 2007. Aimed at academics, this is a discussion of how slavery trials were covered in the press as clamor for the abolition of the slave trade rose.

Dillon, Merton L. *Slavery Attacked: Southern Slaves and Their Allies, 1619–1865.* Baton Rouge: Louisiana State University Press, 1990. A discussion of the relation of slave discontent to American political and diplomatic history and to American wars.

Foner, Eric. *Nat Turner.* Englewood Cliffs, NJ: Prentice-Hall, 1971. Sets Turner's Rebellion in the context of the abolition movement.

French, Scot. *The Rebellious Slave: Nat Turner in American Memory.* Boston, MA: Examines how Turner's revolt is viewed by popular culture.

Greenberg, Kenneth. *Nat Turner: A Slave Rebellion in History and Memory.* New York: Oxford University Press, 2003. The definitive study of Turner, reflecting the latest scholarship.

Oates, Stephen B. *The Fires of Jubilee: Nat Turner's Fierce Rebellion.* New York: Harper and Row, 1975. A very readable and well-researched account of the revolt that has become the standard history of the event.

Rodriguez, Junius P., ed. *Encyclopedia of Slave Resistance and Rebellion.* Westport, CT: Greenwood Press, 2006. Contains an entry on Turner and covers many more rebellions.

Styron, William. *The Confessions of Nat Turner.* New York: Vintage, 1992. A fictional work that set off a firestorm of protests upon its publication in

1970 for its portrayal of Turner. The book won the Pulitzer Prize, but Styron also deeply offended many readers by inventing a sexually charged relationship between Turner and a teenage girl whom he later killed. It might be read alongside Melvin J. Friedman, *William Styron's The Confessions of Nat Turner: A Critical Handbook* (New York: Wadsworth, 1970). The latter book is a literary guide.

World Wide Web

"Africans in America: Nat Turner's Rebellion." http://www.pbs.org/wgbh/aia/part3/3p1518.html. Summarizes the rebellion and includes links to primary sources about the event, including a *Richmond Times* article.

"The Confessions of Nat Turner by Nat Turner." http://www.gutenberg.org/etext/15333. Project Gutenberg includes the full text of Nat Turner's confession.

"The Insurrection, by William Lloyd Garrison, *The Liberator,* September 3, 1831." http://fair-use.org/the-liberator/1831/09/03/the-insurrection. Garrison, a newspaper editor and one of the foremost abolitionists of the day, reported on Turner's Rebellion in his paper. This site provides the full text.

"The Southampton Slave Revolt." http://www.historybuff.com/library/refslave.html. Provides an overview of events followed by the reproduction of an 1831 letter to the editor of the *American Beacon of Norfolk* (Virginia) describing the incident.

Multimedia Sources

Africans in America. Boston: PBS, 1998. 2 DVDs. Includes a segment on Turner's Rebellion.

The Confessions of Nat Turner: America's Black Spartacus Remembered. New York: Masterbuy Audiobooks, 1999. 1 Audiocassette. This audiobook recounts Turner's Rebellion and compares it to the revolt of the Roman slave Spartacus.

Nat Turner: A Troublesome Property. San Francisco: California Newsreel, 2003. DVD. Discusses the impact of the revolt and its legacy.

21. American Anti-Slavery Society Is Founded (1833)

The American Anti-Slavery Society (AASS), founded by abolitionists, became one of the most important antislavery organizations in the United States. Part of the radical wing, it called for immediate abolition of slavery and complete integration of African Americans into American society.

At its peak, the AASS counted more than 200,000 members in more than 2,000 chapters.

In December 1833, local antislavery organizations from across the United States gathered in Philadelphia to form a national association that would work for abolition. Arthur and Lewis Tappan, prominent antislavery activists from New York City, served as president and member of the executive committee, respectively. Remarkably for the era, the AASS included women and African Americans among its founding members. To achieve the end of slavery and equal rights for African Americans, the AASS focused on the sinfulness of slavery and inadequacy of colonization as a solution. It distributed antislavery pamphlets, sent petitions to Congress, and sponsored lectures.

In 1839, the Tappan brothers and newspaper editor William Lloyd Garrison split the AASS over the best strategy for ending slavery and the involvement of women in the antislavery movement. Garrison, a radical, viewed the entire political system as corrupt and denounced the Constitution as an illegal document because it denied freedom to blacks. He advocated the secession of the North from the Union if the South failed to abolish slavery. The Tappans, more conservative, wanted to work through the political system to end slavery. They also believed that women should be seen and not heard, in contrast to Garrison, who wanted women to hold leadership positions within the abolitionist movement. The Tappans and their supporters left the AASS to form the American and Foreign Anti-Slavery Society.

The AASS formally disbanded in 1870. With the end of slavery and the promise of Reconstruction to achieve equal rights for blacks, the organization no longer seemed to have a purpose.

TERM PAPER SUGGESTIONS

1. The two major antislavery organizations of the first decades of the nineteenth century were the AASS and the American Colonization Society. Compare and contrast the two groups.

2. Compare and contrast the Tappan brothers with William Lloyd Garrison.

3. Both abolitionists and slaveholders based their arguments on the Bible and the Constitution. Use these two sources to show the pros and cons of each side's argument.

4. Discuss the role of women, such as AASS members Angelina and Sarah Grimke, in the abolitionist movement.

ALTERNATIVE TERM PAPER SUGGESTIONS

1. Assume that you are Lewis Tappan trying to persuade abolitionists to work through the political system or William Lloyd Garrison trying to persuade abolitionists that the Constitution and the rest of the political system are corrupt. Design a Microsoft PowerPoint presentation to convince your classmates of the correctness of your view.

2. Assume that you are one of Garrison's supporters and that you strongly believe that women should be permitted to hold leadership positions within the AASS. Prepare a Microsoft PowerPoint presentation to convince the other members of the AASS of the correctness of your view.

SUGGESTED SOURCES

Primary Sources

American Anti-Slavery Society. *Declaration of Sentiments and Constitution of the American Anti-Slavery Society.* Ithaca, NY: Cornell University Library, n.d. This pamphlet, published in 1861 on the eve of the Civil War, details the beliefs of the society.

American Anti-Slavery Society. *The Disunion: Address of the American Anti-Slavery Society; and F. Jackson's Letter on the Pro-Slavery Character of the Constitution.* Ithaca, NY: Cornell University Library, n.d. Originally published in 1845, this pamphlet is produced from digital images from the Cornell University Library Samuel J. May Anti-Slavery Collection.

American Anti-Slavery Society. *First Annual Report of the American Anti-Slavery Society: With the Speeches Delivered at the Anniversary Meeting.* Ithaca, NY: Cornell University Library, n.d. Originally printed in 1834, this pamphlet has been reproduced by Cornell from its holdings.

Quincy, Edmund. *An Examination of the Charges of Mr. John Scoble and Mr. Lewis Tappan against the American Anti-Slavery Society.* Ithaca, NY: Cornell University Library, n.d. Originally printed in 1852, this pamphlet explains the break between founders of the American Anti-Slavery Society that led to the formation of the American and Foreign Anti-Slavery Society. This latter society helped form the Liberty Party that would eventually merge with the Republican Party.

Secondary Sources

Ferrell, Claudine L. *The Abolitionist Movement.* Westport, CT: Greenwood Press, 2006. An excellent reference book on abolitionism that includes biographies of the major figures, primary source documents, and an annotated bibliography.

Ginzberg, Lori D. *Women in Antebellum Reform.* Wheeling, IL: Harlan David-son, 2000. Includes a chapter on women in the antislavery movement that explains life as an abolitionist and involvement with the American Anti-Slavery Society.

Harrold, Stanley. *The Abolitionists and the South, 1831–1861.* Lexington: University Press of Kentucky, 1995. Argues that abolitionists were active in the South, particularly in the upper South, up to the start of the Civil War.

Harrold, Stanley. *American Abolitionists.* Harlow, UK: Longman, 2001. Part of a Seminar Series in History, this is an excellent introduction to the abolitionist movement in the United States.

Kraditor, Aileen S. *Means and Ends in American Abolitionism: Garrison and His Critics on Strategy and Tactics, 1834–1850.* New York: Pantheon, 1969. Kraditor, a noted scholar of intellectual history, examines the differences between respectable and radical political action.

Sklar, Kathryn Kish. *Women's Rights Emerges Within the Antislavery Movement, 1830–1870: A Brief History with Documents.* Boston: Bedford St. Martin's, 2000. Includes an essay and primary source documents that show women's involvement in the antislavery movement, including in the American Anti-Slavery Society.

Stewart, James Brewer. *William Lloyd Garrison and the Challenge of Emancipation.* Arlington Heights, IL: Harlan Davidson, 1992. A succinct and well-written biography of the abolitionist leader.

World Wide Web

"The Abolitionist Movement by James Brewer Stewart." http://afgen.com/abmovement.html. Good overview of the abolitionist movement drawn from *Reader's Companion to American History.*

"American Abolitionism." http://americanabolitionist.liberalarts.iupui.edu/docs.htm. Provides links to primary sources, including government documents, slave narratives, songs, letters, and document collections relating to abolition.

"American Antislavery Society." http://www.ohiohistorycentral.org/entry.php?rec=832. This project of Ohio History Central contains an excellent summary of the AASS with a bibliography and links to related topics.

"The Antislavery Literature Project." http://antislavery.eserver.org. The Antislavery Literature Project includes antislavery documents, including hymns. It views the antislavery movement as the beginning of a multicultural society.

Multimedia Source

Arizona State University Antislavery Ensemble Performing Jairus Lincoln's 1843 collection, Anti-Slavery Melodies: For the Friends of Freedom. http://
antislavery.eserver.org/video/antislaveryensemble/arizona-state-
university-antislavery-ensemble.html/. This is a video, available in Real
Player format, of the performance of antislavery songs.

22. *Amistad* Mutiny (1839)

On June 18, 1839, the Spanish ship *Amistad* sailed from Havana, Cuba
with a cargo of 54 illegally imported Africans belonging to José Ruiz
and Pedro Montes. The Africans were to be sold as slaves in Puerto Prin-
cipé in east-central Cuba. Four nights later, the Africans freed themselves
from their chains, mutinied, killed the ship's captain and cook, sent two
crewmen overboard, and instructed two surviving crewmen to sail for
Africa. The mutineers were led by Joseph Cinque.

The *Amistad* landed at Long Island, New York on August 26, after
being seized in the Atlantic by a U.S. Coast Guard brig under the command of Lieutenant Thomas Gedney. The U.S. State Department recommended that the Spanish minister take custody of the *Amistad* and its
jailed cargo. When the Africans were indicted for piracy, Lewis Tappan
and other abolitionists established the Amistad Committee to raise money
for their defense. Meanwhile, the Spanish government claimed the
Africans as its property and demanded their return. The case moved from
district court to circuit court and arrived before the Supreme Court in late
1840.

Antislavery activists took an interest in the case and convinced former
president John Quincy Adams to defend the Africans. Adams had not
practiced law in years. He hesitated to take such an emotional case in part
because he feared that his antislavery zealotry would diminish his ability
to provide a cool, rational defense. Nevertheless, Adams stood before the
Supreme Court for over four hours on February 24, 1841 and again on
March 1 to present arguments that ranged from the minute wording of
shipping laws to the ideals of the Declaration of Independence.

On March 9, 1841, Chief Justice Roger B. Taney, a Maryland slaveowner who later decided the 1857 *Dred Scott* case, found the Africans
innocent of murder and piracy. He ruled that they were free and should

be allowed to return to Africa. The 35 surviving Africans, aided by the defense committee and Yale University's Divinity School, sailed for Sierra Leone in November 1841 to serve as Christian missionaries and provide positive examples of returned-to-Africa blacks for the American Colonization Society.

Cinque and his African companions remained an important symbolic presence for slaves in the United States because they seized freedom. After the end of slavery, the *Amistad* mutineers continued as examples of the black will to persevere for justice against great odds.

TERM PAPER SUGGESTIONS

1. Discuss how abolitionists used the *Amistad* case to further the antislavery cause, draw attention to the plight of slaves, and raise funds for the defense of the Africans.

2. Outline all the legal issues involved in the *Amistad* case, including maritime salvage rights, criminal law, and international law.

ALTERNATIVE TERM PAPER SUGGESTIONS

1. In the wake of the *Amistad* decision, successive presidents asked Congress to compensate Spain for the loss of property, partly as a way to reduce tensions with the Spanish. Assume that you are a member of the cabinet of an incoming president. Argue for or against giving compensation to Spain.

2. Put yourself in the shoes of an attorney arguing the *Amistad* case before the Supreme Court. Explain why you believe that the Africans should be found innocent and freed to return to Africa.

3. Assume that you are a reporter for a newspaper. Write an op-ed piece to make people aware of the *Amistad* case and the issues surrounding slavery.

4. There are a number of works of art that memorialize the *Amistad* mutiny. Create your own work of art or rap song to illuminate the case.

5. Create a YouTube video that explains the significance of the *Amistad* case.

6. Create a Web page to pay tribute to Joseph Cinque or to John Quincy Adams.

7. Joshua R. Giddings, an antislavery member of the House of Representatives from Ohio, supported both the *Amistad* mutineers and a group of slaves who, in 1842, mutinied and sailed to the Bahamas to get freedom. For his efforts, he was censured by Congress. Assume that you are Giddings. Write a speech to deliver to Congress upon being censured.

SUGGESTED SOURCES

Primary Sources

Adams, John Quincy. *Amistad Argument.* Whitefish, MT: Kessinger, 2004. Reprints Adams's argument before the Supreme Court.

The Amistad Case: The Most Celebrated Slave Mutiny of the Nineteenth Century. New York: Johnson Reprint, 1968. Provides correspondence between the United States and Spanish governments regarding the mutiny as well as John Quincy Adams's Supreme Court argument.

"National Archives Administration—Teaching With Documents: The *Amistad* Case." http://www.archives.gov/education/lessons/amistad/. Contains the full text of many of the documents relating to the mutiny, including the Supreme Court decision.

Tappan, Lewis. *African Captives: Trial of the Prisoners of the Amistad on the Writ of Habeas Corpus* ... Ithaca, NY: Cornell University Press, 2007. Reprints abolitionist Tappan's work in support of the Africans.

Secondary Sources

Cable, Mary. *Black Odyssey: The Case of the Slave Ship Amistad.* New York: Viking Press, 1971. Good overview of the case, including arguments made before the Supreme Court.

Jones, Howard. *Mutiny on the Amistad: The Saga of a Slave Revolt and Its Impact on American Abolition, Law, and Diplomacy.* New York: Oxford University Press, 1987. Provides a scholarly analysis of the case, focusing on the trial testimony and legal briefs presented to the court.

Kromer, Helen. *Amistad: The Slave Uprising Aboard the Spanish Schooner.* Philadelphia, PA: Pilgrim Press, 1997. Brief overview of the case.

Martin, Christopher. *The Amistad Affair.* New York: Abelard-Schuman, 1970. Brief history of the case and an epilogue that charts the reemergence of the *Amistad* case in public memory.

Myers, Walter Dean. *Amistad.* New York: Puffin, 2001. Aimed at high school students, this work uses letters, speeches, and other primary sources to tell the story of the *Amistad* mutiny along with a summation of its moral and legal outcomes.

Nagel, Paul C. *John Quincy Adams: A Public Life, A Private Life.* New York: Random House, 1997. In one of the best accounts of Adams's life, the author uses the former president's diaries to cover his role in arguing the *Amistad* mutiny.

Osagie, Iyunola Folayan. *The Amistad Revolt: Memory, Slavery, and the Politics of Identity in the United States and Sierra Leone.* Athens: University of

Georgia Press, 2000. Addresses the lives of the *Amistad* mutineers in Sierra Leone.

Owens, William A. *Black Mutiny: The Revolt on the Schooner Amistad.* Philadelphia, PA: Pilgrim Press, 1968. A re-creation of the mutiny and court case using primary source dialogue.

Williams, John, et al. *Amistad.* New York: Cherry Lane Music, 1998. This is sheet music for piano and voice with selections drawn from the John Williams soundtrack to the Steven Spielberg film. Color photos from the film, as well as historical background and commentary from both Williams and Spielberg are included.

Zeinert, Karen. *The Amistad Slave Revolt and American Abolition.* North Haven, CT: Linnet Books, 1997. Sets the revolt in the context of the abolition movement.

World Wide Web

"The *Amistad* Case." http://www.npg.si.edu/col/amistad/index.htm. Provides an overview of the mutiny and biographies of the leading characters, including Joseph Cinque and John Quincy Adams.

"The *Amistad* Revolt." http://usa.usembassy.de/etexts/soc/amistad.pdf. Provides a lengthy history of the case as well as quotes from primary sources and links to other sites. It includes a letter from Kali, the only male child among the *Amistad* captives.

"*Amistad* Story Ties Into Roots of United Methodist Church in Africa." http://gbgm-umc.org/umhistory/sierra-leone/amistad2.html. Gives a brief account of the role played by Methodist missionaries in the *Amistad* case.

"Famous American Trials—*Amistad* Trials, 1839–1840." http://www.law.umkc.edu/faculty/projects/ftrials/amistad/AMISTD.HTM. One of the best sites devoted to the case, this site provides all available primary materials related to the case as well as a timeline, biographies, and maps.

Multimedia Sources

Amistad. Universal City, CA: DreamWorks, 1997. 2 DVDs. Fictional and very powerful account of the *Amistad* case directed by Steven Spielberg.

Amistad Slave Revolt Case Documents. N.P.: Paperless Archives, 2008. CD. 260 pages of printed text and documents related to the *Amistad* slave revolt case.

The Voyage of La Amistad. Oak Forest, IL: MPI Home Video, 1998. DVD. The most historically accurate visual source on the *Amistad* case, this documentary explores the issues surrounding the case.

23. *Narrative of the Life of Frederick Douglass, Written by Himself* Is Published (1845)

Frederick Douglass was the most famous African American activist of the nineteenth century. A former slave, he wrote and spoke of his experiences with slavery while arguing for the freedom of those still in bondage.

Born into slavery in 1818 near Easton, Maryland as Frederick Bailey, he never knew his white father and only occasionally visited his mother. At the age of six, he was sent to work on a wheat plantation. Two years later, he became a house slave in Baltimore. As there were laws against teaching slaves to read and write, Douglass managed to teach himself these skills. He began studying discarded newspapers and learned of the growing national debate over slavery. Moved by the sight of black men reading and speaking in church, Douglass bought a rhetoric book. He would later be known as one of the best public speakers of the era.

Increasingly resistant to being captive, Douglass started a secret school for slaves that a mob of local whites destroyed. Shipped out to a local farmer with a reputation for being a "slave breaker," Douglass refused to allow himself to be whipped. He then started a second school for slaves that was also discovered. After being sent by his master to work in a Baltimore shipyard, Douglass tried to purchase his freedom but failed. Disguised as a sailor with the papers of a free black seaman, he escaped by train and boat to New York City.

He adopted the name of Douglass to confuse slavecatchers. While attending antislavery meetings, he occasionally spoke about his experiences as a slave. Impressed by Douglass's eloquence, the Massachusetts Anti-Slavery Society hired him as a lecturer. Speaking out against slavery could be dangerous. Such lecturers were often the targets of insults, thrown objects, and mob violence. As a fugitive slave, Douglass had the added risk of being caught. To ensure his continued freedom, he had to change or omit details in his life story, including names, dates, and locations.

Douglass's skill as a speaker combined with his reluctance to provide specifics about his slave past prompted critics to question whether he had ever indeed been a slave. Some white abolitionists advised him to be less eloquent and more like the stereotype of a slave. In response, Douglass published his autobiography with the full details of his life.

The *Narrative of the Life of Frederick Douglass, Written by Himself* appeared in 1845.

It sold more than 30,000 copies in the United States and Britain within five years and was translated into French, German, and Dutch. Along with his public lectures, the book made Frederick Douglass the most famous black person in the world.

Now a famous fugitive slave, Douglass risked being caught by slave-catchers. He went to Europe for two years. English antislavery activists eventually purchased his freedom, permitting Douglass to return home. In 1848, he started a weekly newspaper, *North Star,* which promoted abolitionism, African Americans' rights, temperance, women's rights, and a host of related reforms. He worked for the Underground Railroad, urged violent resistance to the Fugitive Slave Act, and suggested that slaves use violence to gain their freedom. When the antislavery Republican Party formed in 1856, he backed it. After the Civil War, he worked to gain equal citizenship for African Americans. He died in 1895.

TERM PAPER SUGGESTIONS

1. Douglass suggested that slaves use violence to gain their freedom. Discuss the merits and faults of this approach.

2. Frustrated at the inability of blacks to gain full freedom in the United States, Douglass once considered moving to Haiti. The island nation had become the first in the Western Hemisphere to end slavery, and it long served as a model to many African Americans. Investigate the history of slavery in Haiti.

3. Black and white abolitionists occasionally disagreed over tactics. Compare and contrast Douglass with his one-time friend and mentor, abolitionist William Lloyd Garrison.

4. Douglass used his autobiography to argue that blacks deserved freedom. Discuss how he presented this argument.

5. Douglass gained his freedom in two ways: by running away and through purchase. Discuss the many ways in which slaves could become free.

ALTERNATIVE TERM PAPER SUGGESTIONS

1. One of Douglass's best-known speeches is "What, to the Slave, is the Fourth of July?" It can be found at www.teachingamericanhistory.org/library/index.asp?document. Create a speech arguing that in the land of the free, slavery should be immediately abolished.

2. Compare and contrast life as a slave with life as a free person of color in the North. Create a podcast urging slaves to flee to the North.

SUGGESTED SOURCES

Primary Sources

Blassingame, John W., ed. *The Frederick Douglass Papers.* New Haven, CT: Yale University Press, 1979. Many of Douglass's papers were lost in a fire in his home in the 1870s. His surviving letters, speeches, interviews, and other papers are reprinted in this collection.

Douglass, Frederick. *Life and Times of Frederick Douglass: His Early Life as a Slave, His Escape from Bondage, and His Complete History: An Autobiography.* New York, Gramercy Books, 1993. Douglass updated his autobiography toward the end of his life. It can also be found at http://metalab .unc.edu/docsouth/douglasslife/menu.html.

Douglass, Frederick. *My Bondage and My Freedom.* New York: Penguin, 2003. Douglass wrote a second autobiography in 1855. It is less well known and had less impact than his *Narrative.* The entire text of this book is available through Google at http://books.google.com/books?id=rak-JAAAAIAAJ&dq=%22my+bondage+and+my+freedom%22+frederick&pg=PP1&ots=z2–KT4qxD&sig=x_Gt-_l29V9xRt2QPOYtA6u Ouo0&hl=en&sa=X&oi=book_result&resnum=1&ct=result, or type the title and author into the search engine.

Gates, Henry Louis, Jr. *The Classic Slave Narratives.* New York: Signet, 2002. Gates, one of the foremost historians of the black experience, provides a good introduction to Douglass's narrative.

Meltzer, Milton, ed. *Frederick Douglass in His Own Words.* San Diego: Harcourt Brace, 1995. Reprints many of Douglass's speeches and writings.

Meyer, Michael. *The Narrative and Selected Writings of Frederick Douglass.* New York: Modern Library, 1983. A good edition of Douglass's works. The original version of the autobiography can be found at http://metalab .unc.edu/docsouth/douglass/menu.html.

Secondary Sources

Factor, Robert L. *The Black Response to America: Men, Ideals, and Organization, from Frederick Douglass to the NAACP.* Reading, MA: Addison-Wesley, 1970. A bit dated in that it does not consider the contributions of black women, but still a good study of forms of resistance to oppression.

Kendrick, Paul, and Stephen Kendrick. *Douglass and Lincoln: How a Revolutionary Black Leader and a Reluctant Liberator Struggled to End Slavery and Save the*

Union. New York: Walker, 2008. Shows that Douglass shaped Lincoln's thinking about slavery and influenced the Emancipation Proclamation.

McFeely, William S. *Frederick Douglass.* New York: W.W. Norton, 1991. A good standard biography of Douglass.

Oakes, James. *The Radical and the Republican: Frederick Douglass, Abraham Lincoln, and the Triumph of Antislavery Politics.* New York: W.W. Norton, 2007. Similar to the Kendrick book but more readable.

Stauffer, John. *The Black Hearts of Men: Radical Abolitionists and the Transformation of Race.* Boston: Harvard University Press, 2002. Discusses a convention of abolitionists held in 1855 that attracted John Brown, Gerrit Smith, Frederick Douglass, and James McCune-Smith. Douglass backed Brown and nearly joined his attack on Harper's Ferry in 1859.

Sweeney, Fionnghuala. *Frederick Douglass and the Atlantic World.* Liverpool, UK: Liverpool University Press, 2007. Discusses Douglass's interactions with British opponents of slavery.

Wu, Jin-Ping, *Frederick Douglass and the Black Liberation Movement: The North Star of American Blacks.* New York: Routledge, 2000. Focuses on Douglass's impact upon other African American leaders.

World Wide Web

"Africans in America: Frederick Douglass." http://www.pbs.org/wgbh/aia/part4/4p1539.html. A biographical sketch of Douglass with links to related primary sources.

"Frederick Douglass National Historic Site." http://www.nps.gov/archive/frdo/freddoug.html. Includes a link to an online museum exhibit about Douglass.

"The Frederick Douglass Papers." http://lcweb2.loc.gov/ammem/doughtml/doughome.html. This Library of Congress site permits Douglass's papers to be searched by keyword or name.

Multimedia Sources

Black Americans of Achievement: Frederick Douglass. Bala Cynwyd, PA: Schlessinger, 1992. VHS. A simple biography of Douglass aimed at secondary school students.

The Black Press: Soldiers Without Swords. San Francisco: CA: Half Nelson, 1998. Shows the impact of the black press, including Douglass's newspaper.

Frederick Douglass: When the Lion Wrote History. Atlanta, GA: Turner Home Entertainment, 1994. VHS and DVD. Very good biography of Douglass.

24. Sojourner Truth Gives "Ain't I a Woman?" Speech (1850)

Sojourner Truth combined activism on women's rights with abolitionism to become one of the best-known African American women of the nineteenth century. Only Harriet Tubman rivaled her for fame, but the shy Tubman never took public positions. Truth is most famous for her public utterings, including the speech, "Ain't I a Woman?"

Born into slavery in New York as Isabella Baumfree, Truth suffered both physical and sexual abuse at the hands of several owners. She was sold four times during her life and was forced to marry a slave named Thomas. The couple had five children together. Truth purchased her freedom in 1826 and successfully sued to gain the freedom of one of her children. Deeply religious by this time, she preached while working as a maid.

In 1843, Baumfree changed her name to Sojourner Truth and became a traveling preacher. The new name symbolized her calling to travel the land while spreading the word of God. After becoming friends with abolitionists such as Frederick Douglass and William Lloyd Garrison, Truth published her memoir, *The Narrative of Sojourner Truth*. By 1850, Truth spoke across the North on behalf of women's rights, abolitionism, religion, and temperance. In 1851, she spoke at the Annual Ohio Women's Rights Convention, where she reportedly delivered "Ain't I a Woman?" The speech may have been created subsequently by a biographer. Nevertheless, it does capture the sentiments of a woman who was accorded none of the privileges presumably due her sex and all the penalties forced upon her race.

Truth spent the Civil War procuring supplies for African American troops and campaigning for President Abraham Lincoln's reelection. After the war, she raised money for the Freedman's Aid Society and successfully challenged segregation on the streetcars in Washington, D.C. By the time of her death in 1883, Truth had became a public celebrity as well as an enormously admired woman.

TERM PAPER SUGGESTIONS

1. Discuss life as a female slave.
2. Compare and contrast the lives of the two most famous African American women of the nineteenth century, Sojourner Truth and Harriet Tubman.
3. Discuss the challenges unique to women who were abolitionists.

ALTERNATIVE TERM PAPER SUGGESTIONS

1. Create a virtual art gallery of images that illustrate Sojourner Truth's life and times. Include text that describes the images and how they illuminate Truth's era.

2. Every schoolchild for generations has learned about Harriet Tubman. Fewer students are familiar with Sojourner Truth, perhaps because she is a more complicated figure. Pay Truth her due. Create a Web site that explains who this woman was and why we should care about her.

SUGGESTED SOURCES

Primary Sources

"Ain't I a Woman? Delivered by Sojourner Truth." http://afroamhistory .about.com/library/blsojourner_truth_womanspeech.htm. This About .com: African American History site includes Truth's speech and historical background on the speech.

"Modern History Sourcebook: Sojourner Truth: 'Ain't I a Woman?', December 1851." http://www.fordham.edu/halsall/mod/sojtruth-woman.html. Reprints Truth's famous speech in its entirety.

Truth, Sojourner. *Narrative of Sojourner Truth.* New York: Penguin, 1998. Truth's autobiography introduced by historian Nell Irvin Painter.

Secondary Sources

McKissack, Patricia C. *Sojourner Truth: Ain't I a Woman.* New York: Scholastic, 1994. Aimed at junior high students, this is a good biography of Truth that places her in the context of the antislavery movement.

Painter, Nell Irvin. *Sojourner Truth: A Life, a Symbol.* New York: W.W. Norton, 1997. The definitive biography of Truth by one of the most respected historians of black women.

World Wide Web

"Keeping the Thing Going While Things Are Stirring: Address to the First Annual Meeting of the American Equal Rights Association Delivered by Sojourner Truth on May 9, 1867." http://www.pacifict.com/ron/ Sojourner.html. Reprints a less well-known Truth speech.

"Narrative of Sojourner Truth." http://digital.library.upenn.edu/women/truth/ 1850/1850.html. Reprints the full text of Truth's biography.

"Sojourner Truth Institute." http://www.sojournertruth.org/. A public history organization dedicated to spreading knowledge about Truth and continuing her mission.

"Sojourner Truth, the Libyan Sibyl, by Harriet Beecher Stowe." http://etext.virginia
.edu/etcbin/toccer-new2?id=StoSojo.sgm&images=images/modeng&data
=/texts/english/modeng/parsed&tag=public&part=1&division =div1.
Reprints an April 1863 *Atlantic Monthly* essay on Truth by the most famous
white female abolitionist.

"Women in History: Sojourner Truth." http://www.lkwdpl.org/wihohio/trut-soj.
htm. Extensive biography of Truth prepared by Lakewood Public
Library.

"Women in Slavery: USA." http://www.vgskole.net/prosjekt/slavrute/
slavwomen.htm. Part of a UNESCO series on Women and Families in
Slavery, this site includes links to primary and secondary source documents.

Multimedia Sources

Black Americans of Achievement: Sojourner Truth. Wynnewood, PA: Schlessinger,
1992. VHS. A short biography targeted at secondary school students.

Life of Sojourner Truth: Ain't I a Woman? St. Louis, MO: Phoenix Learning
Group, 2008. DVD. Short biography of the political activist.

Side By Side: Reenactments of Scenes from Women's History, 1848 to 1920. Galaxia
Historical Record, 1978. LP. Includes a re-creation of the "Ain't I a
Woman?" speech.

Sojourner Truth: I Sell the Shadow. Las Vegas: Women of Diversity Productions.
VHS. Actor Kim Russell portrays Truth.

What If I Am a Woman?, Vol. 1: Black Women's Speeches by Ruby Dee. Washington,
DC: Smithsonian Folkways Recording, 1977. MP3 recording. Originally
issued as an LP, this album contains re-creations of several of Truth's speeches.

25. Compromise of 1850

The Compromise of 1850 was one of the last attempts by Congress to
end the differences over slavery that divided the nation. In contrast to
the expectations of some of the most prominent political leaders in
American history, the legislation failed magnificently. The collapse of the
compromise pointed out the impossibility of reconciling the North and
the South over the issue of slavery.

The compromise was a series of five pieces of legislation passed
between August and September 1850. The measures, designed by Senator
Henry Clay of Kentucky, chiefly addressed the question of whether slavery would be permitted or prohibited in the lands acquired from Mexico

as a result of the Treaty of Guadeloupe Hidalgo that ended the Mexican-American War. In two of the measures, the South gave ground to the North. Southern legislators agreed to end the slave trade in Washington, D.C. and admit California to the Union as a free state. The admission of another free state ended forever the balance of free and slave states, thereby swinging political power in Congress away from the South. The Texas and New Mexico Act established New Mexico as a territory and paid Texas for its claims upon the lands east of the Rio Grande. Texas received $10 million, enough to pay off its debt. The Utah Act established another territory that might or might not act to exclude slavery.

The final measure destroyed several political careers as well as the compromise. While the Constitution contained a fugitive slave law, it lacked teeth and was generally ignored. The Fugitive Slave Act of 1850 had teeth. It provided for the return of runaway slaves to their masters. It also unintentionally encouraged the kidnapping of free blacks by slavecatchers. The law denied fugitive blacks a jury trial and provided that commissioners received a fee of $10 when they sent an African American to slavery. For freeing an alleged fugitive slave, commissioners received only $5. In addition, federal marshals could require citizens to help capture runaway slaves. Failure to aid marshals could result in imprisonment and fines of up to $1,000. The legislation widened and deepened antislavery sentiment in the North.

TERM PAPER SUGGESTIONS

1. Compare and contrast the Missouri Compromise with the Compromise of 1850. Both tried to settle the dispute over slavery. Did they instead put the nation on the road to the Civil War?

2. Explain the circumstances that prompted legislators to compromise in 1850.

3. The legislators of the antebellum years have been faulted by historians for failing to adequately address the divisions that would ultimately split the nation in 1861, when the Civil War began. Can you propose any compromise on slavery that might have satisfied both sides, or was it too late for compromise? Discuss.

4. Daniel Webster, arguably the most famous statesman of the antebellum era, sought to preserve the Union with the Compromise of 1850. Instead, he resigned from office under a cloud. Examine the career of Webster.

5. Discuss the implementation of the Fugitive Slave Act and its effects upon local law enforcement. You might want to focus on a particular case, such as that of Anthony Burns.

ALTERNATIVE TERM PAPER SUGGESTIONS

1. Create a Microsoft PowerPoint presentation that shows the main components needed to get the Compromise of 1850 passed through Congress. Diagram how the bill proceeded into law.

2. Create a Microsoft PowerPoint presentation to explain to northern whites why they should refuse to cooperate with the Fugitive Slave Act.

3. Write a story, diary, or letter describing how it might feel to suddenly lose personal freedom.

SUGGESTED SOURCES

Primary Sources

Chase, Salmon P. *Union and Freedom, Without Compromise: Speech of Mr. S. P. Chase, of Ohio, in the Senate of the United States, March 26–27, 1850, on the Compromise Resolutions . . . by Mr. Clay on the 25th of January.* Ithaca, NY: Cornell University Library, n.d. Originally printed in 1850, this pamphlet contains the objection to the compromise by the man who would serve in President Lincoln's cabinet during the Civil War.

Webster, Daniel. *Webster and Hayne's Celebrated Speeches in the United States Senate, on Mr. Foot's Resolution of January, 1830: Also Daniel Webster's Speech in the Senate . . . on the Slavery Compromise.* Ithaca, NY: Cornell University Press, n.d. Originally printed in 1863, this volume contains Webster's speech on the Compromise of 1850. Webster was one of the most famous speakers of his day.

Secondary Sources

Hamilton, Holman. *Prologue to Conflict: The Crisis and Compromise of 1850.* Lexington: University Press of Kentucky, 2005. A concise discussion of the compromise and the larger issues that led the United States into the Civil War.

Holt, Michael F. *The Political Crisis of the 1850s.* New York: W.W. Norton, 1983. Examines why slavery became a critical national issue in the 1850s after being on the nation's back burner since the founding of the United States and blames the crisis on a political breakdown.

Potter, David M. *The Impending Crisis, 1848–1861.* New York: Harper Perennial, 1977. A massive work that examines the reasons for the Civil War, including the failure of the Compromise of 1850.

Waugh, John C. *On the Brink of Civil War: The Compromise of 1850 and How It Changed the Course of American History.* Wilmington, DE: SR Books,

2003. Engaging and concise history of the compromise, with a focus on the personalities of the major legislators.

World Wide Web

"Africans in America: The Compromise of 1850 and the Fugitive Slave Act." http://www.pbs.org/wgbh/aia/part4/4p2951.html. Summarizes the legislation and includes a link to a primary source about captured slave Anthony Burns, as well as a link to explanation of the act by historian Eric Foner.

"March 7, 1850 Speech Costs Senator His Seat." http://www.senate.gov/artand history/history/minute/Speech_Costs_Senator_His_Seat.htm. Discusses Daniel Webster's famous speech in which he defended the Fugitive Slave Act.

"Primary Documents in American History: Compromise of 1850." http://www.loc.gov/rr/program/bib/ourdocs/Compromise1850.html. Contains a brief history of the legislation as well as a link to the full text of the compromise.

"Treasures of Congress: Struggles Over Slavery: The Compromise of 1850." http://www.archives.gov/exhibits/treasures_of_congress/page_11.html. Produced by the National Archives and Records Administration, this site includes both a discussion of the compromise and links to primary sources.

26. Underground Railroad Increases Its Efforts to Aid Runaway Slaves (1850)

The Underground Railroad became the most significant and wide-ranging protest against slavery in the United States prior to the Civil War. Not nearly as organized as its name implies, the Underground Railroad aided slaves who were traveling through the South to freedom in the North. In the wake of the Fugitive Slave Act of 1850, many slaves did not stop running until they reached Canada.

The beginnings of the Railroad are very murky, befitting a secret organization. It apparently began during the colonial period, when Quakers acted on their opposition to slavery by assisting blacks who sought to escape to freedom. One of the earliest references to the Underground Railroad appears in a 1797 letter by President George Washington, who blames the Quakers for the escape of one of his slaves. As abolitionist activity increased, the Railroad grew stronger. It reached its peak between 1830 and 1865.

Considerable risks came with escaping from slavery or aiding those who were escaping from slavery. Historians estimate that only 1 of every 40 slaves successfully escaped with the numbers of successfully escaped slaves placed at anywhere from 60,000 to 100,000. Slaves who failed to escape often kept trying until they succeeded. Those slaves who were captured could expect, at minimum, to be whipped as an example to others and as warning to never again try to escape. Slavecatchers were known to track slaves to the homes of reputed members of the Underground Railroad. Several shoot-outs are known to have occurred between slavecatchers and the defenders of slaves.

In accord with the high risks, the Underground Railroad relied upon code words to maintain secrecy. "Conductors" helped slaves travel along their route to freedom, often escorting them to a safe place to rest. The most famous conductor was ex-slave Harriet Tubman, codenamed "Moses" for her uncanny ability to lead her people to safety. "Station keepers" offered food and clothing. "Lines" were established escape routes that took slaves across the Ohio River, into Ohio and north or up to New England or Canada. Slaves sang songs, such as "Follow the Drinking Gourd," that contained messages about how to successfully escape. The reference in this particular song is to astronomy. The Big Dipper in the sky led to the North Star, which pointed the way to the North and freedom. Quilts also contained maps within the designs.

TERM PAPER SUGGESTIONS

1. Harriet Tubman is, by far, the most famous conductor on the Underground Railroad. Discuss Tubman's motivation, the challenges that she faced, and the methods that she used to succeed.

2. Compare and contrast the lives of African American conductor William Still and white conductor Levi Coffin.

3. Report on the history of the Underground Railroad in your hometown.

4. Examine the lives of American slaves who fled to Canada. Did they find a warm welcome?

ALTERNATIVE TERM PAPER SUGGESTIONS

1. Take a look at the "Passage to Freedom" Web site. Create a similar Web page for your city or town listing the local buildings that played a role in the struggle over slavery.

2. Accept the National Park Service's challenge to educate the public about the Underground Railroad by creating a YouTube video to inform your peers about it.

3. Imagine that you are a runaway slave and plan an escape. Choose your route, pick your time, and discuss the other factors that will determine whether or not you succeed.

4. Create a chapter of a graphic novel that features panels relating to the Underground Railroad. (You may want to use "Comic Life" software available from the Plasq.com Company.)

SUGGESTED SOURCES

Primary Sources

Hendrick, George. *Fleeing for Freedom: Stories of the Underground Railroad as Told by Levi Coffin and William Still.* Condenses Coffin's *Reminiscences* (1876) and Still's *Underground Rail Road* (1872). Chicago: Ivan R. Dee, 2004. Coffin was a white Quaker conductor in Indiana, while Still was a free black who aided runaway slaves in Pennsylvania.

Humez, Jean M. *Harriet Tubman: The Life and the Life Stories.* Madison, WI: University of Wisconsin Press, 2003. Contains a biographical sketch of the famed conductor as well as some of her diary entries, letters, and speeches.

Siebert, Wilbur. *The Underground Railroad from Slavery to Freedom: A Comprehensive History.* New York: Dover, 2006. Contains over 500 pages of interviews and excerpts from diaries, letters, biographies, memoirs, speeches, and other firsthand accounts collected by Siebert over the span of his long career.

Still, William. *The Underground Railroad: Authentic Narratives and First-Hand Accounts.* New York: Dover, 2007. A Philadelphia-based conductor, Still helped guide fugitive slaves to safety in the years before the Civil War. This is a collection of documents that he preserved, including letters, newspaper articles, and firsthand accounts about refugees' hardships and narrow escapes.

Secondary Sources

Bordewick, Fergus. *Bound for Canaan: The Underground Railroad and the War for the Soul of America.* New York: Amistad, 2006. Comprehensive and highly readable account of the Railroad by a journalist.

Calarco, Tom. *People of the Underground Railroad: A Biographical Dictionary.* Westport, CT: Greenwood Press, 2008. Profiles 100 important figures involved in the Underground Railroad.

Tobin, Jacqueline L. *From Midnight to Dawn: The Last Tracks of the Underground Railroad.* New York: Anchor, 2008. Examines the Canadian end of the escape route.

Tobin, Jacqueline L., and Raymond G. Dobard. *Hidden in Plain View: A Secret Story of Quilts and the Underground Railroad.* New York: Anchor, 2000. Reports that slaves created coded quilts to help each other escape to freedom. Stitching and knots created maps in the quilts with wagon wheels and log cabins indicating aids to escape.

Wagner, Tricia Martineau. *It Happened on the Underground Railroad.* Guildford, CT: TwoDot, 2007. Provides short biographies of individuals involved with the Railroad.

World Wide Web

"Aboard the Underground Railroad: A National Register of Historic Places Travel Itinerary." http://www.nps.gov/history/nr/travel/underground/. Identifies and describes 64 Underground Railroad sites throughout the United States as well as the most common escape routes.

"Anna L. Curtis's *Stories of the Underground Railroad.*" http://www.shockfamily .net/underground/. Reprints a 1941 book aimed at children that contains biographies of Underground Railroad workers.

"Code Words in the Underground Railroad." http://www.angelfire.com/me2/ ugrrmania/lingo.html. Lists the words used by slaves and conductors.

"History of the Drinking Gourd." http://quest.arc.nasa.gov/ltc/special/mlk/ gourd1.html. Provides the history of a song that helped runaway slaves locate the way to freedom. The words to the song can be found at: http:// www.montgomeryschoolsmd.org/curriculum/socialstd/grade5/Drinking _Gourd.html.

"National Geographic Online Presents the Underground Railroad." http:// www.nationalgeographic.com/railroad/. Interactive site that lets the viewer assume the role of a escaping slave and make choices along the Underground Railroad.

"National Underground Railroad Freedom Center." http://www.freedom center.org/. Provides a history of the Underground Railroad along with a timeline and a link to historic Railroad sites. The center includes a museum about the Railroad.

"National Underground Railroad Network to Freedom." http://www.nps.gov/ history/ugrr/. National Park Service site dedicated to promoting knowledge about the railroad.

"Passage to Freedom: Discovering Ohio's Underground Railroad History." http://passagetofreedomohio.org/. Allows visitors to explore buildings used for the Underground Railroad in cities and towns across Ohio.

Multimedia Sources

American Experience: Roots of Resistance: A Story of the Underground Railroad. Boston: WGBH, 1989. DVD and VHS. Arguably the best representation of the Railroad.

Race to Freedom: The Story of the Underground Railroad. Santa Monica, CA: Xenon, 1994. DVD. Fictionalized account of four slaves who follow the Railroad into Canada.

Steal Away: Songs of the Underground Railroad. West Chester, PA: Appleseed Records, 1998. CD and MP3. Kim and Reggie Harris perform songs used by escaping slaves, including "Follow the Drinking Gourd."

Underground Railroad. The History Channel, 2003. DVD. Very good documentary about the Railroad that blends interpretation by historians with actors reading from primary documents. An extra relates the biography of former slave Frederick Douglass.

Whispers of Angels: A Story of the Underground Railroad. Janson Media, 2004. DVD. Actors Edward Asner and Blair Underwood reenact the story of the Railroad in an entertaining film.

A Woman Called Moses. Santa Monica, CA: Xenon, 1978. DVD and VHS. Cicely Tyson plays conductor Harriet Tubman in an exceptionally well-done fictionalized account of Tubman's life.

27. Harriet Beecher Stowe's *Uncle Tom's Cabin* Is Published (1851)

In 1862, Ohio author and abolitionist Harriet Beecher Stowe met President Abraham Lincoln while she was visiting Washington, D.C. Lincoln reportedly said, "So you're the little woman who wrote the book that started this Great War!" When Stowe published *Uncle Tom's Cabin* in 1852, the book sold 300,000 copies in that year alone. It became the basis of the most popular play in American history. Readers and theatergoers who had never read an antislavery editorial in a newspaper were shocked at scenes of cruelty, violence, and sexual abuse that were well-known to abolitionists. Stowe's book ranks next to the Bible as the most significant literary influence upon American history.

Stowe came from a family famed for its dedication to helping others. Her father, Lyman Beecher, a minister in the Congregational Church, served as president of Lane Theological Seminary in Cincinnati. Stowe's sister, Catherine Beecher, pioneered in the education of girls by opening a female academy. In this atmosphere, it is not surprising that Stowe took up the most pressing issue of her day.

During the 1830s, Stowe became an abolitionist. Cincinnati lay in Ohio, directly across from the Ohio River. The state, next to the slave state of Kentucky, served as beacon of liberty to thousands of slaves who streamed across the Ohio River to freedom. Stowe met some of the runaways through friends and heard their stories. She would later combine these tales with accounts from conductors to form the basis of her book, *Uncle Tom's Cabin*. Although the work is fictional, it is grounded in extensive research.

Stowe might never have picked up her pen if not for the Fugitive Slave Act of 1850. Like many of her friends, Stowe passionately objected to the federal government actively assisting slaveowners in reclaiming their property. In 1850, Stowe and her husband moved to Brunswick, Maine. She realized that few northerners had any experience with slavery and that most northern whites had no idea of the brutality of the practice. *Uncle Tom's Cabin*, which famously featured a young slave mother leaping across ice flows on the Ohio River with her baby in arms and slavecatchers on her heels, brought slavery to vivid life. The book made it easy for whites who had never met a slave to sympathize with slaves and to view slaveholders as despicable creatures who raped, beat, and split families with impunity.

Upon publication of the book, Stowe became an instant celebrity. She took advantage of this fame to encourage other people to protest slavery. Following the Civil War, Stowe continued to write prolifically. She published 30 books before her death in 1893, but none proved as far-reaching as *Uncle Tom's Cabin*.

TERM PAPER SUGGESTIONS

1. Stowe used language that stressed the humanity of African Americans as well as the similarities between whites and blacks. Discuss the ways in which Stowe portrayed blacks.

2. Supporters of slavery criticized *Uncle Tom's Cabin* for being a work of fiction. They argued that Stowe had exaggerated the lives of slaves for dramatic effect. Investigate this claim. Did slaves indeed live as Stowe wrote?

3. Imagine "what if" Stowe had never written her book. Do you believe that Lincoln was correct when he credited her, partly in jest, with starting the Civil War?

ALTERNATIVE TERM PAPER SUGGESTIONS

1. Write a review of Stowe's book for a northern newspaper.
2. Imagine that you a white resident of Maine learning about the truth of slavery for the first time. In a diary entry, describe your reaction to *Uncle Tom's Cabin.*

SUGGESTED SOURCES

Primary Sources

Stowe, Harriet Beecher. *A Key to Uncle Tom's Cabin; Presenting the Original Facts and Documents Upon Which the Story Is Founded. Together With Corroborative Statements Verifying the Truth of the Work.* Bedford, MA: Applewood, 1853. Harriet Beecher Stowe wrote this book in answer to those who questioned the basis of truth of her novel, *Uncle Tom's Cabin.* Includes a comprehensive collection of her research material.

Stowe, Harriet Beecher. *Uncle Tom's Cabin.* New York: W.W. Norton, 1994. This edition, with an introduction by Elizabeth Ammons, includes a collection of responses to the novel.

Secondary Sources

Crozier, Alice C. *The Novels of Harriet Beecher Stowe.* New York: Oxford University Press, 1969. Discusses Stowe's fictional works, including *Uncle Tom's Cabin.*

Hedrick, Joan D. *Harriet Beecher Stowe: A Life.* New York: Oxford University Press, 1994. Pulitzer Prize-winning biography of the author.

Hedrick, Joan D., ed. *The Oxford Harriet Beecher Stowe Reader.* New York: Oxford University Press, 1999. A collection of Stowe's writings from the 1830s through the 1860s with a section devoted to her antislavery writings.

Wagenknecht, Edward. *Harriet Beecher Stowe: The Known and the Unknown.* New York: Oxford University Press, 1965. Although the language is dated, this remains a solid biography of the author.

White, Barbara Anne. *The Beecher Sisters.* New Haven, CT: Yale University Press, 2003. A good history of a famous family of activist women.

World Wide Web

"Harriet Beecher Stowe." http://womenshistory.about.com/od/stoweharriet/ Harriet_Beecher_Stowe.htm. Includes a biography, photographs, and links to writings by and about the author.

"Harriet Beecher Stowe Center." http://www.harrietbeecherstowecenter.org/index_home.shtml. The Stowe Center commemorates the life of the abolitionist author. The Web page includes a biography of Stowe and links to primary sources under "Teacher and Student Resources."

"Harriet B. Stowe." http://www.ohiohistorycentral.org/entry.php?rec=360. Provides a biography of Stowe as well as bibliography of related books and links to related entries, such as the one for *Uncle Tom's Cabin* at http://www.ohiohistorycentral.org/entry.php?rec=1405&nm=Uncle-Toms-Cabin.

"*Uncle Tom's Cabin* and American Culture." http://jefferson.village.virginia.edu/utc/. This extensive University of Virginia site includes texts, images, songs, and film clips that illustrate the impact of *Uncle Tom's Cabin* and its evolution as an American phenomenon.

"Uncle Tom's Cabin Historic Site." http://www.uncletomscabin.org/. Introduces the Ontario, Canada, home of Reverend Josiah Henson, the inspiration behind Uncle Tom.

Multimedia Sources

Josiah Henson—The Real Uncle Tom. RBC Ministries, n.d. The Reverend Josiah Henson inspired part of Stowe's book. This is his biography, filmed partly at Uncle Tom's Cabin Historic Site. It is useful as a good account of a man's movement from slavery to freedom with heavy emphasis on religion.

Uncle Tom's Cabin. Kino Video, 1999. DVD and VHS. This is a reprint of a 1927 silent film, one of the most expensive ever made. While the film has its gripping moments, the stereotypical portrayal of African Americans may be offensive to twenty-first-century eyes. The DVD version includes an essay by historian David Pierce.

Uncle Tom's Cabin. Republic Pictures, 1997. VHS. This version of the book stars Avery Brooks and Phylicia Rashad. It remains faithful to Stowe's work.

28. Kansas-Nebraska Act Establishes Popular Sovereignty (1854)

The Kansas-Nebraska Act, another attempt at a compromise over the expansion of slavery, put the nation on the fast track to the Civil War. In the wake of the passage of Kansas-Nebraska, the Whig Party collapsed and died. Northern Whigs eventually helped to form the antislavery Republican Party. Kansas deteriorated into open warfare between supporters and opponents of slavery, essentially entering the Civil War before it was officially declared.

The legislation began innocently enough as an attempt to build a transcontinental railroad that would link the East with the West. Stephen A. Douglas, a senator from Illinois, wanted the eastern end of the railroad to be located in Chicago. Accordingly, he proposed the Kansas-Nebraska Act to establish territorial government in the lands west of Missouri and Iowa. To gain support for the bill, Douglas needed the support of southerners. To get southern support, he had to offer concessions on slavery. Douglas wrote popular sovereignty into the bill, meaning that the people residing in the territories could vote on whether to permit slavery in those states that would form in the region.

Douglas apparently thought that popular sovereignty would quiet the debate over slavery. However, he failed to appreciate the depth of antislavery feelings. When Douglas proposed to repeal the Missouri Compromise as a further concession to supporters of slavery, six antislavery congressmen publicly attacked him. This protest quickly spread across the North as editorials, sermons, speeches, and petitions all attacked Douglas and his bill. However, Douglas had enough votes to get the measure passed, and he did so.

Everyone agreed that Nebraska would be free. No such agreement existed over Kansas. Antislavery and proslavery organizations sent settlers to Kansas. Many other migrants to Kansas did not want blacks in the territory for reasons of racism. As the dispute grew more heated, both sides armed themselves. In 1856, a proslavery mob attacked the antislavery town of Lawrence to burn down houses and steal property. In response, radical abolitionist John Brown and his supporters hacked five proslavery men to death in front of their screaming families in the Pottawatomie Massacre. "Bleeding Kansas" had begun.

TERM PAPER SUGGESTIONS

1. Senator Douglas served as a director of the Illinois Central Railroad and a land speculator. Discuss what he personally had to gain economically from placing the transcontinental railroad in Chicago and discuss the consequences of his actions.

2. Analyze the political implications of the Kansas-Nebraska Act.

3. Discuss John Brown's antislavery beliefs and his role in the abolition movement.

4. Discuss the clash between antislavery and proslavery forces in Kansas. What role did the state play in the Civil War?

ALTERNATIVE TERM PAPER SUGGESTIONS

1. Write a newspaper editorial in opposition to Senator Douglas's Kansas-Nebraska Act.
2. Create an advertisement designed to persuade abolitionists to move to Kansas.

SUGGESTED SOURCES

Primary Sources

"Kansas-Nebraska Act." http://www.loc.gov/rr/program/bib/ourdocs/kansas.html. This Library of Congress site has created one of the best sources on the Kansas-Nebraska Act with maps, images, speeches, and letters.

"Kansas-Nebraska Act 1854." http://www.ourdocuments.gov/doc.php?flash =true&doc+28. Provides the full text of the legislation along with background material.

Malin, James C. "The Motives of Stephen A. Douglas in the Organization of Nebraska Territory: A Letter Dated December 17, 1853." *Kansas Historical Quarterly* 19 (November 1951): 321–53. (Available in JSTOR.) Explains that Douglas backed the Kansas-Nebraska Act as a means of boosting the economy of his home state by running a transcontinental railroad through Illinois, then on to Kansas and Nebraska.

Seward, William Henry. *Freedom and Public Faith: Speeches of William H. Seward on the Abrogation of the Missouri Compromise, in the Kansas and Nebraska Bills: Delivered in . . . United States, February 17 and May 26, 1854.* Ithaca, NY: Cornell University Library Press, 2006. Includes the full text of Seward's attack on the Kansas-Nebraska Act.

"Territorial Kansas—Online 1854–1861." http://www.territorialkansas .online.org/cgiwrap/imlskto/index.php. This is an excellent site with primary source documents, maps, lesson plans, links, a timeline, a bibliography, and images of historic sites related to the Kansas-Nebraska Act.

"Transcript of the Kansas-Nebraska Act 1854." http://www.ourdocuments.gov/ doc.php?flash=false&doc=28&page=transcript. Provides the full text of the legislation.

Secondary Sources

Gienapp, William E. *The Origins of the Republican Party, 1852–1856.* New York: Oxford University Press, 1987. Examines the collapse of the Whig Party and the rise of the Republican Party out of the ashes of the Know-Nothing Party.

Holt, Michael F. *The Political Crisis of the 1850s.* New York: W.W. Norton, 1978. Explores the social and economic factors that contributed to the 1850s crisis and the start of the Civil War.

Johannsen, Robert W. *Stephen A. Douglas.* New York: Oxford University Press, 1973. The standard biography of the senator from Illinois.

McArthur, Debra. *The Kansas-Nebraska Act and Bleeding Kansas in American History.* Berkeley Heights, NJ: Enslow, 2003. Written for secondary school students, this is an excellent overview of the issues and personalities involved with the legislation.

McPherson, James W. *Battle Cry of Freedom: The Era of the Civil War.* New York: Oxford University Press, 1988. One of the greatest historians of the Civil War discusses the issues, including the Kansas-Nebraska Act, that led to the war.

Morrison, Michael. *Slavery and the American West: The Eclipse of Manifest Destiny and the Coming of the Civil War.* Chapel Hill: University of North Carolina Press, 1999. Explains the connection between slavery, the Kansas-Nebraska Act, and the coming of the Civil War.

Nichols, Roy Franklin. "The Kansas-Nebraska Act: A Century of Historiography." *Mississippi Valley Historical Review* 43 (September 1956): 187–212. (Available in JSTOR.) Discusses the legislative history, debates, and consequences of the legislation.

Waugh, John C. *On the Brink of Civil War: The Compromise of 1850 and How It Changed the Course of American History.* Washington, DC: Scholarly Resources, 2003. Analyzes the Compromise of 1850 and how it sowed the seeds for future clashes over popular sovereignty in the admission of new states to the Union.

Wolff, Gerald. *The Kansas-Nebraska Bill: Party, Section, and the Coming of the Civil War.* New York: Revisionist Press, 1977. Examines how the breakdown of the two-party system over the Kansas-Nebraska Act contributed mightily to the Civil War.

World Wide Web

"Kansas: Its Interior and Exterior Life." http://www.kancoll.org/books/robinson/r_intro.htm. Written in 1856 by Sara L. Robinson, wife of the first governor of the free state of Kansas, this online book describes life in the state during the era of Bleeding Kansas.

"The Kansas-Nebraska Act and the Rise of the Republican Party, 1854–1865." http://lincoln.lib.niu.edu/biography6text.html. Contains an overview of the legislation and describes how it helped give rise to the Republican Party.

Multimedia Source

The Civil War: A Nation Divided. Silver Spring, MD: Discovery Channel, 2005.
DVD. This documentary includes coverage of the passage of the Kansas-Nebraska Act.

29. Senator Charles Sumner Is Attacked in the Senate (1856)

In 1854, an uneasy truce created by the Compromise of 1850 collapsed when Senator Stephen Douglas introduced the Kansas-Nebraska Act. Douglas aimed to aid the rapid settlement of the West by allowing the people of the Kansas and Nebraska territories to determine the slavery question by popular vote. As the time for the vote in Kansas approached, opponents and proponents of slavery moved into the territory and armed themselves to persuade others to vote "correctly." A guerilla war then began in 1855 in which over 200 people lost their lives.

Violence over the Kansas issue spread to Congress. In May 1856, Massachusetts Senator Charles Sumner delivered a speech before the Senate popularly known as "The Crime Against Kansas." A noted abolitionist, Sumner harshly criticized South Carolina Senator Andrew P. Butler with highly inflammatory words that reflected his disgust with slavery. The speech precipitated an assault upon Sumner a few days later by Butler's nephew, Representative Preston Brooks. Brooks came up behind Sumner when the latter was seated at his desk in the Senate. Brooks struck the unsuspecting Sumner repeatedly with a metal-topped cane as Sumner tried to rise from his seat and defend himself. After only a minute or so, the Massachusetts man lay unconscious in a pool of blood. Brooks then walked out of the Senate as stunned onlookers did nothing. So seriously injured that he did not return to the Senate for three years, Sumner became a "living martyr" to the antislavery cause as well as a symbol of the brutality of supporters of slavery. For their part, southerners sent new canes to Brooks, now a hero in that region.

The assault seemed to prove the Republican charge that the South would stop at nothing to spread slavery and would not even allow civilized debate on the issue. The violence directed at Sumner convinced many northerners to abandon the Know-Nothing Party for the Republican cause, as it seemed to indicate that the "Slave Power" posed a more immediate menace than immigrants and Catholics. This helped the Republicans replace the Know Nothings as the most powerful party in the North, initiating the second phase of the slavery crisis.

TERM PAPER SUGGESTIONS

1. Analyze why Preston Brooks and the southerners who sent him replacement canes approved of a physical attack upon an abolitionist senator.
2. Explain how this attack marked a step in the march toward the Civil War.
3. Sumner delivered a speech that definitely qualified as the rhetoric of a radical abolitionist. Research Sumner's life to explain why he took a radical stance toward slavery.
4. Explore the risks taken by abolitionists who made their views public.

ALTERNATIVE TERM PAPER SUGGESTIONS

1. Assume that you are a fellow senator, an abolitionist, and a friend to Charles Sumner. Prepare a speech that is a response both to the "Crime Against Kansas" speech and the attack upon Sumner.
2. Prepare a podcast that reports on the crime for a northern audience. Explain what happened, why it happened, and what the assault means for the United States.

SUGGESTED SOURCES

Primary Source

Sumner, Charles. *The Crime Against Kansas: The Apologies for the Crime, the True Remedy, Speech of Hon. Charles Sumner, in the Senate of the United States, 19th and 20th May, 1856.* Ithaca, NY: Cornell University Library, n.d. Reprint of a holding in the Cornell University Library.

Secondary Sources

Donald, David Herbert. *Charles Sumner and the Coming of the Civil War.* New York: Random House, 1960. Covers Sumner's life through the Kansas-Nebraska Act and up to the start of the Civil War.

Donald, David Herbert. *Charles Sumner and the Rights of Man.* New York: Knopf, 1970. A companion book to *Charles Sumner and the Coming of the Civil War,* this work addresses Sumner's philosophy.

Potter, David M. *The Impending Crisis: 1848–1861.* New York: Harper and Row, 1976. A exhaustive study of the causes, including the Crime Against Sumner, that led to the Civil War.

World Wide Web

"Africans in America: Bleeding Kansas." http://www.pbs.org/wgbh/aia/part4/ 4p2952.html. Sets the attack upon Sumner in the context of the Kansas-Nebraska Act.

"Charles Sumner." http://www.nndb.com/people/458/000050308/. A biography of the senator.

"Charles Sumner of Massachusetts." http://www.iath.virginia.edu/seminar/ unit4/sumner.html. Reprints the "Crime Against Kansas" speech that prompted Brooks's attack.

"May 22, 1856: The Caning of Senator Charles Sumner." http://www.senate .gov/artandhistory/history/minute/The_Caning_of_Senator_Charles _Sumner.htm. Created by the U.S. Senate, this site contains a summary of the event.

30. George Fitzhugh of Virginia Argues the Benefits of Slavery (1857)

As the antislavery movement gained strength, supporters of slavery developed their own arguments for the maintenance of the peculiar institution. George Fitzhugh, a Virginia attorney and slaveholder, became the most vocal proponent of slavery. With several publications, especially *Cannibals All!* in 1857, he argued that slavery served the public good.

Supporters of slavery generally offered four major arguments to justify keeping human beings in bondage. First, the Bible appears to offer support for slavery. In the Old Testament, Ham is cursed into slavery for seeing Noah naked, and the people of Israel owned slaves. In the New Testament, Paul advises slaves to obey their masters and accept their lot in life. Secondly, the Constitution mentions slavery in the 3/5 Compromise, with respect to the slave trade, and by including a fugitive slave law. Since the Constitution is the law of the land, the legal framework of the United States supports slavery. Third, the science of the nineteenth century appeared to demonstrate that African people were racially inferior with smaller brains and shapes. (Obviously, there were major flaws with the research designs of these "scientific" studies.) Slavery supporters argued that these physical differences meant that Africans were a separate species made to serve whites. Lastly, slavery proponents used sociological arguments by suggesting that people of African ancestry were not educated or capable of living on their own. Therefore, they needed the guidance and protection of whites. Slavery, in essence, served as a means of protecting blacks.

Fitzhugh became the major advocate of the sociological view of slavery. Born in 1806 to a slaveholding family, he became distressed in the 1840s by the increasing numbers of free blacks in Virginia and the resistance to the extension of slavery into the territories gained as a result of the Mexican-American War. In 1849, he published his first pamphlet, *Slavery Justified.* He spent the next few years justifying slavery through essays in newspapers and magazines. In 1854, he published the first book with sociology mentioned in the title, *Sociology for the South.* The book suggested that slavery was both natural and beneficial. It proved especially popular with southern readers.

Fitzhugh had traveled through the North and had read about the poor treatment given to factory workers in England. In response to Harriet Beecher Stowe's novel *Uncle Tom's Cabin* and the growth of abolition in the North, he published *Cannibals All! Or, Slaves Without Masters.* In this book, he argued that slavery proved more humane than the factory system prevalent in the North. In the factories, the employer assumed no responsibility for the worker beyond the payment of wages since labor was a commodity. In the South, the master took responsibility for the well-being of the slaves by providing food, medical care, and caring for the aged. While Fitzhugh defined blacks as belonging to the human race in *Cannibals All!,* he changed his mind within a few years to designate blacks as members of an inferior species.

An ardent supporter of the Confederacy, Fitzhugh survived the Civil War, possibly to his regret. After the war, he became a judge in the Freedmen's Court, which was part of the Freedmen's Bureau. He did not change his views toward blacks, thereby illustrating some of the problems with the Freedmen's Bureau.

TERM PAPER SUGGESTIONS

1. Contrast Fitzhugh's claims about slavery with the accounts of slavery from ex-slaves and historians.
2. Challenge Fitzhugh's notion that slavery served as a means of protecting blacks.

3. While supporters of slavery cited the Bible, many of the most dedicated abolitionists also drew inspiration for their activism from the Bible. Investigate the religious beliefs of antislavery activists, perhaps with a focus on the Quakers.

4. Compare and contrast Harriet Beecher Stowe's *Uncle Tom's Cabin* with one of Fitzhugh's writings.

5. Compare and contrast the views of George Fitzhugh with those of a white southerner opposed to slavery, perhaps Hinton Rowan Helper, Sarah Grimke, or Angelina Grimke.

ALTERNATIVE TERM PAPER SUGGESTIONS

1. Write a review of *Cannibals All!* for a northern newspaper in a city with many factory workers.

2. Fitzhugh died in Kentucky in 1877. Write his obituary for an African American newspaper.

SUGGESTED SOURCES

Primary Sources

"Africans in America: George Fitzhugh Advocates Slavery." http://www.pbs.org/wgbh/aia/part4/4h3141t.html. Reprints Fitzhugh's "The Universal Law of Slavery."

Finkelman, Paul, ed. *Defending Slavery: Proslavery Thought in the Old South: A Brief History with Documents.* New York: Bedford/St. Martin's, 2003. A very readable discussion of proslavery beliefs accompanied by letters and essays from defenders of slavery.

Fitzhugh, George. "The Blessings of Slavery." 1857. http://occawlonline .pearsoned.com/bookbind/pubbooks/divine5e/medialib/timeline/docs/sources/theme_primarysources_Slavery_16.html. Provides the full text of this essay.

Fitzhugh, George. *Cannibals All! Or, Slaves Without Masters.* Cambridge, MA: Belknap Press of Harvard University Press, 1960. Edited by noted historian of the South C. Vann Woodward, this is Fitzhugh's best-known work.

Fitzhugh, George. *Sociology for the South; Or, The Failure of Free Society.* New York: B. Franklin, 1965. A good edition of Fitzhugh's influential book.

McKitrick, Eric L., ed. *Slavery Defended: The Views of the Old South.* Englewood Cliffs: Prentice-Hall, 1963. Fifteen leaders of the antebellum South defend slavery as a system of labor and as a social institution through letters, essays, and poetry.

Wish, Harvey, ed. *Antebellum Writings of George Fitzhugh and Hinton Rowan Helper on Slavery.* New York: Capricorn, 1960. Helper was a southerner who harshly criticized slavery.

Secondary Sources

Berlin, Ira, Marc Favreau, and Steven F. Miller, eds. *Remembering Slavery: African Americans Talk about Their Personal Experiences of Slavery and Emancipation.* New York: The New Press, 1998. Based largely on the interviews with former slaves conducted by the Works Progress Administration in the 1930s, this is a good counterpoint to Fitzhugh's claims.

Faust, Drew Gilpin. *The Ideology of Slavery: Proslavery Thought in the Antebellum South, 1830–1860.* Baton Rouge: Louisiana State University Press, 1981. An intellectual history of slaveholding designed for an advanced audience.

Owens, Leslie Howard. *This Species of Property: Slave Life and Culture in the Old South.* New York: Oxford University Press, 1976. Uses plantation records and the autobiographies of former slaves to provide a full description of slave life.

White, Deborah Gray. *Ar'n't I a Woman?: Female Slaves in the Plantation South.* New York: W.W. Norton, 1999. This is the standard history of what it meant to be a female slave.

World Wide Web

"George Fitzhugh." http://www.faculty.fairfield.edu/faculty/hodgson/Courses/City/fitzhugh/george.html. Includes an essay by Eugene Genovese about Fitzhugh as well as excerpts from Fitzhugh's *Sociology for the South.*

"George Fitzhugh, 1806–1881." http://docsouth.unc.edu/southlit/fitzhughcan/bio.html. Contains a biography of Fitzhugh as well as links to the full texts of *Cannibals All!* and *Sociology for the South.*

31. *Dred Scott* Decision (1857)

Dred Scott came before the U.S. Supreme Court in 1856 to request his freedom from slavery. When the Court ruled against him, it set the nation inexorably on the path to the Civil War.

Scott, born in Virginia about 1800, had moved to the territories of the upper Midwest with his master in the 1830s. These territories, above the Ohio River, did not permit slavery according to the provisions of the Northwest Ordinance. Scott married another slave and had two daughters, both of whom belonged to his owner. Upon the death of his master,

Scott and his family became the property of a widow in St. Louis, Missouri. In 1846, Scott petitioned for the freedom of his entire family, charging that their residence in free territory entitled them to free status.

The *Dred Scott* case came before the Supreme Court when Roger B. Taney sat as its chief justice. An elderly slaveowner from Maryland, Taney sought to resolve once and for all the question of whether the United States was a slave country with pockets of freedom or a free country with pockets of slavery. Rejecting all compromise, Taney and six other justices ruled in March 1857 that the United States was a slave country with no pockets of freedom permitted. In his opinion, Taney denied that Scott had any standing to bring the case to court in the first place. He notoriously declared that African Americans were "so far inferior that they had no rights which the white man was bound to respect." Since Scott had never been a citizen, he could not use the courts of the United States. Going further, Taney stated that Congress never possessed the right to restrict slavery in the territories. He then declared the Missouri Compromise to be unconstitutional and void.

The *Dred Scott* decision brought joy to white southerners. To Republicans, the decision meant that slavery could now spread into the states that had abolished the practice as well as those that had never allowed it. The decision enraged supporters of freedom for blacks as well as those Americans who opposed the expansion of slavery on economic grounds.

TERM PAPER SUGGESTIONS

1. Ideally, the Supreme Court is to be free from political considerations. Justices are expected to make their ruling strictly on the basis of the law. Discuss whether Roger B. Taney allowed his personal feelings about slavery and the political situation in 1857 to determine his ruling.

2. Roger B. Taney planned to settle the slavery dispute once and for all. Examine the reaction to the *Dred Scott* case.

3. Discuss the legacy of the *Dred Scott* case with respect to the Civil War.

4. Compare and contrast the majority and minority opinions in *Dred Scott* with those in *Plessy v. Ferguson*. Both cases are examples of ways in which the Constitution can be interpreted to promote inequality.

ALTERNATIVE TERM PAPER SUGGESTIONS

1. Write an editorial for an antislavery newspaper about the *Dred Scott* decision. At this point, what options were left to opponents of slavery?

2. The Republican Party used the *Scott* case to help galvanize supporters. It warned that the transatlantic slave trade would resume and that slavery would return to Massachusetts and New York, among other states. Assume that you a Republican leader in 1857. Create a podcast explaining the significance of the decision to other Republicans.

SUGGESTED SOURCES

Primary Sources

Finkelman, Paul, ed. *Dred Scott v. Sandford: A Brief History with Documents.* New York: St. Martin's Press, 1997. Finkelman, one of the foremost legal historians, provides a wonderful history of *Dred Scott* as well as primary documents relating to the case.

"60 U.S. 393 *Scott v. Sandford.*" http://www.law.cornell.edu/supct/html/historics/ USSC_CR_0060_0393_ZS.html. This stellar site sponsored by Cornell University Law School includes the individual opinions of each justice, including the two dissenters.

Secondary Sources

Allen, Austin. *Origins of the Dred Scott Case: Jacksonian Jurisprudence and the Supreme Court, 1837–1857.* Athens: University of Georgia Press, 2006. Sets the case in context by looking at antebellum legal history.

Fehrenbacher, Don E. *The Dred Scott Case: Its Significance in American Law and Politics.* New York: Oxford University Press, 1978. A classic book that examines the legal ramifications of the case as well as its impact on the movement toward the Civil War.

Fleischner, Jennifer. *The Dred Scott Case: Testing the Right to Live Free.* Brookfield, CT: Millbrook Press, 1997. Aimed at secondary school students, this is the engaging story of Dred Scott and his legal case.

Graber, Mark A. *Dred Scott and the Problem of Constitutional Evil.* New York: Cambridge University Press, 2006. Argues that Taney's Court made a choice to seek peace rather than justice and made the constitutionally correct, but evil, decision.

Huebner, Timothy S. *The Taney Court: Justices, Rulings, and Legacy.* Santa Barbara, CA: ABC-CLIO, 2003. This is the best available study of Taney. It examines the decisions that Taney made during his 28 years on the Supreme Court and provides biographical information about all of the justices in this era.

Kaufman, Kenneth C. *Dred Scott's Advocate: A Biography of Roswell M. Field.* Columbia: University of Missouri Press, 1996. This is a biography of the attorney who presented Scott's case to the Supreme Court.

Maltz, Earl M. *Dred Scott and the Politics of Slavery.* Lawrence: University Press of Kansas, 2007. This publisher is well known for its excellent legal studies. This book sets the *Scott* case in the context of a United States on the brink of war over slavery.

Swisher, Carl B. *Roger B. Taney.* Hamden, CT: Archon, 1961. This is the only full-length biography of Taney that is readily available in libraries and through bookstores. It is good but suffers from the writing style of its day.

World Wide Web

"About the *Dred Scott* Case." http://www.nps.gov/jeff/historyculture/ dredscottsesquicentennial.htm. Includes a link to an electronic field trip about Scott, a short history of the case, and links to teaching materials.

"*Dred Scott* Decision: The Lawsuit That Started the Civil War." http: www.historynet.com/magazines/civil_war_times/3037746.html. Analyzes the *Scott* case and includes links to related sources.

"Dred Scott Trial." http://www.nps.gov/jeff/forteachers/upload/dred4.pdf. Part of the Jefferson National Expansion Memorial site, this page contains a 16-page mock trial transcript that can be used as a classroom resource.

"James Buchanan." http://www.whitehouse.gov/history/presidents/jb15.html. Buchanan hoped that the Supreme Court would settle the *Scott* case and end the slavery dispute before he entered office. Once in the White House, he hoped to exit before the war began. In short, Buchanan did not prove to be one of the more distinguished presidents.

"*Dred Scott v. Sandford.*" http://www.oyez.org/cases/1851-1900/1856/1856_0/. The Oyez project provides a summary of the case, the opinion of the Supreme Court, and a chronological link to similar cases on slavery.

Multimedia Sources

Dred Scott v. Sandford. http://audiocasefiles.com/featured/dredscott. Presents a short summary of the case, the full text of the opinion, and a condensed version of the opinion on audio.

"Slaves and the Court, 1740–1860." http://memory.loc.gov/ammem/sthtml/ sthome.html. This Library of Congress site allows visitors to search for the full text of over 1,000 pamphlets and books published between 1772 and 1889 about the legal concerns of slaves.

The Supreme Court. New York: Ambrose Video Publishing, 2007. DVD. The
    first disc in this series contains a discussion of *Dred Scott.*

32. John Brown's Attack on Harper's Ferry (1859)

Abolitionist John Brown's attack on Harper's Ferry in 1859 helped set the
stage for the Civil War. Brown became one of many abolitionists who
risked their lives in an attempt to end slavery. More successful and more
violent than most, he became a martyr to the antislavery cause.

Raised by an abolitionist family, Brown was a devout Calvinist who
believed that abolition was God's cause. In 1851, Brown helped found
the League of Gileadites, which attracted progressive whites, free blacks,
and runaway slaves. The primary aim of this radical group was to encourage physical resistance to the Fugitive Slave Act of 1850 and to protect
runaway slaves from pursuing slaveowners. Despite this activism, Brown's
violent streak did not fully emerge until his journey to Kansas.

In Kansas, supporters and opponents of slavery debated with guns whether
Kansas would enter the Union as a free or slave state. After one failed attempt
to destroy Lawrence, a free-state town, proslavery forces attacked again on
May 21, 1856, and destroyed it. Three days later, Brown and his group sought
out five southern settlers along Pottawatomie Creek and butchered them.
Brown picked up the nickname of "Pottawatomie Brown" and came to sym-
bolize a holy crusade against slavery. He firmly believed that God had chosen
him for a special destiny, that of ending slavery.

Brown decided that God wanted him to liberate the slaves by invading the
South and inciting a slave uprising. As he gathered a handful of conspirators
behind him, he vindicated his war on slavery on several grounds: the institution
was a barbaric and unjustifiable war on blacks, it violated God's command-
ments, and it contradicted the cherished ideals of the Declaration of Independence. By the late 1850s, Brown contended, slavery had become so entrenched in
the United States that only violent revolution could eradicate it.

The federal armory at Harper's Ferry in northern Virginia was well
stocked with arms and strategically well placed for easy access to the slave
South through the Appalachian Mountains. Brown planned to establish a
free state in the mountains to use as a base to attack slaveowners. With
21 followers, including 2 former slaves, Brown assaulted the arsenal on

October 16, 1859. The raid was well planned but not well executed. Thirty-six hours later and after 15 deaths, including several of his own sons, Brown was captured by Colonel Robert E. Lee. Taken to Charlestown, Brown impressed many people in the South and the North with the courage that he displayed as he went to his death on the scaffold. He predicted just before being hanged that the crimes of the United States would only be purged away by blood.

While most northerners praised Brown's principles, they disagreed with his methods. However, "John Brown's Body," sung to a Methodist hymn tune, became a popular song among the Union troops. In 1862, Julia Ward Howe used some of the lyrics of "John Brown's Body" to create the "Battle Hymn of the Republic." The song, especially the line, "John Brown's body lies a-mouldering in the grave, but his soul goes marching on," became synonymous with the Union cause.

TERM PAPER SUGGESTIONS

1. The Union soldiers who wrote and sung "John Brown's Body" viewed the abolitionist as a martyr to the antislavery cause whose soul marched along with them. Discuss whether Brown should be admired for his willingness to use violence to end slavery. Was he the same as the Union soldiers?

2. John Brown never succeeded in any public endeavor until he decided to massacre supporters of slavery in Kansas. Discuss Brown's impact on Kansas and the increasingly ugly national climate over slavery.

3. The most famous painting of Brown portrays him with a Bible in one hand and a gun in the other. Many abolitionists, such as the Reverend Henry Ward Beecher, urged that abolitionists spill the blood of slaveholders. Discuss the role of religion in the radical abolitionist movement.

4. Many southerners were stunned that a white man would be willing to sacrifice himself and his sons to free slaves. Examine the southern reaction to Brown's raid on Harper's Ferry.

5. Famed abolitionist and former slave Frederick Douglass nearly joined John Brown at Harper's Ferry. Other black men did fight and die alongside Brown. Investigate why these men supported Brown.

ALTERNATIVE TERM PAPER SUGGESTIONS

1. The songs that emerged from the Civil War are some of the most moving in U.S. history. Many of these songs are readily available on MP3. Download some of these songs, including "John Brown's Body." Provide context for each song and explain its importance.

2. Create a Web site that uses music and illustrations from the nineteenth century to illustrate Brown's life.

3. Create a Microsoft PowerPoint presentation that explains the reasons behind the attack at Harper's Ferry, sketches the events that day, and covers the aftermath of the raid.

SUGGESTED SOURCES

Primary Sources

DeCaro, Louis A. *John Brown—The Cost of Freedom: Selections from His Life and Letters.* New York: International, 2007. Explores the various historical interpretations of John Brown.

Quarles, Benjamin, ed. *Blacks on John Brown.* Urbana: University of Illinois Press, 1972. Includes letters, poems, and essays written about Brown from 1858 to 1972 by Langston Hughes, Frederick Douglass, W. E. B. Du Bois, and Countee Cullen.

Ruchames, Louis, ed. *A John Brown Reader: The Story of John Brown in His Own Words, in the Words of Those Who Knew Him and in the Poetry and Prose of the Literary Heritage.* New York: Abelard-Schuman, 1959. Contains Brown's views on slavery and his autobiography.

Secondary Sources

Benet, Stephen Vincent. *John Brown's Body.* Chicago, IL: Elephant, 1990. An epic poem about Brown.

Boyer, Richard O. *The Legend of John Brown: A Biography and a History.* New York: Alfred A. Knopf, 1972. Places Brown's life within the context of his times.

DeCaro, Louis A., and Louis DeCaro Jr. *Fire From the Midst of You: A Religious Life of John Brown.* New York: New York University Press, 2005. Focuses on the effect of Brown's religious beliefs upon his abolitionist activities.

Finkelman, Paul, ed. *His Soul Goes Marching On: Responses to John Brown and the Harpers Ferry Raid.* Charlottesville: University of Virginia Press, 1995. A collection of essays that examines Brown's raid and modern responses to it.

Goodrich, Thomas. *War to the Knife: Bleeding Kansas, 1854–1861.* Lincoln, NE: Bison, 2004. Examines Brown's role in the civil war in Kansas.

Oates, Stephen B. *Our Fiery Trial: Abraham Lincoln, John Brown, and the Civil War Era.* Amherst: University of Massachusetts Press, 1979. Historian Oates has a reputation as an exceptional writer. This is an entertaining account of how Nat Turner, John Brown, and Abraham Lincoln were linked in the fight against slavery.

Oates, Stephen B. *To Purge This Land With Blood: A Biography of John Brown.* Amherst: University of Massachusetts Press, 1984. The standard biography of Brown.

Peterson, Merrill D. *John Brown: The Legend Revisited.* Charlottesville: University of Virginia, 2004. Discusses the changes that Brown's reputation has undergone in light of the rise of the civil rights movement of the late twentieth century.

Renehan, Edward J. *The Secret Six: The True Tale of the Men Who Conspired with John Brown.* New York: Crown, 1995. Details the lives of the men— Thomas Wentworth Higginson, Theodore Parker, Samuel Howe, Gerrit Smith, Franklin Sanborn, and George Luther Stearns—who helped plot Brown's raid on Harper's Ferry.

Reynolds, David S. *John Brown, Abolitionist: The Man Who Killed Slavery, Sparked the Civil War, and Seeded Civil Rights.* New York: Alfred A. Knopf, 2005. Despite a title that exaggerates Brown's significance, this is a solid biography of a religious man who railed against the evils of slavery.

Stauffer, John. *The Black Hearts of Men: Radical Abolitionists and the Transformation of Race.* Cambridge, MA: Harvard University Press, 2002. Tells how abolitionists, including Frederick Douglass, responded to the raid on Harper's Ferry.

Toledo, Gregory. *The Hanging of Old Brown: A Story of Slaves, Statesmen, and Redemption.* Westport, CT: Praeger, 2002. A good biography of Brown that explains his actions by setting them in the context of his times.

World Wide Web

"Documents Resource: Harper's Ferry." http://www.dickinson.edu/departments/ hist/NEHworkshops/NEH/resource/profiles3.htm. Provides a collection of letters and images relating to Brown's raid on Harper's Ferry as a well as biographical profiles of some of the attackers.

"The Father of American Terrorism." http://www.americanheritage.com/articles/ magazine/ah/2000/1/2000_1_81.shtml. An *American Heritage* article that portrays John Brown as a terrorist.

"John Brown and the Valley of the Shadow." http://www3.iath.virginia.edu/ jbrown/master.html. Contains a biographical sketch of Brown.

"John Brown State Historic Site." http://www.kshs.org/places/johnbrown/index.htm. An online exhibit with links to resources about Brown's experiences in Kansas.

"The Last Days of John Brown by Henry David Thoreau." http://www .walden.org/Institute/thoreau/writings/essays/Last_Days.htm. Contains the full text of an essay on Brown by one of the most famed nineteenth-century advocates of civil disobedience.

Multimedia Source

John Brown's Holy War. Alexandria, VA: PBS Home Video, 1999. DVD.
A superb documentary on Brown that uses letters, speeches, and interviews with historians to make the man come alive.

33. Abraham Lincoln Issues the Emancipation Proclamation (1862)

When Abraham Lincoln issued the Emancipation Proclamation, he did not end slavery throughout the United States. He ended slavery only in the states that still remained "in rebellion against the United States" as of January 1, 1863. Thus, slavery ended in Virginia but continued to exist in Maryland until passage of the Thirteenth Amendment in 1865.

At the start of the Civil War, Lincoln promised to restore the Union but accept slavery. With several border states that permitted slavery, such as Kentucky and Maryland, still loyal to the Union, Lincoln could not afford to offend the white people of these states. The Confiscation Act of 1861 freed only the slaves used by Confederates for military purposes. The Second Confiscation Act, passed in 1862, liberated the slaves of all people who aided the Confederacy. In an action that recognized the extreme reluctance of Union commanders to return runaways to slavery, a third piece of legislation prohibited the army from sending slaves back to their owners in the border states. Finally Lincoln resolved to end slavery for war-related reasons: slave labor supported the Confederate military effort, the North needed the morale-boosting effect of a moral cause, and public opinion in the North had swung toward emancipation.

In July 1862, Lincoln privately announced plans to issue the Emancipation Proclamation. An advisor warned him to wait for a Union victory to avoid any scent of desperation. The Union victory at Antietam gave the president his opening. On September 22, 1862, he declared that all people held as slaves in the Confederacy would be forever free.

TERM PAPER SUGGESTIONS

1. Historian Benjamin Quarles stated that, "in a document proclaiming liberty, the unfree never bother to read the fine print." Do you believe that this is why Lincoln is categorized as the Great Emancipator even though he did not free all of the slaves? Discuss.

2. Describe the reaction of the South to the Emancipation Proclamation.

3. Describe the reaction of northerners—both abolitionists and the other opponents of slavery—to the Emancipation Proclamation.

4. Examine the legal powers that Lincoln used to take property away from slaveholders.

5. Describe the reaction of African Americans in the North and the South to the Emancipation Proclamation.

6. Juneteenth is the only formalized celebration of the end of slavery. The holiday originated in Texas when slaves received the news in 1865 that they had been freed nearly two years earlier by the Emancipation Proclamation. Discuss the history of Juneteenth.

ALTERNATIVE TERM PAPER SUGGESTIONS

1. Imagine that you are a slave in Virginia who has just received confirmation of the Emancipation Proclamation. Create a blog that describes your feelings about the proclamation, about Lincoln, and about the Civil War.

2. Many northerners, especially the Irish in New York City, opposed the Emancipation Proclamation. The document is identified as one of the causes of the New York City Draft Riots of 1863. Create a podcast that explains to non-abolitionist northerners why they should support emancipation.

3. Design a storyboard that shows a black person's passage through slavery to emancipation.

4. Assume that Abraham Lincoln has asked you to create a Web site for him. Introduce the visitor to Lincoln's life, to his views on slavery, and to his reasons for issuing the Emancipation Proclamation. A sample Web site for a historical figure can be found at http://www.webquests.comptonhistory.com/Equiano%20webquest.htm.

SUGGESTED SOURCES

Primary Sources

Cuomo, Mario M., and Harold Holzer, eds. *Lincoln on Democracy.* New York: HarperCollins, 1990. Collects Lincoln's speeches, letters, and diary entries about freedom and equality.

"Emancipation Proclamation." http://www.loc.gov/rr/program/bib/ourdocs/EmanProc.html. This Library of Congress site is one of the best on the document, giving its full text, biographical sketches, images, and more.

"Emancipation Proclamation, 1863." http://www.archives.gov/exhibits/american
_originals_iv/sections/emancipation_proclamation.html. Provides the full
text of the proclamation, images, and letters about it.

"I Will Be Heard: Abolitionism in America." http://rmc.library.cornell.edu/aboli-
tionism/index.htm. Contains a summary and the full text of the proclamation as well as letters, newspaper articles, and diary entries relating to it.

Secondary Sources

Beschloss, Michael. *Presidential Courage: Brave Leaders and How They Changed
America 1789–1989.* New York: Simon and Schuster, 2007. Includes a
discussion of the risks involved with issuing the Emancipation
Proclamation.

Donald, David Herbert. *Lincoln.* New York: Simon and Schuster, 1995. A solid
biography of Lincoln that shows him as a man plagued by self-doubts.

Ewan, Christopher. "The Emancipation Proclamation and British Public Opinion." *The Historian* 67 (March 22, 2005): 1–19. Also available at http://
www.encyclopedia.com/doc/1G1-135466323.html. This journal is aimed
at undergraduate history majors, making it more readable than most historical journals. This article shows that Lincoln, by making the Civil War
into a fight against slavery, forced the British to reconsider their support
of the South. Great Britain had abolished slavery decades earlier.

Franklin, John Hope. *The Emancipation Proclamation.* Garden City, NJ: Doubleday, 1963. One of the most distinguished African American historians
sets the document within historical context.

Gienapp, William E. *Abraham Lincoln and Civil War America: A Biography.* New
York: Oxford University Press, 2002. Examines Lincoln's life during the war.

Guelzo, Allen C. *Lincoln's Emancipation Proclamation: The End of Slavery in
America.* New York: Simon and Schuster, 2004. Winner of the Lincoln
Prize, this book examines why the Emancipation Proclamation has raised
doubts among African Americans about Lincoln's motives and why its
language is bland compared with Lincoln's other proclamations.

Holford, David M. *Lincoln and the Emancipation Proclamation.* Berkeley
Heights, NJ: Enslow, 2002. Aimed at the secondary school market, this
is a good overview of the various issues surrounding the document.

Holzer, Harold, et al. *The Emancipation Proclamation: Three Views.* Baton
Rouge: Louisiana State University Press, 2006. Presents opinions by
three historians about the reaction and impact of the Emancipation Proclamation on the North and the South.

McPherson, James M. *Abraham Lincoln and the Second American Revolution.*
New York: Oxford University Press, 1990. McPherson is one of the

foremost historians of the Civil War. This book is a collection of his essays comparing the Civil War to the American Revolution.

McPherson, James M. *The Struggle for Equality: Abolitionists and the Negro in the Civil War and Reconstruction.* Princeton, NJ: Princeton University Press, 1964. Shows how abolitionists pressured Lincoln to free the slaves.

Neely, Mark E., Jr. *The Last Best Hope of Earth: Abraham Lincoln and the Promise of America.* Cambridge, MA: Harvard University Press, 1993. Examines how Lincoln developed as a national leader and preserved the Union.

Roberts, Russell. *Lincoln and the Abolition of Slavery.* San Diego, CA: Greenhaven, 2000. Reviews Lincoln's role in freeing the slaves.

Silvana, R. Siddali. *From Property to Person: Slavery and the Confiscation Acts, 1861–1862.* Baton Rouge: Louisiana State University Press, 2005. Discusses the relationship between the Confiscation Acts and the Emancipation Proclamation.

World Wide Web

"Juneteenth.com." http://www.juneteenth.com/. This site is devoted to promoting Juneteenth by providing a short history of it, links to celebrations throughout the United States, and a gift store.

"Mr. Lincoln and Freedom." http:www.mrlincolnandfreedom.org/home.html. Aimed at teachers, this site provides lesson plans along with related links, biographical sketches, and a summary of the debate over the proclamation.

Multimedia Sources

Abraham and Mary Lincoln: A House Divided. New York: PBS, 2001. DVD. Biography of the Lincolns that shows challenges over the issue of slavery.

The Civil War—A Film by Ken Burns. New York: PBS Paramount, 2004. DVD. Contains segments on the Emancipation Proclamation and the New York City Draft Riots.

The Fight for Freedom. New York: Ambrose Video, 2005. DVD. Short segment of the series A History of Black Achievement in America that focuses on the Emancipation Proclamation.

34. Blacks Enlist in the 54th Massachusetts Regiment (1863)

Unwanted at first, treated poorly by the Union, and in danger of being enslaved or slaughtered if captured by the Confederates, African

American men nevertheless rushed to join the fight against slavery and for the preservation of the United States. When they were permitted to fight, black soldiers helped make a strong case for equal rights by proving that they could match white men on the battlefield.

Black men tried to volunteer for service as soon as President Abraham Lincoln called for troops in April 1861. Participation in military service had long been viewed as a sacred rite of citizenship reserved for white men only. Local recruiters rejected black volunteers. Only after the Emancipation Proclamation of 1863 did the Union admit African American soldiers.

The popular 1989 movie *Glory* immortalized the Civil War's 54th Massachusetts Regiment and depicted New England as the heart of the U.S. Colored Troops (USCT) movement. Most African American men who served with the Union did not enlist in New England. Of the roughly 180,000 men in the USCT, only about 38,000 belonged to units raised in northern free states. A greater number, about 42,000, joined in the slave states loyal to the Union: Maryland, Delaware, Missouri, and Kentucky. The remainder of the USCT soldiers came from Confederate territory. Slaves fled their homes in such great numbers to enlist in black Union regiments that the institution of slavery began to dissolve throughout the South.

Many men, black and white, enlisted to find glory on the battlefield. They discovered that a soldier's life consisted chiefly of boredom. Most days were spent either marching or in camp. The tedium would be broken only infrequently by the terror of combat. The Confederates refused to grant prisoner-of-war status to captured African American soldiers, either enslaving them or summarily executing them on the battlefield. White Union soldiers and officers routinely belittled black soldiers as unfit for combat. Black men quickly realized that only extraordinary heroism in battle would help to erode the prejudice against them. Black troops brought themselves honor at Vicksburg, Milliken's Bend, Port Hudson, and Fort Wagner. At the 1864 Battle of New Market Heights in Virginia, five black men earned the Medal of Honor for heroism.

TERM PAPER SUGGESTIONS

1. Trace the history of black soldiers in one state, perhaps Massachusetts or Ohio, in the Civil War.
2. Discuss the history of the Medal of Honor. What did winning the medal mean for African Americans?

3. Discuss the difficulties facing African American soldiers in the Civil War. You might want to focus on the Battle of Saltville, also known as the Saltville Massacre. Details of this case can be found on http://members.home.net:80/5thuscc/.

4. Explore why black men joined the military during the Civil War. What did they hope to achieve? Did they succeed in reaching their goals?

5. Discuss how white citizens in the South and in the North viewed black soldiers.

ALTERNATIVE TERM PAPER SUGGESTIONS

1. Create a poster to persuade African American men to join the Union military.

2. Create a Web site to challenge the idea that most of the U.S. Colored Troops came from the state of Massachusetts and to honor the men who served from other states. If your state played a role in the Civil War, you might want to focus on the men from your state.

3. Write an editorial for an African American newspaper urging black men to volunteer for military service with the Union.

SUGGESTED SOURCES

Primary Sources

Adams, Virginia M., ed. *On the Altar of Freedom: A Black Soldier's Civil War Letters from the Front: Corporal James Henry Gooding.* Boston: University of Massachusetts Press, 1991. Gooding belonged to the 54th Massachusetts.

Emilio, Luis F. *A Brave Black Regiment.* Cambridge, MA: Da Capo Press, 1995. Captain Luis F. Emilio (1844–1918) emerged as the acting commander of the 54th Massachusetts after the rest of the unit's officers were left dead or wounded at the 1863 Battle of Fort Wagner.

"Freedmen and Southern Society Project: The Black Military Experience." http://www.inform.umd.edu/ARHU/Depts/History/Freedman/bmepg.htm. Provides only a few documents relating to the black troops, but the selected documents are very powerful, including a letter from the mother of a member of the 54th Massachusetts to President Lincoln condemning the Confederate practice of killing black prisoners.

Redkey, Edwin S. *A Grand Army of Black Men: Letters from African-American Soldiers in the Union Army, 1861–1865.* New York: Cambridge University Press, 1992. Nineteenth-century Americans who wrote letters often expected that the letters would be preserved as part of family history. This collection shows both how black men felt about their service and what they wanted to share with a broader audience.

Ward, Andrew. *The Slaves' War: The Civil War in the Words of Former Slaves.* Boston: Houghton Mifflin, 2008. This is the only book to create a narrative history of the war told by the very people it freed. It is also exceptionally well written and a riveting read. While African American soldiers are not the focus, the book does include discussion of black troops.

Secondary Sources

Buckley, Gail Lumet. *American Patriots: The Story of Blacks in the Military from the Revolution to Desert Storm.* New York: Random House, 2002. This is a general history of the military involvement of African Americans.

Cornish, Dudley Taylor. *The Sable Arm: Negro Troops in the Union Army, 1861–1865.* Lawrence: University Press of Kansas, 1987. The standard history, first published in 1966, of black troops in the Union.

Haskins, Jim. *Black, Blue, and Gray: African Americans in the Civil War.* Aimed at younger high school students, this book is a good history of blacks, with coverage of African Americans who served in Confederate units.

Washington, Versalle F. *Eagles on Their Buttons: A Black Infantry Regiment in the Civil War.* Columbia: University of Missouri Press, 1999. Examines the first black regiment from Ohio, the Fifth Regiment of Infantry, United States Colored Troops.

World Wide Web

"The African American Experience in Ohio, 1850–1920." http://dbs.ohiohistory.org/africanam. Created by the Ohio Historical Society, this site contains a database of materials related to black Ohioans. It includes material on the USCT and its legacy, although patience is needed with the cumbersome search and browse functions. The documents in the site are not related to each other in any formal way, and little context is provided.

"The African American Odyssey: A Quest for Full Citizenship." http://memory.loc.gov/ammem/aaohtml/exhibit. The Library of Congress drew on its extensive American Memory digital collection to build this online exhibit. The Civil War section contains much material on the USCT, including Frederick Douglass's orders to recruit black soldiers in the Union-held areas around Vicksburg, Mississippi. The site also includes USCT regimental flags and coverage of Christian A. Fleetwood of the Fourth USCT, who won the Medal of Honor for heroism at the Battle of New Market Heights.

"The Battle of Olustee." http://extlab1.entnem.ufl.edu/olustee. Three USCT units fought in this battle. The site provides an informative account of the battle and an analysis of the contribution of the black soldiers.

"5th Regimental Cavalry, United States Colored Troops." http://members
.home.net:80/5thuscc/. Outlines the experiences of the Fifth USCT, lists
the engagements in which it participated, and links to the regimental roster. Four of the battles are linked to detailed information from the
National Park Service or historic newspapers. This site is notable for its
extraordinarily good discussion of the Battle of Saltville.

"The Fight for Equal Rights: Black Soldiers in the Civil War." http://www/
nara.gov/education/teaching/usct/home.html. Aimed at teachers, this site
includes a good history of the USCT with links to primary documents.

"Fort Scott National Historic Site." http://www.nps.gov/fosc/. A small site but one
of the few battlefield sites with good coverage of African American troops.
Kansas became the first state to officially mobilize black troops. The
site explains how the units were raised and later incorporated into the
USCT.

"Museum of the Kansas National Guard: Historic Units." http://skyways
.lib.ks.us/kansas/museums/kng/kngunits.html. Developed by the Kansas
National Guard, this site contains the histories of the First Kansas
(Colored) Volunteer Infantry and the Second Kansas (Colored) Volunteer Infantry, which are considered to be the first officially-raised troops
of African American soldiers in the Civil War.

"National Park Service Civil War Soldiers and Sailors System: History of African
Americans in the Civil War." http://www.itd.nps.gov/cwss/info.htm. This
is an online database of military service records of all men in the U.S. Army
and Navy during the Civil War. While some records may not be available,
all USCT records are on the site. This is the most extensive record of individuals who served in the USCT on the Web.

"The Valley of the Shadow: Two Communities in the American Civil War." http://
valley.vcdh.virginia.edu. This site is a multimedia archive created by the
University of Virginia. It focuses on Augusta County, Virginia and Franklin County, Pennsylvania and includes an in-depth analysis of Franklin
County men in the USCT. The "Newspapers" section details how black
soldiers were perceived by white citizens in the South and North.

Multimedia Sources

The Civil War—A Film by Ken Burns. Los Angeles: PBS Paramount, 1990. VHS
and DVD. This may be the best documentary film ever created. Shown
initially on television, it captured a vast audience with a gripping story.

Glory. Los Angeles: Sony Pictures, 1989. VHS and DVD. This award-winning
movie stars Matthew Broderick, Denzel Washington, and Morgan Freeman in a fictionalized account of the 54th Massachusetts. It is one of
the very best films about the Civil War.

35. Congress and President Lincoln Devise Rival Forms of Reconstruction (1864)

The end of the Civil War offered the promise of an America in which racial equality ruled. These hopes for a better nation were dashed by disagreements in Washington, D.C. over Reconstruction that encouraged massive white resistance on the part of southerners.

When Andrew Johnson learned of President Abraham Lincoln's plan to issue the Emancipation Proclamation, he said: "Damn the Negroes, I am fighting their masters." A former slaveholder, he had absolutely no interest in protecting the rights and freedoms of African Americans. As a result, he resisted a Reconstruction that involved more than simply reuniting the Union. In the seven-month span between Lincoln's assassination and he time that Congress went into session, Johnson implemented "Presidential Reconstruction." He offered amnesty to former Confederates who took an oath of loyalty to the Union. He offered nothing to former slaves.

When former Confederates who had their full political rights restored used their return to political office to enact the Black Codes, many in the North reacted with rage. The South seemed to be attempting to deny that it had lost the Civil War. Congress returned in December 1865. It immediately issued support for civil rights legislation and backed constitutional amendments guaranteeing citizenship and voting rights for blacks. Johnson urged the South to resist, which the region did. Johnson then toured the country in the fall of 1866 to denounce the Republicans. Congress retaliated by passing a Reconstruction Act in 1867 that placed the South under military control. This "Radical Reconstruction" banned former Confederates from voting, encouraged black voting, and forced the former states of the Confederacy to write state constitutions that accepted the Fourteenth Amendment. Johnson tried to challenge the Republicans. As a result, he just missed being removed from office.

TERM PAPER SUGGESTIONS

1. Compare and contrast Presidential Reconstruction with Radical Reconstruction.
2. Johnson argued that his form of Reconstruction offered the best hope for bringing the South back into the Union with minimal difficulty. Do you agree or disagree? Discuss.

3. Discuss what white northerners, white southerners, and black southerners wanted from Reconstruction.

4. Examine Andrew Johnson's life. Why did he have a failed presidency?

5. Discuss the key political issues involved with the impeachment of Andrew Johnson.

ALTERNATIVE TERM PAPER SUGGESTIONS

1. Go to http://www.andrewjohnson.com/ and put yourself in the shoes of a *Harper's Weekly* reader of the 1860s. Follow the editorials, cartoons, and stories from week to week. Write an editorial for *Harper's* arguing for or against the impeachment of Johnson.

2. Using "African American Perspectives: Pamphlets from the Daniel A. P. Murray Collection" at http://memory.loc.gov/ammem/aap/aaphome.html, examine three of the major problems facing African Americans. Assume that you are a member of Congress and write a speech proposing solutions to these problems. The Web site can be searched by keyword, subject, or author.

SUGGESTED SOURCES

Primary Source

"The Impeachment of Andrew Johnson." http://www.andrewjohnson.com/. A wonderful and extensive site about Johnson's difficulties with Reconstruction that includes contemporary editorials and cartoons from *Harper's Weekly* magazine.

Secondary Sources

Benedict, Michael Les. *The Impeachment and Trial of Andrew Johnson.* New York: W.W. Norton, 1973. Benedict, a legal scholar, argues that Johnson bears responsibility for the collapse of Reconstruction but that his disagreeable nature did not constitute sufficient grounds for impeaching him.

Carter, Dan T. *When the War Was Over: The Failure of Self-Reconstruction in the South, 1865–1867.* Baton Rouge: Louisiana State University Press, 1985. A history of the South during Presidential Reconstruction.

Perman, Michael. *Reunion Without Compromise: The South and Reconstruction, 1865–1868.* New York: Cambridge University Press, 1973. Shows how the South resisted Radical Reconstruction with the aid of Johnson.

Trefousse, Hans L. *Andrew Johnson.* New York: American Political Biography Press, 1998. A very readable biography of a man out of step with his times.

Trefousse, Hans L. *Background for Radical Reconstruction.* New York: Little, Brown, 1970. Describes both the anger in the North towards Johnson's policies that prompted Congress to push for stronger Reconstruction measures as well as the riots triggered by resistance to Reconstruction in Memphis and New Orleans.

Trefousse, Hans L. *Impeachment of a President: Andrew Johnson, the Blacks, and Reconstruction.* New York: Fordham University Press, 1999. Explains how Johnson's poor treatment of African Americans and unpopular plan for Reconstruction led to efforts to remove him from office.

World Wide Web

"American President: An Online Reference Resource." http://millercenter.org/academic/americanpresident/johnson. Contains in-depth essays on Johnson's presidency by scholars from the University of Virginia.

"Andrew Johnson." http://www.whitehouse.gov/history/presidents/aj17.html. Good discussion of the president and his difficulties during Reconstruction.

"The Impeachment of Andrew Johnson." http://www.impeach-andrewjohnson.com/11biographieskeyindividuals/AndrewJohnson.htm. Chiefly a biography of Johnson that touches on his trial before Congress.

"Reconstruction and Its Aftermath." http://afroamhistory.about.com/gi/dynamic/offsite.htm?zi=1/XJ&sdn=afroamhistory&cdn=education&tm=2156&gps=209_28_1020_599&f=11&tt=2&bt=1&bts=1&zu=http%3A//lcweb2.loc.gov/ammem/aaohtml/exhibit/aopart5.html. This Library of Congress site is illustrated heavily with primary documents relating to Reconstruction.

"Reconstruction by Jessica McElrath." http://afroamhistory.about.com/cs/reconstruction/a/reconstruction.htm. Good general history of Reconstruction with a timeline of events.

Multimedia Source

Reconstruction: The Second Civil War. Boston: WGBH, 2004. The only documentary film on Reconstruction beautifully explores the difficulties in bringing the Union back together.

36. Sharecropping Is Established (1865)

With the end of the Civil War, many African Americans in the South found themselves without money and a place to live but in possession of farming skills. Southern whites had land but did not have enough field hands to pick the cotton. Sharecropping became the compromise. Sharecroppers received a designated portion of the crops that they raised, with the landowner controlling the crop until it was divided. The system quickly became abusive and reminiscent of slavery.

Most southerners earned a living through agriculture, with cotton as the chief crop in the region. To succeed as cotton growers, farmers needed a cheap labor force to pick enough cotton to make up for decreasing prices as the result of increasing world production. Sharecroppers received food, clothing, farm equipment, and seed from a merchant—often the owner of the old plantation—with the promise that they would pay after harvest. To safeguard the merchant's investment, southern states passed crop lien laws that the merchant could claim the crop if the farmer could not make enough money to pay off his debt. Often, the merchant kept the books and simply informed the ex-slaves of how much money they owned. The system, ripe for abuse, became a way of locking African Americans into debt and tying them to the land as cheap labor. Sharecropping gradually faded as mechanization reduced the need for workers. It disappeared by about 1940, after drawing both poor black and poor white workers into perpetual debt.

TERM PAPER SUGGESTIONS

1. Explain why African Americans were drawn to sharecropping and how they became trapped in it.
2. Compare and contrast Alabama sharecroppers several generations removed from slavery with slaves in the antebellum era. Information can be found at http://memory.loc.gov/cgi-bin/query/r?ammem/fsaall:@FILREQ(@field (SUBJ+@band(Sharecroppers–Alabama+))+@FIELD(COLLID+fsa)).

ALTERNATIVE TERM PAPER SUGGESTIONS

1. Assume that a series of photographs of sharecroppers has just appeared in a major magazine to considerable outrage. You are hired by a group of landowners and merchants to do damage control. Create a podcast that explains why sharecropping became popular and why it is the best available choice for some southerners.
2. Design a Web site that explains why poor workers were drawn to sharecropping and what it was like to be a sharecropper.

SUGGESTED SOURCES

Primary Source

Sterling, Dorothy, ed. *The Trouble They Seen: The Story of Reconstruction in the Words of African Americans.* New York: Da Capo Press, 1994. Good collection of accounts of sharecropping from the mouths of sharecroppers.

Secondary Sources

Davis, Ronald L. F. *Good and Faithful Labor: From Slavery to Sharecropping in the Natchez District, 1860–1890.* Westport, CT: Greenwood Press, 1982. Aimed at a scholarly market and first published in 1974, this book is a detailed examination of sharecropping in Mississippi.

Nieman, Donald G. *From Slavery to Sharecropping: White Land and Black Labor in the Rural South, 1865–1900.* New York: Garland, 1994. This collection of essays examines the origins of sharecropping, the economic impact of racism, and the transition from slavery to sharecropping on one southern plantation.

Royce, Edward. *The Origins of Southern Sharecropping.* Philadelphia: Temple University Press, 1993. A good general study of the sharecropping system.

Saville, Julie. *The Work of Reconstruction: From Slave to Wage Laborer in South Carolina 1860–1870.* New York: Cambridge University Press, 1994. Excellent study of the economic system of a southern state during the Civil War and in the immediate aftermath of the conflict.

World Wide Web

"American Experience: Fatal Flood." http://www.pbs.org/wgbh/amex/flood/. Focusing on a 1927 Mississippi disaster that pitted white landowners against black farmers, this site includes information on sharecropper migration out of the South in the early twentieth century.

"America's Reconstruction: Free Labor." http://www.digitalhistory.uh.edu/reconstruction/section3/section3_free.html. The Digital History web site, a collaboration between the University of Houston, the Gilder Lehrman Institute of American History, and other institutions, presents an online version of Eric Foner and Olivia Mahoney's exhibit on Reconstruction. This section describes the transition from slave labor to free labor and includes a gallery of photographs.

"Economic and Social Conditions of North Carolina Farmers." http://docsouth.unc.edu/nc/ncfarmers/farmers.html. Part of the University of

North Carolina–Chapel Hill's Documenting the American South archive, this survey of 1,000 farmers in three North Carolina counties was published in 1922. It details family food supplies, cash income and credit, education, and other aspects of tenant farmers' lives.

"Farm Security Administration Photographs." http://memory.loc.gov/cgi-bin/query/r?ammem/fsaall:@FILREQ(@field (SUBJ+@band (Sharecroppers–Alabama+))+@FIELD(COLLID+fsa)). The Library of Congress's American Memory web site contains 78 photographs showing Alabama sharecroppers, several generations removed from slavery.

"Sharecropping." http://www.digitalhistory.uh.edu/database/article_display.cfm? HHID=130. Provides a good general history of sharecropping

"Sharecropping." http://www.georgiaencyclopedia.org/nge/Article.jsp ?id=h-3590. This entry from the *New Georgia Encyclopedia* is a superb introduction to sharecropping despite its focus on the system in one state.

"Sharecropping by Trudier Harris." http://www.english.uiuc.edu/maps/poets/a_f/brown/sharecropping.htm. This excerpt from *The Oxford Companion to Women's Writing in the United States* discusses the representation of sharecropping in literature.

"Slave to Sharecropper." http://www.pbs.org/wgbh/amex/reconstruction/sharecrop/index.html. This American Experience site includes a mini-documentary on sharecropping and two sharecropping contracts.

Multimedia Source

Reconstruction: The Second Civil War. Boston: WGBH, 2004. Contains a superb short film on sharecropping in the years after the Civil War.

37. Thirteenth Amendment Is Ratified (1865)

The Thirteenth Amendment to the U.S. Constitution finally abolished slavery throughout all of the United States. While the Emancipation Proclamation only ended slavery in the states still in rebellion as of January 1, 1863, this constitutional amendment stopped the practice in the border states, as well as in slave states like Maryland that had never left the Union.

When President Abraham Lincoln issued the Emancipation Proclamation, he realized that it would have to be succeeded by a constitutional amendment to guarantee the end of slavery. Without such an amendment, the United States would remain part slave and part free.

The Thirteenth Amendment passed the Senate on April 8, 1864, during the Civil War. The absence of representatives from southern states should have assured relatively quick and easy passage of the bill. However, the House of Representatives did not approve it until January 31, 1865. The delay infuriated Lincoln. He insisted that passage of the amendment be added to the Republican Party platform for the upcoming presidential elections in November 1864. Lincoln's promotion of the legislation helped it pass the House by a vote of 119 to 56.

The Thirteenth Amendment is listed alongside the Fourteenth and Fifteenth Amendments as the pieces of the Constitution that greatly expanded the civil rights of African Americans. The amendment could not give equal rights to blacks without the full support of the courts and the wider society, though. Full political equality would require another 100 years to achieve.

TERM PAPER SUGGESTIONS

1. Discuss the history of the Thirteenth Amendment following its passage. In what situations has the amendment been held by the courts to be inapplicable?

2. The Thirteenth Amendment may provide constitutional support for congressional actions against racial discrimination by private individuals and businesses. The U.S. Supreme Court has been divided on this point. Examine the long-term significance of the amendment.

3. Compare and contrast the Emancipation Proclamation with the Thirteenth Amendment.

ALTERNATIVE TERM PAPER SUGGESTIONS

1. Create a Microsoft PowerPoint presentation to show the passage of the Thirteenth Amendment to the Constitution, from birth through ratification, with a discussion of the amendment's impact upon African Americans.

2. The American Anti-Slavery Group, found at iabolish.org, has the motto "Slavery Is Not History." Create a Web site that compares the form of slavery

abolished by the Thirteenth Amendment with the forms of slavery that still exist in the world.

SUGGESTED SOURCES

Primary Sources

"13th Amendment to the U.S. Constitution." http://www.loc.gov/rr/program/ bib/ourdocs/13thamendment.html. This Library of Congress site provides an original copy of the amendment as well as a brief legislative history of it and links to related documents.

"13th Amendment to the U.S. Constitution: Abolition of Slavery." http:// www.ourdocuments.gov/doc.php?flash=true&doc=40. This National Archives and Records Administration site includes a history of the amendment and an original copy of it that can be viewed in a larger size.

Secondary Sources

Fletcher, George C. *Our Secret Constitution: How Lincoln Redefined American Democracy.* New York: Oxford University Press, 2003. One of the best studies of Lincoln's support for the Thirteenth Amendment and how that amendment changed the United States.

Hoemann, George H. *What God Hath Wrought: The Embodiment of Freedom in the Thirteenth Amendment.* New York: Garland, 1987. A challenging discussion of the ideas behind the amendment.

Holzer, Harold, and Sara Vaughn Gabbard, eds. *Lincoln and Freedom: Slavery, Emancipation, and the Thirteenth Amendment.* Carbondale: Southern Illinois University Press, 2007. A scholarly examination of the president and his use of law to oppose slavery.

Maltz, Earl M. *Civil Rights, the Constitution, and Congress, 1863–1869.* Lawrence: University Press of Kansas, 1990. A very good legal study of the three Reconstruction amendments.

Schleichert, Elizabeth. *The Thirteenth Amendment: Ending Slavery.* Springfield, NJ: Enslow Publishers, 1998. Aimed at secondary school students, this is a good discussion of the impact of the amendment.

Tsesis, Alexander. *The Thirteenth Amendment and American Freedom: A Legal History.* New York: New York University Press, 2004. Aimed at an audience that is well versed in the law, this is a challenging book to read though a well-researched one.

Vorenberg, Michael. *Final Freedom: The Civil War, the Abolition of Slavery, and the Thirteenth Amendment.* New York: Cambridge University Press, 2001. A readable and well-researched examination of the amendment.

World Wide Web

"Constitution of the United States." http://www.gpoaccess.gov/constitution/
index.html. Provides a downloadable copy of the Constitution with
analysis.

"The End of Slavery: The Creation of the 13th Amendment." http://13
thamendment.harpweek.com/. Provides a history of the amendment,
with considerable focus on the ratification process, as well as a timeline
and biographies of significant individuals.

"The Thirteenth Amendment." http://www.greatamericanhistory.net/
amendment.htm. Compares the amendment with the Emancipation
Proclamation.

"The United States Constitution." http://www.usconstitution.net/const.html.
The U.S. Constitution Online provides the primary document as well
as a copy of the Constitution of China for comparison.

38. Freedmen's Bureau Is Created (1865)

When President Abraham Lincoln issued the Emancipation Proclamation
to free the slaves in the Confederacy during the Civil War, he did not provide a way for the former slaves to make a living away from the plantation.
To ease the transition from slavery to freedom, Congress created the
Bureau of Refugees, Freedmen, and Abandoned Lands, popularly known
as the Freedmen's Bureau, on March 3, 1865.

In the wake of the tremendous upheaval caused by the Civil War,
immediate measures were needed to help the poor of the South. The
Freedmen's Bureau provided food, clothing, and transportation to freed
blacks as well as to whites displaced by the war. It also set up schools, distributed lands, and attempted to monitor employment contracts—
documents which were never needed during the age of slavery. The
bureau mediated labor and land disputes while supervising trials involving
African Americans. The Freedmen's Bureau suffered from poor leadership
that drastically hampered its effectiveness. Andrew Johnson, a man notorious for his hostility to African Americans and who became president
upon Lincoln's assassination, opposed the Freedmen's Bureau throughout
his brief term in office. General Oliver Otis Howard, the bureau's commissioner, was well meaning and sympathetic, as were a number of field
agents. However, many of the regional and local officers were more concerned with gaining the approval of the white communities in which they

worked. These bureau officials viewed their main responsibility as persuading the former slaves to accept contracts with their former masters and preventing the blacks from drifting into the towns. Additionally, some of the more dedicated officers who genuinely sought to help the African Americans were removed from office by Johnson.

The president's resistance to the Freedmen's Bureau and Reconstruction killed the agency. Johnson challenged Congress by vetoing a bill in 1866 that would have extended the life of the bureau. He argued that the bill violated the Constitution by making the federal government responsible for indigents, by being passed by a Congress that denied seats to the 11 states that had belonged to the Confederacy, and by being vague in its definition of civil rights. In early 1866, Johnson still had sufficient prestige to persuade the Senate to uphold his veto. However, Johnson then attacked congressional leaders with a fiery speech. Moderate Republicans began to abandon the president. When Johnson vetoed an 1866 civil rights act on the grounds that giving citizenship to native-born blacks went beyond the scope of federal power, Congress overrode his veto. Congress then enacted a revised Freedmen's Bureau bill on April 9, 1866, overriding Johnson's veto.

However, the battle over the bureau and the lack of presidential support left the agency severely weakened. By 1872, it was dead. In the brief years of its existence, it fed about 4,000 people and educated many southerners, but it achieved little more. The Freedmen's Bureau was a temporary relief measure, yet it still served as the only program of Reconstruction that ever incorporated more than constitutional and legal rights for African Americans.

TERM PAPER SUGGESTIONS

1. An old interpretation of Reconstruction claimed that it victimized whites by giving power to blacks. Using the Freedmen's Bureau as an example, challenge this argument.

2. Imagine "what if" the Freedmen's Bureau had received stronger support from the federal government. Would the lives of former slaves have changed dramatically for the better?

3. Using the Freedmen and Southern Society site at http://www.history.umd.edu/Freedmen/, discuss the impact of the bureau upon either African Americans or whites in the South.

ALTERNATIVE TERM PAPER SUGGESTIONS

1. Use the Freedmen's Bureau Online at http://freedmensbureau.com/ to search for the name of an ancestor. Discuss your family member's experiences with the bureau and place these experiences in historical context.

2. Imitate Thomas Nast by designing an editorial cartoon about the Freedmen's Bureau.

SUGGESTED SOURCES

Primary Sources

Berlin, Ira, and Leslie S. Rowland. *Families and Freedom: A Documentary History of African-American Kinship in the Civil War Era.* New York: The New Press, 1997. Shows how black families responded to the challenge of newfound freedom.

Fields, Barbara J., et al. *Free At Last: A Documentary History of Slavery, Freedom, and the Civil War.* New York: The New Press, 1992. Provides documents relating to the Freedmen's Bureau.

"Freedmen's Bureau Online." http://freedmensbureau.com/. Contains all available records of the Freedmen's Bureau in a searchable form with links to related sites.

Holt, Thomas C., and Elsa Barkley Brown, eds. *Major Problems in African-American History: From Slavery to Freedom, 1619–1877.* Boston: Houghton Mifflin, 2000. Contains several documents showing the interaction of former slaves with their ex-masters, with Union officials, and with the Freedmen's Bureau.

Secondary Sources

Benedict, Michael Les. *The Impeachment and Trial of Andrew Johnson.* New York: W.W. Norton, 1973. The best book on the president who attacked the Freedmen's Bureau and seriously damaged Reconstruction.

Finley, Randy. *From Slavery to Uncertain Freedom: The Freedmen's Bureau in Arkansas, 1865–1869.* Fayetteville: University of Arkansas Press, 1996. A good state study of the impact of the bureau upon African Americans.

Keller, Morton. *The Art and Politics of Thomas Nast.* New York: Oxford University Press, 1968. One of the greatest of political cartoonists, Nast created a number of illustrations that critiqued the Freedmen's Bureau and other aspects of Reconstruction.

Nieman, Donald G., ed. *The Freedmen's Bureau and Black Freedom.* New York: Garland, 1994. A collection of scholarly essays about the bureau.

Nieman, Donald G., ed. *To Set the Law in Motion: The Freedmen's Bureau and the Legal Rights of Blacks, 1865–1868.* New York: KTO, 1979. A legal study of the bureau by a noted scholar of the Constitution.

Oubre, Claude F. *Forty Acres and a Mule: The Freedmen's Bureau and Black Land Ownership.* Baton Rouge: Louisiana State University Press, 1978. Shows how the bureau struggled to help blacks achieve part of the American Dream.

World Wide Web

"Freedmen and Southern Society." http://www.history.umd.edu/Freedmen/. The Freedmen and Southern Society Project began in 1976 to capture the voices of all the Freedmen's Bureau participants—liberated slaves and defeated slaveholders, soldiers and civilians, common folk and the elite, northerners and southerners. Many of the documents gathered by the Project are in books, listed under this site. A number of documents are also accessible from the site.

"The Freedmen's Bureau." http://afroamhistory.about.com/cs/reconstruction/a/freedmensbureau.htm. A good but brief history of the bureau.

"The Freedmen's Bureau, 1865–72." http://www.archives.gov/research/african-americans/freedmens-bureau/. There are no records on this site, but the page provides information about how and where to examine the microfilmed records about the bureau that are held by the National Archives and Records Administration. This is an especially good site for genealogists.

"The Freedmen's Bureau Act, March 3, 1865." http://www.history.umd.edu/Freedmen/fbact.htm. Offers the full text of the legislation that established the bureau.

"The Freedmen's Bureau by W. E. B. Du Bois." http://afroamhistory.about.com/library/bldubois_freedmens_bureau1.htm. Reprints the full text of an essay on the bureau by this famed historian and civil rights activist of the late nineteenth and early twentieth centuries.

"Handbook of Texas Online: Freedmen's Bureau." http://www.tshaonline.org/handbook/online/articles/FF/ncf1.html. Everything you ever wanted to know about the Freedmen's Bureau in Texas along with an extensive Texas-focused bibliography.

"The Rise and Fall of Jim Crow: Jim Crow Stories." http://www.pbs.org/wnet/jim-crow/stories_events_freed.html. Provides a history of the bureau and a link to a short video about the agency and its leader, General Oliver Howard.

Multimedia Source

Reconstruction: The Second Civil War. Boston: WGBH, 2005. DVD. This American Experience documentary has a full-length video about Reconstruction plus a mini-documentary that addresses the Freedmen's Bureau.

39. Black Codes Are Passed (1865–1866)

The Black Codes came in response to the end of slavery. Southern legislatures, in passing legislation that restricted the freedom of blacks, indicated that they had no intention of abandoning slavery. Some conservative northern states, notably Ohio, enacted similar legislation to control free blacks.

The Black Codes emphasized the distinction between blacks and whites. While they extended new rights to African Americans, they also marked African Americans as a separate class subject to unique restraints. Details varied from state to state, but many of the codes were similar. Under slavery, marriages between blacks were not legally recognized. The codes recognized common-law marriages, although interracial relationships were still banned. African Americans could testify in court but only in six states. In the other five states of the Old Confederacy, blacks could only testify in cases involving other blacks. African Americans could own property, except for farm lands in Mississippi and city lots in South Carolina. They could pursue lawsuits, but they could not carry firearms in most states of the Old Confederacy without a license to do so. (Whites did not need a license anywhere.) African Americans were also required to buy licenses to practice certain trades, such as barbering.

The Civil Rights Act of 1866 passed Congress in an effort to stop the Black Codes, and the Fourteenth Amendment further supported civil rights. However, by the 1880s, Republicans concerned about civil rights no longer controlled Congress. At the same time, the Supreme Court was becoming increasingly hostile to federal civil rights legislation based on the Fourteenth Amendment. This hostility led the Court to invalidate the Civil Rights Act of 1875 in 1883. The act, the last piece of Reconstruction civil rights law, proclaimed the equality of all persons before the law. The Supreme Court decision meant that racial segregation could be imposed by private businesses. The South moved quickly to ensure that African Americans would be unequal before the law. The Black Codes were reinstated.

TERM PAPER SUGGESTIONS

1. Why did white southerners believe that a separate code of laws applying only to "persons of color" was necessary?
2. Northerners protested that the Black Codes of South Carolina and other southern states attempted to restore slavery. Do you agree or disagree? Why?

3. The Fourteenth Amendment, ratified in 1868, attempted to prevent discriminatory state laws such as those that made up the Black Codes. Compare the amendment with the laws included in the Black Codes in Louisiana, Mississippi, and Ohio. These codes can be found at http://www.ipoaa.com/black _codes_louisians_miss_ohio.htm.

4. Discuss why Congress believed that amendments to the Constitution were preferable to civil rights acts as a means for protecting African Americans.

ALTERNATIVE TERM PAPER SUGGESTIONS

1. Assume that you are a member of Congress and you have been asked to persuade your colleagues to support the Civil Rights Act of 1866. Create a Microsoft PowerPoint presentation that urges Congress to support the bill.

2. Assume that you are a reporter for National Public Radio. Create a podcast that discusses the implications of the South Carolina Black Code.

SUGGESTED SOURCES

Primary Sources

"Black Codes." http://www.ipoaa.com/black_codes_louisians_miss_ohio.htm. Reprints the Black Codes of Louisiana, Mississippi, and Ohio.

"Black Codes." http://www.spartacus.schoolnet.co.uk/USASblackcodes.htm. Contains excerpts of primary documents relating to the Black Codes, such as Senator Charles Sumner's attack on the regulations.

"Mississippi Black Codes." http://chnm.gmu.edu/courses/122/recon/code.html. Reprints Mississippi's regulations.

"The Southern Black Codes of 1865–66." http://www.crf-usa.org/brown50th/ black_codes.htm. Reprints the South Carolina Black Code in its entirety.

Secondary Sources

Litwack, Leon F. *Been in the Storm So Long: The Aftermath of Slavery.* New York: Vintage, 1980. Won the Pulitzer Prize and the National Book Award for blending analysis with interviews with ex-slaves and accounts by former slaveholders.

Smith, Page. *Trial by Fire: A People's History of the Civil War and Reconstruction.* New York: McGraw-Hill, 1982. This is a 1,000-page discussion of the Civil War and Reconstruction that is aimed at the college textbook market. The focus is on social and cultural history, not the political and military aspects of the era.

Wilson, Theodore Brantner. *The Black Codes of the South.* Tuscaloosa: University of Alabama Press, 1965. A bit dated but still an excellent discussion of the codes.

World Wide Web

"Black Code." http://www.pbs.org/wnet/aaworld/reference/articles/black _code.html. This essay traces the history of the Black Codes from their roots in the slave codes that were in effect prior to the Civil War.

"Black Codes in the Former Confederate States." http://www.civilwarhome .com/blackcodes.htm. A good introduction to the codes taken from Page Smith's *Trial By Fire: A People's History of the Civil War and Reconstruction.*

"The Black Codes of 1865." http://afroamhistory.about.com/od/blackcodes/a/ blackcodes1865.htm. A general introduction to the restrictions.

"The Post-War Years: Free at Last." http://xroads.virginia.edu/%7ECAP/SCAR TOONS/caremanc.html. A superb discussion of life after the Civil War for African Americans that is heavily illustrated with political cartoons of the era.

40. Ku Klux Klan Is Formed (1866)

The Ku Klux Klan (KKK) is a white supremacist organization that has shifted slightly in its ideology and choice of targets since its incarnation in 1866. While it has remained viciously antiblack in every era, the later Klan targeted Catholics, immigrants, and elements of modernization in the 1920s, as part of a nationwide backlash. It also had a considerable number of women members. The KKK lost much steam by the end of World War II, only to revive to combat the civil rights movement of the 1950s and 1960s.

The KKK began in Pulaski, Tennessee in 1866 when six Confederate veterans decided to create a social club. The Klan expanded within a year to fight for the maintenance of white supremacy. It grew into a mighty "invisible empire" that spread throughout the states of the Old Confederacy under the leadership of former Confederate General Nathan Bedford Forrest. The Klan targeted blacks, carpetbaggers, northern schoolteachers, Republicans, and other perceived threats to the southern way of life. Klan members beat, lynched, shot, and generally terrorized opponents. The KKK aimed to preserve the privileged status of whites by driving away any potential leaders of African Americans. Forrest officially disbanded the Klan in 1869, for reasons that remain murky. Federal legislation passed in 1870 and 1871 in the form of the Ku Klux Acts also helped destroy the Klan, as did the ultimate failure of Reconstruction.

TERM PAPER SUGGESTIONS

1. Discuss whether the Ku Klux Klan rose in response to the political and economic gains made by African Americans.

2. Until about 1970, the Ku Klux Klan was typically portrayed in history books as a logical response to the indignities visited upon white southerners by Reconstruction. The flowering of the civil rights movement forced historians to reconsider the Klan. Consider how the present shapes our understanding of the past, using African American history as the base of your paper.

3. A race riot in Colfax, Louisiana in 1873 resulted in the deaths of over 200 African Americans. Report on the causes and events of the Colfax Massacre.

4. Many of the KKK's targets were white political leaders from the Republican Party who supported civil rights. Investigate the KKK's attacks upon whites in the South.

5. The KKK appears to have been strongest in areas that were hotly contested by both Democrats and Republicans. Use the Historical Census Browser at http://fisher.lib.virginia.edu/collections/stats/histcensus to research and write on this theory.

ALTERNATIVE TERM PAPER SUGGESTIONS

1. Assume that you are a white northerner who has moved to the South to help it recover from the Civil War. You support civil rights for blacks. Create a storyboard showing a clash between you and the KKK.

2. You are African American and well-respected enough in your community that your black neighbors are urging you to run for political office. Write an opinion piece for a northern newspaper explaining why you are entering politics or why you are refusing to do so.

SUGGESTED SOURCES

Primary Sources

"Organization and Principles of the Ku Klux Klan, 1868." http://www .albany.edu/faculty/gz580/his101/kkk.html. Presents the guiding beliefs of the first KKK.

Tourgee, Albion W. *The Invisible Empire: A Fool's Errand and a Concise History of Events.* New York: Fords, Howard and Hulbert, 1880. Tourgee, perhaps best known as the plaintiff's attorney in *Plessy v. Ferguson,* writes of his experiences as a white northern supporter of civil rights who moved to the South. As the title of the book indicates, Tourgee had the unfortunate experience of encountering the KKK. Various reprints of this book are readily available.

Winegarten, Ruthe *Black Texas Women: A Sourcebook.* Austin: University of Texas Press, 1996. Reprints accounts of encounters with the Klan.

Secondary Sources

Budiansky, Stephen. *The Bloody Shirt: Terror after Appomattox.* New York: Viking, 2008. Describes the use of terror as a political strategy.

Chalmers, David M. *Hooded Americanism: The History of the Ku Klux Klan.* New York: New Viewpoints, 1981. One of the most detailed and comprehensive books available on the KKK.

Lowe, David. *Ku Klux Klan: The Invisible Empire.* New York: W.W. Norton, 1967. This is a print version of a 1965 CBS Reports documentary that won an Emmy; it highlights Klan history through the mid-1960s.

Maclean, Nancy. *Behind the Mask of Chivalry: The Making of the Second Ku Klux Klan.* New York: Oxford University Press, 1994. The best general history of the 1920s KKK.

Newton, Michael, and Judy Ann Newton. *The Ku Klux Klan: An Encyclopedia.* New York: Garland, 1991. Covers all three versions of the Klan, Klan leaders, Klan victims, and other white supremacist groups that have grown out of the KKK.

O'Donnell, Patrick, and David Jacobs. *Ku Klux Klan: America's First Terrorists Exposed.* Seattle, WA: Booksurge, 2006. Provides a history of the rise of the Reconstruction-era Klan and the legislation that tried to halt the organization.

Rice, Arnold S. *The Ku Klux Klan in American Politics.* New York: Haskell House, 1972. Traces the political involvement of the KKK from 1915 to 1970.

Trelease, Allen W. *White Terror: The Ku Klux Klan Conspiracy and Southern Reconstruction.* New York: Harper and Row, 1971. Traces the development of the Klan.

World Wide Web

"History of the Ku Klux Klan: A Brief Biography." http://www.african americans.com/KuKluxKlan.htm. Provides a history of the Klan as well as a description of KKK titles and a full-text copy of the KKK creed.

"The Ku Klux Klan Act of 1871." http://education.harpweek.com/KKKHear ings/AppendixA.htm. Provides the full text of the legislation passed by Congress in an effort to halt the Klan.

"Ku Klux Klan History." http://www.spartacus.schoolnet.co.uk/USAkkk.htm. Provides a brief hyperlinked history of the Klan.

"The Ku Klux Klan in the Reconstruction Era." http://www.georgiaen cyclopedia.org/nge/Article.jsp?id+h-694. This essay, from the online *New Georgia Encyclopedia,* is a good study of the Klan in the Peach State.

Multimedia Source

The Ku Klux Klan—A Secret History. New York: A&E Home Entertain ment, 1998. DVD. Traces the rise of the Klan from 1866 to the present.

41. Fourteenth Amendment Is Ratified (1868)

In the immediate aftermath of the Civil War, Republicans introduced sev eral amendments to the Constitution. The Fourteenth Amendment, intro duced in 1866 and ratified in 1868, made all native-born persons into American citizens and prohibited the states from denying any citizen equal protection under the law. Congress devised the amendment chiefly to show the constitutionality of the 1866 Civil Rights Act, but the amendment extended protections far beyond those given by that legislation.

The Fourteenth Amendment reaffirmed state and federal citizenship for anyone born or naturalized in the United States. It forbade any states to restrict the privileges of citizenship; to deprive any person of life, lib erty, or property without due process of law; or to deny any person the equal protection of the law. Southerners strongly opposed the Fourteenth Amendment and attempted to maintain second-class status for African Americans with various challenges to the amendment. A conservative U.S. Supreme Court cooperated in restricting the privileges of citizenship for African Americans. In 1896, the Court ruled in *Plessy v. Ferguson* that the Fourteenth Amendment did not intend to require mixing of the races in social situations. The amendment mandated legal equality, not social equality. Accordingly, "separate but equal" facilities for blacks and whites were permitted.

Not until the 1938 did the Supreme Court begin to enforce Fourteenth Amendment protections for blacks. In that year, *Missouri ex rel. Gaines v. Canada* involved a black applicant who was denied admission to the University of Missouri Law School. The state of Missouri, which had no law schools for blacks, attempted to fulfill its separate-but-equal obligations by offering to pay for the black applicant's tuition at a comparable out-of-state school. The Court held that this arrangement violated the applicant's rights guaranteed by the Equal Protection Clause of the Fourteenth Amendment.

Since this decision, the Fourteenth Amendment has proved to be one of the most effective tools for social and legal change in the United States. The efforts of civil rights activists to end the state-mandated segregation of public facilities and racial discrimination in all areas of American life were aided immeasurably by the Supreme Court's determination that the Equal Protection Clause could be read liberally. This change in the Court's thinking led to the development of standards of judicial review that put certain types of legislation under strict scrutiny and spelled out suspect classifications. Ultimately, the concept of equal protection led to the overturning of "separate but equal" schools in the 1954 *Brown v. Board of Education.*

TERM PAPER SUGGESTIONS

1. Discuss the history of the Fourteenth Amendment.
2. Examine why the Supreme Court did not interpret the amendment in a way that benefitted African Americans until about 60 years after its creation.
3. In 1896, the Supreme Court decided in *Plessy v. Ferguson* that the Fourteenth Amendment required legal equality but not social equality. Explore this decision and either defend or challenge the reasoning of the Court.

ALTERNATIVE TERM PAPER SUGGESTIONS

1. Create a Microsoft PowerPoint presentation to show the impact of the Fourteenth Amendment to the Constitution from ratification to the present, focusing on the amendment's impact upon African Americans.
2. Create a Web page that explains the Fourteenth Amendment. Include an annotated bibliography with links to articles and books on the amendment.

SUGGESTED SOURCES

Primary Source

"14th Amendment to the U.S. Constitution." http://www.loc.gov/rr/program/bib/ourdocs/14thamendment.html. Contains a brief summary of the amendment and a link to an 1868 copy of it.

Secondary Sources

Curtis, Michael Kent. *No State Shall Abridge: The Fourteenth Amendment and the Bill of Rights.* Durham, NC: Duke University Press, 1990. Like most of the books on the Fourteenth Amendment, this work is aimed at legal scholars. Curtis examines whether the framers of the amendment intended to incorporate the Bill of Rights guarantees and thereby inhibit state action.

Epps, Garrett. *Democracy Reborn: The Fourteenth Amendment and the Fight for Equal Rights in Post-Civil War America.* New York: Holt, 2007. A very readable account of the creation and impact of the Fourteenth and Fifteenth Amendments by a legal scholar who is also a novelist.

Hall, Kermit L., ed. *Freedom and Equality: Discrimination and the Supreme Court: The Supreme Court and American Society.* New York: Garland, 2000. Examines the impact of Supreme Court decisions on American life.

Nelson, William E. *The Fourteenth Amendment: From Political Principle to Judicial Doctrine.* Cambridge, MA: Harvard University Press, 1998. Explains why the Supreme Court eventually gave an expansive interpretation to the amendment.

Perry, Michael J. *We the People: The Fourteenth Amendment and the Supreme Court.* New York: Oxford University Press, 2001. Examines whether the Supreme Court has made rulings on the Fourteenth Amendment because of political considerations.

World Wide Web

"United States Constitution." http://www.law.cornell.edu/constitution/constitution.amendmentxiv.html. This is a Cornell University Law School page that reprints the amendment and contains a link to the rest of the Constitution.

"The United States Constitution." http://www.usconstitution.net/const.html. The U.S. Constitution Online presents the Constitution as a series of individual pages, in plain text, in standard Palm DOC, and in enhanced TealDoc to make it as readable as possible.

Multimedia Source

Foner, Philip, ed. "Fourteenth and Fifteenth Amendments," in *The Autobiography of Frederick Douglass*. Vol. 2, Washington, DC: Smithsonian Folkways, 1966. MP3. Actor Ossie Davis reads Douglass's autobiography, including the chapters devoted to these amendments.

42. Fifteenth Amendment Is Ratified (1870)

The Fifteenth Amendment, the last of the three Reconstruction amendments, declared that race or color could not be used as a reason to deny a citizen the right to vote. Once Ulysses S. Grant won the presidency in 1868, Republicans began pushing for this amendment. Legislative approval came in February 1869 with ratification taking place almost exactly a year later.

As Republicans designed, the amendment limited the legal ability of the former states of the Confederacy to block African Americans from voting. Former slaves had been registering to vote and voting in large numbers in state elections since 1867. The amendment gave them the right to vote in national elections while threatening the ability of southern whites to regain control over state and local governments. Democrats attacked the amendment as an attempt to centralize and consolidate power, while Republicans argued that one nation needed one voting law. State legislatures outside of the South quickly endorsed the amendment, making it law.

The amendment contained significant weaknesses. It did not guarantee blacks the right to hold political office, nor did it address the restrictions that northern states had imposed on the right of other males to vote. These limits included literacy tests and property qualifications. To the furor of women who had worked for decades in support of rights for African Americans, the amendment did not give women the right to vote. As a result, some white advocates of women's rights, such as Susan B. Anthony and Elizabeth Cady Stanton, publicly opposed the amendment. Other activist white women endorsed the amendment and began to work at the state level to give women the right to vote. Black women largely remained silent on the issue, unwilling to break ranks with African American men. Black women did not gain the right to vote until the Nineteenth Amendment passed in 1920, giving the ballot to women of all races.

TERM PAPER SUGGESTIONS

1. Discuss the aims of Congress in creating the three Reconstruction amendments to the Constitution. Were these goals achieved?
2. The right to vote is the most powerful right accorded to a citizen because it brings control over government. Discuss the history of African Americans and the vote.

ALTERNATIVE TERM PAPER SUGGESTIONS

1. African Americans traditionally do not vote in percentages as high as whites. Create a Web site to persuade blacks to register to vote and to cast ballots. On the site, include a history of the Fifteenth Amendment and the struggle for blacks to be able to vote.
2. Frederick Douglass defended the exclusion of women from the Fifteenth Amendment by famously proclaiming that "this hour belonged to the Negro." Assume that you are a woman in 1870. Write an editorial urging support for the amendment.
3. Write an editorial urging rejection of the amendment because it will not permit women to vote.

SUGGESTED SOURCES

Primary Source

"15th Amendment to the U.S. Constitution." http://www.loc.gov/rr/program/bib/ourdocs/15thamendment.html. Contains a brief summary of the amendment and a link to an 1870 copy of it.

Secondary Sources

Banfield, Susan. *The Fifteenth Amendment: African-American Men's Right to Vote.* Berkeley Heights, NJ: Enslow, 1998. Examines the amendment and discusses the struggle that took place for black men to regain the right to vote when it was denied.

Darling, Marsha. *Race, Voting, Redistricting, and the Constitution: Sources and Explorations of the Fifteenth Amendment.* New York: Routledge, 2001. Aimed at legal scholars, this is a discussion of whether the Fifteenth Amendment blocks redistricting that appears to be based upon the race of the majority of voters in an area. By making blacks, who traditionally vote Democratic, into a minority or a majority in a district, political leaders can help a Republican or a Democrat gain office.

Epps, Garrett. *Democracy Reborn: The Fourteenth Amendment and the Fight for Equal Rights in Post-Civil War America*. New York: Holt, 2007. A very readable account of the creation and impact of the Fourteenth and Fifteenth Amendments by a legal scholar who is also a novelist.

Hall, Kermit L., ed. *Freedom and Equality: Discrimination and the Supreme Court: The Supreme Court and American Society*. New York: Garland, 2000. Examines the impact of Supreme Court decisions on American life.

World Wide Web

"(1870) Henry O. Wagoner, Jr., Celebrates the Ratification of the 15th Amendment to the United States Constitution." http://www.blackpast.org/?q=1870-henry-o-wagoner-jr-celebrates-ratification-15th-amendment-united-states-constitution. Reprints a speech delivered by Wagoner, the son of a Denver, Colorado African American civil rights activist.

"15th Amendment: Ratification." http://15thamendment.harpweek.com/HubPages/CommentaryPage.asp?Commentary=03Ratification. Discusses the process of ratification, with links to nineteenth-century editorials and cartoons about the approval of the amendment.

"Passage of the Fifteenth Amendment." http://www.pbs.org/wgbh/amex/grant/peopleevents/e_fifteenth.html. An excellent discussion of the creation of the amendment and the difficulties that proponents faced.

"United States Constitution." http://www.law.cornell.edu/constitution/constitution.amendmentxv.html. This is a Cornell University Law School page that reprints the amendment and contains a link to the rest of the Constitution.

"The United States Constitution." http://www.usconstitution.net/const.html. The U.S. Constitution Online presents the Constitution as a series of individual pages, in plain text, in standard Palm DOC, and in enhanced TealDoc to make it as readable as possible.

Multimedia Source

Foner, Philip, ed. "Fourteenth and Fifteenth Amendments," in *The Autobiography of Frederick Douglass*. Vol. 2, Washington, D.C.: Smithsonian Folkways, 1966. MP3. Actor Ossie Davis reads Douglass's autobiography, including the chapters devoted to these amendments.

43. First Black Men Elected to the U.S. Congress (1870)

In the wake of the Civil War, southern states were required to give voting rights to blacks in their constitutions as a prerequisite for rejoining the Union. Once the new constitutions had been enacted, African American men began to win elections to public office. By the end of Reconstruction in 1877, African Americans numbered over 600 state legislators, including lieutenant governors, treasurers, superintendents of education, and secretaries of state, while countless others served as members of school boards, mayors, justices of the peace, county commissioners, and sheriffs.

South Carolina had a majority black population throughout Reconstruction and, as a result, blacks took control of government. In this state, African Americans achieved their most impressive political gains. In the 1870 elections, blacks won four of South Carolina's eight executive offices and sent three of their own to the U.S. Congress. Louisiana and Mississippi, other black majority states, also elected large numbers of black politicians. Only Texas, Tennessee, and Arkansas failed to send blacks to the U.S. Congress.

Hostile whites responded to black elected officials with a wave of violence that aimed to drive blacks and their white allies from office. Yet as Reconstruction collapsed, southern blacks continued to hold public office. African Americans served in every session of the Virginia Assembly through 1891, North Carolina blacks served in the state legislature until 1894, and South Carolinians voted blacks into state offices until 1902. However, black voting power was clearly diminishing rapidly. After Republican George Henry White of North Carolina left the House of Representatives in 1901, no African American was elected to Congress until Oscar De Priest (R-IL) in 1928.

TERM PAPER SUGGESTIONS

1. Research the life of the first African American from your state elected to the U.S. Congress.
2. Research the life of an African American who has held political office, perhaps as a mayor or governor, in your state.
3. Trace the history of the Congressional Black Caucus.
4. Trace the history of African Americans and the vote.

ALTERNATIVE TERM PAPER SUGGESTIONS

1. Pay tribute to the one of the first African Americans to serve in the U.S. Congress by creating a Web page that honors this man.
2. Create a Web site for the first black elected official in your state.

SUGGESTED SOURCES

Primary Source

Middleton, Stephen, ed. *Black Congressmen During Reconstruction: A Documentary Sourcebook.* Westport, CT: Praeger, 2002. The only collection of primary documents about these men.

Secondary Sources

Barker, Lucius, and Mack H. Jones. *African Americans and the Political System.* Englewood Cliffs, NJ: Prentice Hall, 1994. A general history of blacks in politics, including a history of black political power.

Clay, William L. *Just Permanent Interests: Black Americans in Congress, 1870–1991.* New York: Amistad Press, 1992. Despite the title, this book focuses on the years after 1965. It contains a good history of the Congressional Black Caucus.

Dodd, Lawrence C., and Bruce I. Oppenheimer, eds. *Congress Reconsidered.* Washington, DC: CQ Press, 1997 Contains an essay by Carol H. Swain on women and blacks in Congress from 1870 to 1996.

Dray, Philip. *Capitol Men: The Epic Story of Reconstruction through the Lives of the First Black Congressmen.* New York: Houghton Mifflin, 2008. Covers Reconstruction politicians with exceptional breadth and depth.

Patterson, William L. *The Gentleman from Mississippi, Our First Negro Congressman, Hiram R. Revels.* New York: N.P., c. 1960. Hiram Revels took the Senate seat previously occupied by Jefferson Davis, president of the Confederacy.

Zuczek, Richard, ed. *Encyclopedia of the Reconstruction Era.* Westport, CT: Greenwood Press, 2006. In the A–Z entries gives profiles of the key players.

World Wide Web

"African American Members of the U.S. Congress, 1870–2008." http://www.senate.gov/reference/resources/pdf/RL30378.pdf. Contains the full text of a July 2008 Congressional Research Service report to the U.S. Congress about black representation in Congress. The report provides short biographical sketches and committee assignments of the legislators.

"African Americans of the Senate." http://www.senate.gov/pagelayout/history/
h_multi_sections_and_teasers/News_More_Black_History_Month.htm.
The Senate Historical Office maintains this site, which provides short biographical essays about past and present senators.

"Black Legislators During Reconstruction." http://www.georgiaencyclopedia.org/
nge/Article.jsp?id=h-635. This essay, part of the *New Georgia Encyclopedia,* examines black Georgian legislators.

"The Congressional Black Caucus Foundation." http://www.cbcfinc.org/. The
Congressional Black Caucus (CBC), born in 1969, is the chief network
for black members of Congress. The Congressional Black Caucus Foundation, created in 1976, is a public policy, research, and education institute that focuses on the improvement of the socioeconomic
circumstances of African Americans and other underserved communities.
This site provides a short history of the CBC.

"Outstanding African Americans of Congress." http://uschscapitolhistory
.uschs.org/articles/uschs_articles-07.htm. This essay, part of the Capitol
History Web site, is a very good overview of the history of black legislators at the federal level.

"Reconstruction: A State Divided." http://lsm.crt.state.la.us/cabildo/cab11.htm.
Provides a history of Reconstruction in Louisiana, including mentions
of several African American pioneers such as John Willis Ménard, the
first African American to speak from the floor of Congress, and Charles
E. Nash, the only African American to actually represent Louisiana in the
U.S. Congress during the Reconstruction period.

44. Compromise of 1877

The presidential election of 1876 between Republican Rutherford
B. Hayes and Democrat Samuel B. Tilden threatened to renew hostilities
between the North and the South. Neither candidate had enough electoral votes to win, although Tilden had the majority of the popular vote
and needed only one more electoral vote to become president. The resulting compromise gave the White House to Hayes and removed federal
troops from the South, thereby ending Reconstruction.

When the election results came in, the votes from three southern
states—Louisiana, Florida, and South Carolina—remained in doubt.
The states had enough electoral votes to swing the election to Hayes. Both
parties began maneuvering to control how the votes of these states were
counted. The Constitution is silent on how a contested presidential

election should be decided. To resolve the problem, Congress created an electoral commission. In a series of votes along party lines, the commission gave the disputed electoral votes to Hayes. Democrats strongly protested.

To prevent a crisis, both Democrats and Republicans began to negotiate. Southerners, most of whom were Democrats, wanted an end to Reconstruction. Hayes agreed and ended federal military intervention in the South shortly after entering the White House on March 2, 1877.

TERM PAPER SUGGESTIONS

1. Compare and contrast the disputed election of 1876 with the disputed election of 2000.
2. Discuss the impact of the compromise upon African Americans in the South.
3. Explore why northerners such as President Rutherford B. Hayes were willing to end Reconstruction.
4. Compare and contrast Samuel B. Tilden with Rutherford B. Hayes.
5. Evaluate Rutherford B. Hayes's accomplishments as president.

ALTERNATIVE TERM PAPER SUGGESTIONS

1. Create a Web page that explains the end of Reconstruction.
2. Create a Microsoft PowerPoint presentation that explains the electoral college system and discusses whether it plays a valuable role in political governance.

SUGGESTED SOURCES

Primary Sources

"Diary and Letters of Rutherford B. Hayes." http://www.ohiohistory.org/online-doc/hayes/index.cfm. This site contains 3,000 pages of digitized text drawn from the 1922 published collection of Hayes's diary and letters. Researchers can search by volume and keyword or browse through the five volumes page by page.

Williams, Charles Richard, ed. *The Diary and Letters of Rutherford B. Hayes, Nineteenth President of the United States.* Columbus, OH: Ohio State Archeological and Historical Society, 1922. Hayes kept a diary from age 12 until his death at age 70 in 1893, making him one of only three presidents to keep a diary while in office.

Secondary Sources

Foner, Eric. *A Short History of Reconstruction.* New York: Harper Perennial, 1990. This is an abridged version of Foner's *Reconstruction: America's Unfinished Revolution.* The latter book is arguably the best study ever written about Reconstruction, and it won an unprecedented number of awards, including the Bancroft Prize.

Hoogenboom, Ari. *The Presidency of Rutherford B. Hayes.* Lawrence: University Press of Kansas, 1988. Part of a superb series on the American presidency, this is an excellent study of Hayes's term in office.

Hoogenboom, Ari. *Rutherford B. Hayes: Warrior and President.* Lawrence: University Press of Kansas, 1995. The best biography of Hayes, a Union veteran and one-term president.

Rehnquist, William H. *Centennial Crisis: The Disputed Election of 1876.* New York: Alfred A. Knopf, 2004. This book, by a former U.S. Supreme Court chief justice, focuses on the legal aspects of the election.

Woodward, C. Vann. *Reunion and Reaction: The Compromise of 1877 and the End of Reconstruction.* New York: Oxford University Press, 1991. Originally published in 1951, this is a study by the premiere historian of the American South.

Zuczek, Richard, ed. *Encyclopedia of the Reconstruction Era.* Westport, CT: Greenwood Press, 2006. Gives a thorough overview of the period in the A–Z entries.

World Wide Web

"American President, an Online Resource: Rutherford Birchard Hayes." http://millercenter.org/academic/americanpresident/hayes. This is the best site on Hayes, with essays on Hayes and his administration as well as summary of the president's life and suggested reading.

"The Compromise of 1877." http://compromiseof1877.com/index.htm. This is an exceptionally well-done Web site that, although lacking in images, examines the issue of, relevance of, and people involved with the electoral dispute. It contains a quiz, links to images, and links to other Web sites.

"Compromise of 1877." http://www.cusd.chico.k12.ca.us/~bsilva/ushist/02-CivilWar/handout/compromise_of_1877.htm. Consists of an essay that sets the compromise within the context of Reconstruction.

"The Compromise of 1877." http://www.fandm.edu/x2335.xml. This site, created by the Franklin and Marshall College Center for Politics and Public Affairs, summarizes the electoral dispute.

"Hayes vs. Tilden: The Electoral College Controversy of 1876–1877." http://elections.harpweek.com/controversy.htm. Using original Thomas Nast cartoons and articles from *Harper's Weekly* magazine, this site shows how the dispute was viewed in the nineteenth century.

"Politics and Public Service, Samuel J. Tilden, 1814–1886." http://www.u-s-history.com/pages/h397.html. Provides a short biography of Tilden. This is a problematic Web site because it makes several broad claims—for example, that the choice of Hayes was clearly counter to the will of the voters—that are not supported by the evidence.

"Rutherford B. Hayes—Nineteenth President of the United States." http://americanhistory.about.com/od/rutherfordbhayes1/p/phayes.htm. Provides a good biography of Hayes.

"Rutherford B. Hayes Presidential Center." http://www.rbhayes.org/hayes/links/. Includes an introduction to Hayes, information about conducting research in the Hayes library, and an introduction to the Hayes museum in Fremont, Ohio.

"Rutherford Birchard Hayes." http://www.ipl.org/div/potus/rbhayes.html. A good site on Hayes's presidency with links to his inaugural speech and related sites.

Multimedia Sources

Charlie Rose with William Rehnquist (March 11, 2004). Charlie Rose, 2006. DVD. Originally broadcast on PBS, former Chief Justice of the U.S. Supreme Court William Rehnquist discusses constitutional law and his book, *Centennial Crisis: The Disputed Election of 1876*.

Reconstruction: The Second Civil War. Boston: WGBH, 2004. This video explains the difficulties of Reconstruction and includes a short film on why it ended. It is one of the better history documentaries on the Civil War and Reconstruction eras.

45. Kansas Exodus Joint Stock Company Sends Emigrants West (1879)

As conditions in the South worsened for African Americans, many sought better opportunities in the West. Thousands of blacks left Louisiana, Mississippi, and Texas for Kansas in 1879. The exact number of "Exodusters" is estimated at anywhere from 6,000 to 20,000.

The Kansas Exodus reflected the failure of Reconstruction to bring economic and political equality to African Americans in the South. White southerners reacted with rage at the loss of their cheap labor supply. Rather than improve conditions for blacks, whites beat and threatened migrants. In the spring of 1880, Democrats in Congress ordered an investigation into the exodus, fearing that Republicans were enticing blacks to move to northern areas to vote Republican. African Americans called as witnesses spoke to the committee about the virulent racism in the South that prompted them to pack up and head to Kansas. Benjamin "Pap" Singleton informed the committee that he bore sole responsibility for the migration. Singleton, although a leader of black migrants, exaggerated his role, and some historians have repeated his embellishment as fact.

Not all African Americans supported the Kansas Exodus. Frederick Douglass opposed it because he viewed the migration as an abandonment of the fight for justice in the South. While life in Kansas brought enormous challenges, most Exodusters stayed in the state rather than return to the racism of the Deep South. As many of them stated, they preferred to starve in Kansas rather than be shot and killed in Mississippi.

TERM PAPER SUGGESTIONS

1. Describe how the racial situation in the South prompted African Americans to flee to Kansas.
2. Discuss the challenges facing immigrants to Kansas.
3. Frederick Douglass opposed the black exodus because he believed that migrants were abandoning the fight to improve the South. Ida B. Wells and other black leaders, however, supported migration as a means of using economics to force the South to improve. Wells theorized that the loss of black workers might prompt whites to try to entice blacks to stay in the South. Which argument do you support? Discuss.

ALTERNATIVE TERM PAPER SUGGESTIONS

1. Assume that you are one of the leaders of the exodus. Create a podcast in which you attempt to persuade African Americans to leave the South for Kansas.
2. Design a travel brochure that could be distributed to African Americans in Louisiana to persuade them to join the migration to Kansas. Include directions on the best route to Kansas.

SUGGESTED SOURCES

Primary Source

"The Exodus to Freedom." http://www.nps.gov/untold/banners_and_backgrounds/expansionbanner/exoduster.htm. Filled with the statements of blacks who moved to Kansas and urged other African Americans to do so as well.

Secondary Sources

Jack, Bryan M. *The St. Louis African American Community and the Exodusters.* St. Louis: University of Missouri Press, 2008. Many Exodusters left their homes with little money. Some ran out of funds in St. Louis. Jack tells how the city's African American community came to the aid of the migrants after city officials refused to do so for fear of encouraging more migrants.

Painter, Nell Irvin. *Exodusters: Black Migration to Kansas after Reconstruction.* New York: W.W. Norton, 1992. Focuses on the conditions that led to the movement of the Exodusters and not on what they found there, nor how they adapted to life in a strange land.

World Wide Web

"Escaping Jim Crow." http://www.jimcrowhistory.org/history/escaping.htm. This essay, by Ronald L. F. Davis, briefly explains how blacks sought to escape the indignities of segregation by migrating to Kansas.

"Exodus to Kansas: The 1880 Senate Investigation of the Beginnings of the African American Migration from the South." http://www.archives.gov/publications/prologue/2008/summer/exodus.html. This essay by Damani Davis, reprinted in full, first appeared in the magazine *Prologue*.

"Kansas Exodus." http://www.slaveryinamerica.org/scripts/sia/glossary.cgi?term=k&letter=yes. An encyclopedia article from Slavery in America.

"Reconstruction and Its Aftermath." http://lcweb2.loc.gov/ammem/aaohtml/exhibit/aopart5.html. Contains a paragraph on the black exodus to Kansas as well as a photograph of a settler and a map.

"To Kansas." http://www.inmotionaame.org/migrations/topic_body.cfm;jsessionid=f8302725271222879896126?migration=6&topic=4&bhcp=1. A short summary of the exodus is included alongside links to book chapters that have longer discussions of the migration. This site is especially valuable for its links to primary sources, including an interview with Bill Sims, an Exoduster.

46. Tuskegee Institute Is Founded (1881)

Booker T. Washington founded Alabama's Tuskegee Institute in 1881 to teach industrial skills and character building to African Americans. With black staff and faculty as well as black students, the school became one of the leading institutions of black higher learning.

In the era of slavery, numerous African Americans defied laws against black literacy to teach themselves and others to read. When freedom came, black leaders touted education as a means of advancing the race. Education for blacks would counter white supremacy while also providing economic help. By education, black leaders typically meant preparing the black masses for the rights and responsibilities of citizenship. The majority of uneducated blacks, just out of slavery, viewed education as a practical necessity and a social advantage. The ability to read and write, to understand labor contracts, to calculate payments, and to read the Bible would make them self-sufficient and give them status within the black community.

Nearly the entire system of black higher education sprang up after the Civil War. Many of the black schools focused on the liberal arts, reflecting the higher goals of the black elite. While many African American educators supported this liberal arts model, white philanthropists backed industrial education. Industrial courses such as agriculture, building trades, and domestic science would keep blacks in their place. Students would learn the skills needed to take a subservient place in society but would not develop their minds to serve as leaders. The Tuskegee Institute, run by blacks but dependent on white support, focused on industrial education. It equipped students for jobs in trade and agriculture while also training a large number of teachers. Tuskegee also taught cleanliness, table manners, and moral character. Washington recognized the practical value of education to farmers as well as the necessity of appeasing whites. He hoped that eventually educators trained by Tuskegee would help African Americans bring new ideas into the intellectual, moral, and religious lives of black people. In the meantime, he accommodated the racist attitudes of the people who paid Tuskegee's bills. By the time of Washington's death in 1915, Tuskegee had become an internationally famous institution of vocational learning.

TERM PAPER SUGGESTIONS

1. Discuss the industrial education movement.

2. Examine Booker T. Washington's contributions to the field of education.

3. Explore why so many blacks were infuriated by individuals such as Washington, who encouraged young African Americans to pursue industrial

education rather than a degree in the liberal arts. What does a liberal arts degree mean?

ALTERNATIVE TERM PAPER SUGGESTIONS

1. Assume that you are giving a presentation to a group of African Americans and their parents about the value of a degree from the Tuskegee Institute. Design a Microsoft PowerPoint presentation to persuade these students to enroll at Tuskegee.

2. Create a Booker T. Washington avatar in Second Life as well as a platform where he can speak. Advertise one of his speeches, then have the avatar give the speech. Report on the modern reaction to Washington's ideas. Does he still have any relevance today?

SUGGESTED SOURCES

Primary Sources

Washington, Booker T. *The Story of My Life and Work*. Atlanta, GA: J. L. Nichlos, 1901. There are numerous editions of Washington's autobiography, which first appeared in 1901. Washington describes the founding of Tuskegee.

Washington, Booker T., ed. *Tuskegee and Its People: Their Ideals and Achievements*. New York: Negro Universities Press, 1969. A discussion of the importance of Tuskegee to the African American community.

Washington, Booker T., ed. *Tuskegee: Its Story and Its Work*. New York: Negro Universities Press, 1969. An examination of Tuskegee that is not especially impartial.

Secondary Sources

Butler, Addie Louise Joyner. *The Distinctive Black College—Talladega, Tuskegee, and Morehouse*. Metuchen, NJ: Scarecrow Press, 1977. Compares Tuskegee with two of its peers.

Jackson, Clyde Owen. *Come Like the Benediction: A Tribute to Tuskegee Institute and Other Essays*. Smithtown, NY: Exposition Press, 1981. Describes the importance of Washington's school to the black community.

World Wide Web

"Jim Crow Stories: Tuskegee Institute Founded." http://www.pbs.org/wnet/jim-crow/stories_events_tuskegee.html. Complements the video *The Rise and Fall of Jim Crow* and includes a video clip on the reasons why Tuskegee became a trade school.

Tuskegee Institute. "In Industry the Foundation Must Be Laid." http://www
.nps.gov/archive/bowa/tuskin.html. This essay discusses the history and
impact of the Tuskegee Institute.

"Tuskegee Institute Class Roster 1915." http://www.afrigeneas.com/library/school-
rosters/tuskegee1915.html. Lists names, degrees, and lives after college.

"Tuskegee Institute National Historic Site." http://www.nps.gov/tuin/. Tuskegee
Institute National Historic Site is nestled on the campus of historic
Tuskegee University. The site includes the George W. Carver Museum
and The Oaks, home of Booker T. Washington.

"Tuskegee University." http://www.tuskegee.edu/Global/category.asp?
C=56172&nav=menu200_2. The Web page of the school founded by
Booker T. Washington.

Multimedia Source

The Rise and Fall of Jim Crow. New York: Quest, n.d. VHS. Includes a segment
on the Tuskegee Institute.

47. Colored Farmers' Alliance Representatives Help Found the Populist Party (1892)

In the 1870s, farmers' alliances began to grow in size and significance. Like older farm groups, they offered social and recreational opportunities, but they also emphasized political action. Farmers throughout the South and the Midwest joined the alliance movement to collectively seek relief from the hardships created by chronic debt, decreasing prices, and devastating droughts.

The Colored Farmers' Alliance, an organization of southern black farmers, began in Texas in 1886 under a white minister who reacted to the Southern Farmers' Alliance's rejection of African Americans as members. The organization spread to include thousands of black farmers in a dozen states. It negotiated lower rates from railroads as well as cheaper bulk purchases of farm supplies. White farmers' alliances then began to include black cotton growers in their sales agreements to prevent African Americans from undercutting wholesale prices. Once united, poor white and black farmers began to push for political changes to protect small growers. The coalition eventually led to the Populist or People's Party in 1892. The Knights of Labor, the Colored Farmers' Alliance, and the Dakota Alliance united to form the group to work for the redistribution of wealth as well as restrictions on the power of corporations and railroads. The party proved short-lived, fading away in 1896 following a merger with the Democratic Party.

TERM PAPER SUGGESTIONS

1. Examine the reforms sought by the alliance movement.
2. What reforms did the Populists seek, and to what extent did the movement succeed?
3. What factors prompted whites and blacks to unite in the Populist Party? Why did this effort at interracial unity collapse?
4. The Populists have been portrayed as farmers resisting the forward march of progress as well as modern people with a different vision for what America could become. Discuss which analysis is more credible.

ALTERNATIVE TERM PAPER SUGGESTIONS

1. Suppose you have been asked to persuade white farmers to unite with the Colored Farmers' Alliance. Create a Microsoft PowerPoint presentation that explains the benefits of joining the alliance and the benefits of cooperating across racial lines.
2. Assume there is some discussion about placing a historical marker about the Populist Party in your town or city. Design a Microsoft PowerPoint presentation to persuade city officials of the importance of the Populists.

SUGGESTED SOURCES

Primary Source

"Populist Party Platform, 1892 (July 4, 1892)." http://www.pinzler.com/ushistory/popparplatsupp.html. Provides the Populist plan for the future.

Secondary Sources

Gilbert, Charlene. *Homecoming: The Story of African American Farmers.* Boston: Beacon Press, 2002. Gilbert, an independent filmmaker, documents the historical importance of land and farming for blacks through photographs, historic accounts, and oral histories.

Postel, Charles. *The Populist Vision.* New York: Oxford University Press, 2007. Portrays the Populists as forward-looking individuals who had an alternate vision for what the United States could become.

Schwartz, Michael. *Radical Protest and Social Structure: The Southern Farmers' Alliance and Cotton Tenancy, 1880–1890.* Chicago: University of Chicago Press, 1988. Sociological study of the cotton tenancy system, institutionalized racism, and one-party politics that produced resistance in the form of the alliance.

Vincent, Stephen A. *Southern Seed, Northern Soil: African-American Farm Communities in the Midwest, 1765–1900.* Bloomington: Indiana University Press, 1999. Explores the history of the Beech and Roberts settlements, two African American and mixed-race farming communities in Indiana that managed to prosper.

World Wide Web

"Colored Farmers' Alliance." http://www.tshaonline.org/handbook/online/articles/CC/aac1.html. Good history of the alliance in Texas along with a bibliography.

"1896: The Populist Party." http://projects.vassar.edu/1896/populists.html. Otherwise good history of the Populist Party that completely misses the participating blacks.

"Farmers' Alliances." http://www.ohiohistorycentral.org/entry.php?rec=588. Brief history of all the alliances, not just the one dedicated for African Americans.

"Politics and Public Service: Populist Party, The People's Party." http://www.u-s-history.com/pages/h876.html. Simple history of the party that includes links to related sites, including the Populist Party platform.

"Preliminary Research for Writing a History of the Colored Farmers Alliance in the Populist Movement: 1886–1896, by Omar Ali, May 11, 1998, Department of History, Columbia University." http://www.geocities.com/SoHo/Workshop/4275/part1.html. Explores the Colored Farmers' Alliance and its role in the Populist movement.

48. Ida B. Wells Denounces Lynching (1892)

Journalist Ida B. Wells led the fight against the lynching of African Americans in the late nineteenth century. Common knowledge held that lynchings were a way of defending white women from the lust of black men. In the 1892 pamphlet *Southern Horrors,* she disputed this belief.

A fiery woman unafraid to challenge authority, Wells began her activist career by confronting Jim Crow segregation. In 1883, she refused to move to the segregated section of a railroad car and bit the conductor who tried to force her out of her seat. Wells won a lawsuit against the railroad in the lower courts, only to see the state supreme court overturn the verdict in 1887. A request to write about this episode for a Memphis newspaper launched her journalism career.

Established as a respected voice with the African American community of Memphis, Wells picked up her pen when a close friend died alongside two other black men at the hands of a lynch mob in 1892. Much more than a murder, a lynching aimed to intimidate an entire African American community, with local and state authorities either cooperating in the murder or turning a blind eye to it. Faced with white support for lynching, Wells advised blacks in Memphis to arm for self-defense and abandon the South for the newly opened territory of Oklahoma. She also embarked on an investigation of lynching. Wells combed through newspaper accounts, visited murder sites, and interviewed witnesses to determine that most lynchings could be credited to economic competition and racial control rather than the defense of southern white womanhood. In *Southern Horrors,* which mocked southern honor as the commonly cited justification for lynching, Wells documented that only a third of the 728 lynching victims between 1884 and 1892 were even accused of rape. She revealed that most "rapes" were in fact often consensual liaisons between black men and white women. Wells spent the rest of her life in the North to avoid being lynched in the South.

TERM PAPER SUGGESTIONS

1. *Southern Horrors* did not reduce the number of lynchings. For many decades, the U.S. Congress refused to pass an anti-lynching law despite the best efforts of lobbyists. Why do you think that lynching proved so difficult to stop?

2. What risks did Wells take by so boldly challenging the southern way of life?

3. It is easy to measure the legacy of someone who participated in an event that changed history. Wells died in 1931, before any major civil rights victories were achieved. What is her legacy?

ALTERNATIVE TERM PAPER SUGGESTIONS

1. Suppose a student has written an editorial for your school newspaper in which he states that he does not understand the fuss that African Americans have made over nooses. He argues that white men were lynched plenty of times

in the Old West and there was nothing racial about it. Write a response in which you explain the history of lynchings of African Americans.

2. Wells and other African American activists had no luck in persuading Congress to pass a federal anti-lynching law. Write such a law and create a Web-based marketing plan to persuade Congress to pass it.

SUGGESTED SOURCES

Primary Sources

Allen, James, ed. *Without Sanctuary: Lynching Photography in America.* Santa Fe, NM: Twin Palms, 2000. Reprints historic photographs of lynchings. Warning: This book contains images that are extremely disturbing.

Royster, Jacqueline Jones, ed. *Southern Horrors and Other Writings: The Anti-Lynching Campaign of Ida B. Wells, 1892–1900.* Boston: Bedford Books, 1997. Jones offers a biography of Wells and includes copies of her major writings, included the full text of *Southern Horrors.*

Wells, Ida B. *Crusade for Justice: The Autobiography of Ida B. Wells.* Chicago: University of Chicago Press, 1991. Wells writes of her efforts to change laws and attitudes oppressing blacks.

Wells-Barnett, Ida B. *On Lynchings.* New York: Humanity, 2002. Reprints Wells's three major pamphlets on lynching: *Southern Horrors, A Red Record,* and *Mob Rule in New Orleans.*

Secondary Sources

Davidson, James West. *"They Say": Ida B. Wells and the Reconstruction of Race.* New York: Oxford University Press, 2008. Examines the first 30 years of Wells's life, as well as the meaning of race in post-emancipation America.

Giddings, Paula J. *Ida: A Sword Among Lions: Ida B. Wells and the Campaign Against Lynching.* New York: Amistad, 2008. This is an eagerly anticipated book by one of the major historians of African American women's lives. Giddings tells the story of Wells's crusade against lynching, a practice that threatened both the lives of African Americans and the notion of a nation based on law.

McMurry, Linda O. *To Keep the Waters Troubled: The Life of Ida B. Wells.* New York: Oxford University Press, 1998. An excellent biography of the crusading journalist.

Schechter, Patricia A. *Ida B. Wells-Barnett and American Reform, 1880–1930.* Chapel Hill: University of North Carolina Press, 2001. Sets Wells in the context of civil rights reform in the nadir of American race relations.

Thompson, Mildred I. *Ida B. Wells-Barnett: An Exploratory Study of an American Black Woman, 1893–1930.* Brooklyn, NY: Carlson Publishing, 1990. Reviews Wells's life after the publication of *Southern Horrors,* when she had fled the South.

Tolnay, Stewart. *A Festival of Violence: An Analysis of Southern Lynchings, 1882–1930.* Urbana: University of Illinois Press, 1995. Builds on Wells's work by extending her study of lynching.

Zangrando, Robert. *The NAACP Crusade Against Lynching, 1909–1950.* Philadelphia: Temple University Press, 1989. Traces the unsuccessful effort to get a federal anti-lynching law passed.

World Wide Web

"History of Lynching in the United States." http://www.umass.edu/complit/aclanet/ACLAText/USLynch.html. Lists information related to lynching, including justifications and numbers.

"Ida Wells." http://memory.loc.gov/ammem/aap/idawells.html. The Library of Congress provides several links to background on the life of Ida B. Wells and her article, "Lynch Law in Georgia" (1899), exposing the myths and realities of lynching.

Multimedia Sources

Ida B. Wells: A Passion for Justice. Boston: WGBH Educational, 1990. VHS. Part of PBS's American Experience series, this is an excellent biography of a fascinating civil rights activist and her campaign against lynching.

Ida B. Wells: A Woman of Courage. History on Video, 2008. DVD. A good study of the activist by one of her descendents. A 1993 30-minute version is available on VHS.

49. Booker T. Washington Delivers Atlanta Compromise Speech (1895)

In the speech known as the Atlanta Compromise, African American educator Booker T. Washington told an audience of mostly whites at the Atlanta Cotton States and International Exposition that African Americans should not demand equal rights. He advised that blacks should concentrate on economic improvement and education. The speech serves as an example of accommodationist thought, drawing praise from whites and criticism from blacks, especially black educator W. E. B. Du Bois.

Washington became the most prominent black leader of the late nineteenth century. In the South, he focused on strategies that would allow blacks to move up the economic ladder. Partly because of his dependence on white money to finance his school, the Tuskegee Institute, Washington refused to publicly challenge a political and social system that oppressed blacks. By the time of Washington's speech in 1895, blacks had entered a period of history known as the nadir, because the situation could not get much worse for African Americans.

In Atlanta, Washington advised blacks to maintain peace with white southerners even if doing so meant abandoning their rights as citizens. They should stop agitating for political and social equality while accepting Jim Crow segregation. As part of this compromise, whites would work with blacks on common economic interests and support black efforts at self-improvement through education and work. Washington advised blacks to accept low-level jobs rather than demand equal treatment and equal opportunity. He emphasized that black education should not match the education afforded to whites. Instead of liberal arts, blacks should learn agriculture and the skilled trades. By promoting the accommodation in a way designed to make whites support black progress, he also made it clear that he would not fight against segregation. Although Washington's personal feelings about accommodation indicate that he did not entirely like the concept, he felt that it was politically wiser to publicly appear to be nonthreatening to whites.

TERM PAPER SUGGESTIONS

1. Booker T. Washington grew up in the South and spent his life in the region during an era known for extreme hostility toward African Americans. Research Washington's background and discuss how his experiences shaped his philosophy of accommodation to racism.

2. Compare and contrast Washington's philosophy for advancement with that offered by his harshest critic, W. E. B. Du Bois.

3. Ida B. Wells, a southerner like Washington who had similar experiences with racial hostility, urged African Americans to rage against discrimination. Compare and contrast Wells with Washington.

4. Washington delivered the Atlanta Compromise speech in part to gain white support for his Tuskegee Institute. He sought to appear as nonthreatening as possible. Discuss the white reaction to Washington's philosophy of accommodation.

5. Discuss why many African Americans resisted the advice offered by Washington in the Atlanta Compromise speech.

6. Analyze Washington's accommodationist strategy. Did it offer the best chance for success for blacks in the South?

ALTERNATIVE TERM PAPER SUGGESTIONS

1. Assume that there is an online poll to name the most significant African American leader of the period 1890–1920. Create a Web site to promote Booker T. Washington for this honor.

2. Washington promoted technical education as a means of advancing the black race, while W. E. B. Du Bois advocated a liberal arts education for African Americans. This debate over the best form of education still continues. Research technical education and liberal arts education. Design a Web page that compares and contrasts the costs and benefits of both.

SUGGESTED SOURCES

Primary Sources

"The Booker T. Washington Papers." http://www.historycooperative.org/btw/. Contains Washington's correspondence to donors, newspapers, and others concerning African American matters.

"Booker T. Washington's Atlanta Compromise Speech." http://www.crm-essentials.com/Atlanta_Compromise.pdf. Provides the full text of the famous speech.

"Books by Booker T. Washington in Project Gutenberg." http://www.gutenberg.org/author/Booker+T.+Washington.. Provides the full text of Washington's *Up From Slavery* autobiography as well as several of his other books.

Washington, Booker T. *Up From Slavery.* Rocky Mount, NC: Gardner's, 2007. Available in many editions, this is Washington's autobiography. He discusses the events leading to the Atlanta Compromise speech as well as the entire address.

Secondary Sources

Baker, Houston A., Jr. *Turning South Again: Re-Thinking Modernism/Re-Reading Booker T. Washington.* Durham, NC: Duke University Press, 2001. Challenges Washington's view that confrontation with whites would result in the weakening of the Tuskegee Institute and diminish possibilities for black advancement.

Bontemps, Arno. *Young Booker T. Washington's Early Days.* New York: Dodd, Mead, 1972. Exceptionally well-written story of Washington's life up to the 1895 Atlanta speech.

Brundage, Fitzhugh, ed. *Booker T. Washington and Black Progress: "Up From Slavery" One Hundred Years Later.* Gainesville: University Press of Florida, 2003. Contains essays that examine Washington from various angles. Some of the scholars place Washington's Atlanta speech within a nineteenth-century economic context.

Carroll, Rebecca, ed. *Uncle Tom or New Negro? African Americans Reflect on Booker T. Washington and* Up From Slavery *One Hundred Years Later.* New York: Broadway Books, 2006. Discusses the controversy that has swirled around Washington since 1895.

Du Bois, W. E. B. *The Souls of Black Folk.* New York: Pocket Books, 2005. Available in many editions, this book sets out Du Bois's disagreement with Washington's philosophy of success for African Americans.

Franklin, John Hope, and Alfred A. Moss Jr. *From Slavery to Freedom: A History of African Americans.* New York: Alfred A. Knopf, 1994. Discusses Washington and his views.

Harlan, Louis R. *Booker T. Washington: The Making of a Black Leader, 1865–1901.* New York: Oxford University Press, 1972. Discusses the effect of Washington's Atlanta speech.

Hawkins, Hugh, ed. *Booker T. Washington and His Critics: The Problem of Negro Leadership.* Lexington, MA: D.C. Heath, 1962. Many whites and blacks regarded Washington as the leader of the African American community. Yet many prominent blacks, especially W. E. B. Du Bois, challenged Washington's direction as self-destructive. This set of essays examines the dispute over Washington's leadership.

Meier, August. *Negro Thought in America, 1880–1915: Racial Ideologies in the Age of Booker T. Washington.* Ann Arbor: University of Michigan Press, 1963. Meier, one of the best-known and most prolific scholars of black history, examines black intellectual responses to the severe racism of the post-Reconstruction era.

Moore, Jacqueline M. *Booker T. Washington, W. E. B. Du Bois, and the Struggle for Racial Uplift.* Wilmington, DE: Scholarly Resources, 2003. Compares and contrasts the accommodationist Washington with the more aggressive Du Bois.

Verney, Kevern. *The Art of the Possible: Booker T. Washington and Black Leadership in the United States, 1881–1925.* New York: Routledge, 2001. Compares Washington with other major black leaders while discussing his views on segregation and accommodation.

World Wide Web

"Booker T. Washington." http://memory.loc.gov/ammem/aap/bookert.html. Contains a biographical sketch of Washington and a link to an audio clip of his Atlanta address.

"Booker T. Washington National Monument." http://www.nps.gov/archive/bowa/home.htm. Contains a brief biography of Washington as well as essays about the Atlanta Compromise and the reaction to it.

"Booker T. Washington's West Virginia Boyhood." http:www.wvculture.org/history/journal_wvh/wvh32-1.html. Brief discussion of Washington's youth in West Virginia.

"Legends of Tuskegee." http://www.nps.gov/museum/exhibits/tuskegee/intro.htm. Biographical sketch of Washington and selected bibliography.

Multimedia Sources

Black Americans of Achievement: Booker T. Washington. Wynnewood, PA: Schlessinger Media, 1992. VHS. Short documentary of Washington aimed at grade school students.

Booker T. Washington, the Life and Legacy. Huntsville, TX: Educational Video Network, 2005. VHS. Short biography that depicts Washington in a positive light and focuses on his commitment to education.

50. *Plessy v. Ferguson* (1896)

When the U.S. Supreme Court decided against Homer A. Plessy in 1896, it put a stamp of approval upon segregation as a legal doctrine. In a landmark case that set back the cause of justice, the Court ruled that "separate but equal" facilities for blacks and whites were acceptable under the Constitution.

Louisiana in the 1890s required separate-but-equal accommodations for whites and blacks on railroad cars. A group of New Orleans African Americans decided to challenge this law. Part of the strategy was to have someone of mixed blood violate the law, to allow a legal challenge to the arbitrariness by which people were classified as black. Plessy, a resident of New Orleans, had one-eighth African blood, therefore qualifying as white under Louisiana law. Light-skinned enough to pass for white, Plessy probably could have ridden in the white railroad car without trouble, but he wanted to challenge the law. The railroad company also sought to have the law overturned because of the added business expense of providing separate cars for the races. By prearrangement, the railroad conductor and a detective detained Plessy in June 1892 when he sat in the forbidden place.

In court, Plessy's attorney Albion Winegar Tourgee argued that the law deprived him of equal protection rights under the Fourteenth Amendment. He insisted that the real intention of the law was not promote the public good but to promote the happiness of whites at the expense of blacks. Additionally, Tourgee noted that people of mixed race were so common that it was virtually impossible to determine race in any fair manner and such a difficult determination should not be left to a railroad conductor. By a vote of seven to one, the Court ruled against Plessy. Writing for the majority, Justice Henry Billings Brown stated that the Fourteenth Amendment could not be used to abolish distinctions based on color, to enforce social equality, or require the mixing of the races. Justice John Marshall Harlan, the lone dissenter, argued that the Constitution was color-blind. The *Plessy* case would not be overturned until the 1954 *Brown v. Board of Education* decision ended school segregation.

TERM PAPER SUGGESTIONS

1. Businesses suffered from the costs of providing separate-but-equal facilities right up until the passage of the Civil Rights Act in 1964 that outlawed discrimination in public accommodations. The Louisiana railroad in *Plessy* did not want to bear the burden of providing separate railroad cars for the races. Examine the impact of the "separate but equal" doctrine upon businesses.

2. When Justice John Marshall Harlan dissented, he warned that the *Plessy* decision would prove to be as "pernicious" as the *Dred Scott* decision. Was Harlan correct? Compare and contrast the impact of *Dred Scott* with the impact of *Plessy*.

3. Homer Plessy, with only one-eighth black blood, did not look like an African American. Examine the notion of race. What makes someone black or white?

4. Justice John Marshall Harlan warned that *Plessy* would encourage racial hatred and that no one would be fooled into thinking that separate accommodations were "equal." Was Harlan right? Examine the impact of *Plessy* upon American life.

5. Justice John Marshall Harlan, the son of a Kentucky slaveholding family, almost resigned from the Union Army because of his opposition to Abraham Lincoln's Emancipation Proclamation. Yet, as a Supreme Court justice, Harlan often served as the lone voice in support of equal rights for blacks. Examine Harlan's life. Note that John Marshall Harlan II is the grandson of this Harlan and also served on the Court.

ALTERNATIVE TERM PAPER SUGGESTIONS

1. Assume that Homer Plessy has gone to civil court in the wake of the 1954 *Brown* decision to argue for damages for years of enduring the "separate but equal" doctrine's effects. You are his attorney. Present a case to the jury.

2. There is no monument to Homer Plessy in New Orleans. Assume that you are petitioning the City of New Orleans to erect a historical marker about Plessy. Present an argument for the significance of the man and his legal case.

SUGGESTED SOURCES

Primary Sources

Chafe, William H., et al., eds. *Remembering Jim Crow: African Americans Tell about Life in the Segregated South.* New York: New Press, 2001. Through first-person accounts, this book tells of the effects of *Plessy v. Ferguson* upon everyday Americans.

"*Plessy vs. Ferguson*—1896." http://www.multied.com/Documents/PlessyvsFerguson .html. Provides Harlan's dissenting opinion.

Plessy v. Ferguson, 163 U.S. 537 (1896). http://www.law.cornell.edu/supct/html/ historics/USSC_CR_0163_0537_ZS.html. Provides the full text of the case.

Secondary Sources

Aaseng, Nathan. *Plessy v. Ferguson.* San Diego, CA: Lucent Books, 2003. Written for secondary school students, this is a good discussion of the case.

Anderson, Wayne. *Plessy v. Ferguson: Legalizing Segregation.* New York: Rosen, 2003. This is a readable book for high school students that includes excerpts from the trial and the Supreme Court decision.

Ayers, Edward L. *Southern Crossing: A History of the American South, 1877–1906.* New York: Oxford University Press, 1994. Exceptionally well written account of African American political, social, and cultural life after Reconstruction.

Elliott, Mark. *Color-Blind Justice: Albion Tourgee and the Quest for Racial Equality from the Civil War to Plessy v. Ferguson.* New York: Oxford University Press, 2006. Tourgee, a veteran of the Union Army, spent his life fighting for civil rights. For his efforts, southerners condemned him as a Yankee carpetbagger. This is a richly detailed biography of Plessy's attorney, a man now nearly completely forgotten who deserves to be remembered.

Fireside, Harvey. *Separate and Unequal: Homer Plessy and the Supreme Court Decision That Legalized Racism.* New York: Carroll and Graf, 2004. A scholarly account of the historical impact of the "separate but equal" doctrine upon African Americans.

Lofgren, Charles A. *The Plessy Case: A Legal-Historical Interpretation.* New York: Oxford University Press, 1987. Argues that the Supreme Court simply legally affirmed that segregation had become a fact of American life.

Logan, Rayford W. *The Betrayal of the Negro: From Rutherford B. Hayes to Woodrow Wilson.* New York: Da Capo Press, 1997. First published in 1954, this is an examination of the retreat from racial equality that followed the end of Reconstruction. Logan includes discussion of Supreme Court cases.

Medley, Keith Weldon. *We As Freemen: Plessy v. Ferguson.* Gretna, LA: Pelican, 2003. An engaging narrative history of the famous legal case.

Packard, Jerrold M. *American Nightmare: The History of Jim Crow.* New York: St. Martin's Press, 2004. Details the impact of *Plessy v. Ferguson* throughout the nation.

Przybyszewski, Linda. *The Republic According to John Marshall Harlan.* Chapel Hill: University of North Carolina Press, 1999. The best biography of one of the most significant Supreme Court justices.

Woodward, C. Vann. *The Strange Career of Jim Crow.* New York: Oxford University Press, 1974. First published in 1955, this is the book that made Woodward famous. It has held up exceptionally over the years and remains a readable introduction to segregation.

Wormser, Richard. *The Rise and Fall of Jim Crow.* New York: St. Martin's Press, 2004. An accompaniment to the PBS series of the same name, this book traces the history of segregation to 1954.

World Wide Web

"Landmark Series: Supreme Court: *Plessy v. Ferguson.*" http://www.landmark cases.org/plessy/home.html. This is the best site on the case, with the complete case available for PDF download, as well as other resources and activities.

"*Plessy v. Ferguson.*" http://www.bgsu.edu/departments/acs/1890s/plessy/plessy.html. A brief scholarly essay on the case.

"*Plessy v. Ferguson.*" http://www.oyez.org/cases/1851-1900/1895/1895_210/. This site contains a summary of the decision as well as link to the written opinion.

"*Plessy v. Ferguson.*" http://www.watson.org/~lisa/blackhistory/post-civilwar/plessy.html. A short essay on the case.

Multimedia Sources

Plessy v. Ferguson Today. Washington, DC: Public Affairs Video Archives, 1996. VHS. Not the most exciting of videos, this is a collection of talking heads from various disciplines who consider the ramifications of *Plessy v. Ferguson.* The content is excellent, although the presentation is weak.

Rise and Fall of Jim Crow. Alexandria, VA: PBS Home Video, 2002. VHS. Excellent documentary about the history of segregation from the Civil War to the civil rights movement, with a segment on *Plessy.*

51. Buffalo Soldiers Serve in the American West and Spanish American War (1890s)

African Americans have served in every war fought by the United States, including the Indian Wars in the West and the Spanish American War of 1898. The black men who served in these conflicts were known as "buffalo soldiers," reportedly because Native Americans thought that the hair of African Americans resembled that of the bison.

In 1866, Congress authorized recruitment of African Americans to assist in the pacification of the West. Over the next 40 years, 25,000 African American soldiers passed through the ranks of the 2 black cavalry regiments, the 9th and 10th, and the 2 black infantry regiments, the 24th and 25th. Blacks comprised about 20 percent of the men in the entire U.S. Cavalry. The average recruit signed up for a stable job, a steady income, and the status that came with a uniform. Soldiers learned to read and write, opportunities that they leaped upon despite a shortage of trained teachers.

The army offered reliable, dignified, and rewarding labor, but some African Americans were appalled by the federal government's policies toward Native Americans. In several cases black soldiers protected Indians from bloodthirsty white soldiers, lawmen, or civilians. Some white officers, such as George Armstrong Custer, refused to serve alongside blacks. Others, such as John J. Pershing, were proud to do so. Pershing, nicknamed "Black Jack" when he led the Tenth Cavalry, took his troops into battle on San Juan Hill in Cuba during the Spanish American War.

TERM PAPER SUGGESTIONS

1. Despite discriminatory treatment by white superiors and the federal government, African Americans enlisted in the army by the thousands. Discuss the reasons why blacks volunteered for military service.
2. Discuss the challenges that the buffalo soldiers faced in the American West.
3. Examine the legacy left by the buffalo soldiers.
4. Discuss the treatment of the buffalo soldiers by the federal government.
5. Examine the role played by black soldiers in the Spanish American War.

ALTERNATIVE TERM PAPER SUGGESTIONS

1. Assume that a buffalo soldier has asked you to create a Facebook or MySpace page for him. Introduce the man, capture his daily life, and discuss his goals in life.
2. Assume that you are a young black man applying to West Point in the late nineteenth century. Write an essay persuading the director of admissions to accept you.

SUGGESTED SOURCES

Primary Source

Nalty, Bernard C., and Morris J. Macbregar. *Blacks in the Military: Essential Documents.* Wilmington, DE: Scholarly Resources, 1981. A good reference source for the entire history of blacks in the armed services.

Secondary Sources

Asyot, Gerald. *The Right to Fight, the History of African Americans in the Military.* Novato, CA: Presidio Press, 1998. Focuses on the Spanish American War through Korea with heavy use of personal narratives from black soldiers.
Cunningham, Roger D. *The Black Citizen-Soldiers of Kansas, 1864–1901.* St. Louis: University of Missouri Press, 2008. Examines the lives of buffalo soldiers in Kansas.
Donaldson, Gary. *The History of African-Americans in the Military: Double V.* Malabar, FL: Krieger, 1991. Designed for undergraduates, this is a short history of black soldiers from the colonial era to the present.
Downey, Fairfax. *The Buffalo Soldiers in the Indian Wars.* New York: McGraw Hill, 1969. Interesting examination of how the black man fought the red man in the late nineteenth century.

Field, Ron. *Buffalo Soldiers, 1866–91.* New York: Osprey, 2004. A short but informative book on the black soldier during the Indian Wars.

Field, Ron. *Buffalo Soldiers, 1892–1918.* New York: Osprey, 2004. Succinct history of black soldiers during the Spanish American War, the Philippines War, and World War I.

Katz, William Loren. *Black West: A Documentary and Pictorial History of the African American Role in the Westward Expansion of the United States.* New York: Harlem Moon Broadway Books, 2005. Contains a well-researched and very readable chapter on black soldiers in the West, including a section on a black woman who joined the military during the Civil War and remained in uniform until 1876. Another chapter addresses buffalo soldiers who served overseas.

Leckie, William H., and Shirley A. Leckie. *The Buffalo Soldiers: A Narrative of the Negro Cavalry in the West.* Norman: University of Oklahoma Press, 1967. This is the first book to acknowledge the achievements of the black soldiers in the West.

World Wide Web

"Buffalo Soldiers." http://www.buffalosoldiers.com/. This site appears to be misnamed. It focuses on blacks in the military and cavalry actions in the Guadalupe Mountains. It does, however, include links to notable buffalo soldiers, a buffalo soldiers monument, and photographs. The bibliography appears to list every publication ever created on the buffalo soldiers.

"Buffalo Soldiers and Indian Wars." http://www.buffalosoldier.net/. Essentially an annotated chronology of the involvement of black soldiers in the wars in the West. It includes a video clip of the 25th Infantry in Cuba during the Spanish American War of 1898.

"Buffalo Soldiers National Museum." http://www.buffalosoldiermuseum.com/. The site for this Houston, Texas museum contains a good introduction to both blacks in the military and the buffalo soldiers specifically.

"Buffalo Soldiers on the Western Frontier." http://www.coax.net/people/lwf/BUFFPAGE.HTM. Essentially a listing of the regiments of buffalo soldiers and the duties of the men.

Multimedia Sources

Buffalo Soldiers. Los Angeles: Warner Home Video, 1997. DVD. Fictional account of the soldiers starring Danny Glover.

Crucible of Empire: The Spanish-American War. Boston: PBS, 1999. VHS. This is the only documentary to examine the Spanish American War and is only available on video. It is an excellent and fascinating study of the war from all perspectives.

52. Scott Joplin's "Maple Leaf Rag" Establishes Ragtime as an American Musical Form (1899)

Scott Joplin became one of the earliest and best composers of ragtime, a syncopated (or "ragged time") and improvised style of music of African American origins. With the "Maple Leaf Rag" in 1899, he created an instrumental piece that became the best-selling music of the ragtime era.

Joplin, the Texas-born son of a slave, became a composer and pianist of note in Sedalia, Missouri in the 1890s. He regularly played at a black social club, the Maple Leaf Club. In 1899, he published the "Maple Leaf Rag." The song sold about 500,000 copies and gave Joplin the title "King of Ragtime Writers." Joplin wrote many other ragtime pieces, including "The Entertainer," but he longed to break into opera, ballet, and musical theatre. It is likely that his race blocked him from being viewed as a composer of serious music. Long plagued by financial and health problems, Joplin died in 1917. By the time of his death, ragtime had faded as a musical form to be replaced by jazz.

A rag is an instrumental, syncopated march that follows the same formal conventions as a march. Syncopation is the continuous superimposition of an irregular rhythm over the top of a regular one. In piano rags such as the ones that Joplin wrote, a regular pulse is maintained by the left hand alternating a low bass note with a chord in the midrange. This produces a heavy accent on the first and third beats of the measure. The right hand provides rhythm. Although syncopation is essentially of African origins, its combination with the European musical system created a unique musical form. Ragtime became the first significant musical innovation to evolve from the cultural interchange brought about by the introduction of slavery into the Americas. It is the first African American music as well as the predecessor of jazz, rhythm and blues, and rock.

TERM PAPER SUGGESTIONS

1. Discuss the history of ragtime as a uniquely American musical form.

2. Describe how Joplin's music became so popular that it crossed racial boundaries.

3. Examine the links between ragtime, jazz, and rock and roll.

4. Compare and contrast Scott Joplin with another African American musical pioneer, perhaps his contemporary W. C. Handy.

ALTERNATIVE TERM PAPER SUGGESTIONS

1. Create a Web site that introduces the musical forms created and popularized by African Americans, including ragtime, blues, jazz, reggae, and rap.

2. Create a musical history of black America on your iPod, starting with songs that address slavery and concluding with songs that discuss current urban problems. Provide an introduction to each song to explain how it fits into African American history.

SUGGESTED SOURCES

Primary Sources

Berlin, Edward A. *King of Ragtime: Scott Joplin and His Era.* New York: Oxford University Press, 1994. Contains the three songs missing from *The Complete Works of Scott Joplin* and is the best biography of Joplin.

Joplin, Scott. *The Complete Works of Scott Joplin.* New York: Delta, 1993. These CDs contain the most complete collection of Joplin's music, missing only three songs.

Secondary Sources

Bankston, John. *The Life and Times of Scott Joplin.* Hockessin, DE: Mitchell Lane, 2004. Aimed at secondary school students, this book sets Joplin's life in the context of the challenges facing blacks in post-Reconstruction and early twentieth-century America.

Berlin, Edward A. *Ragtime: A Musical and Cultural History.* Berkeley: University of California Press, 1980. Sets ragtime in historical and cultural context.

Blesh, Rudi, and Harriet Janis. *They All Played Ragtime: The True Story of an American Music.* New York: Oak, 1971. The first Joplin biography, originally published in 1950; it suffers from fictionalizing.

Curtis, Susan. *Dancing to a Black Man's Tune: A Life of Scott Joplin.* Columbia: University of Missouri Press, 1994. Scholarly account of Joplin's life.

Doctorow, E. L. *Ragtime: A Novel.* New York: Random House, 2007. Made into a movie, this entertaining book is marked by considerable historical accuracy about the era of ragtime.

Gammond, Peter. *Scott Joplin and the Ragtime Era.* New York: St. Martin's Press, 1975. Blends chapters on Joplin's life with chapters about the era in which he lived.

Jasen, David A., and Trebor Jay Tichenor. *Rags and Ragtime: A Musical History.* Mineola, NY: Dover, 1989. Good history of ragtime and its background.

Schafer, William J., and Johannes Riedel. *The Art of Ragtime: Form and Meaning of an Original Black American Art.* Baton Rouge: Louisiana State University Press, 1973. Explains the African roots of ragtime.

Waldo, Terry. *This Is Ragtime.* New York: Da Capo, 1991. Probably the best introduction to the musical form by a noted historian of music.

World Wide Web

"A Biography of Scott Joplin." http://www.scottjoplin.org/biography.htm. Provides a long biographical sketch of the composer.

"100 Years of Maple Leaf Rag." http://music.minnesota.publicradio.org/features/9905_ragtime/index.shtml. Provides a biographical sketch of Joplin as well as an audio example of his music.

"Ragtime." http://lcweb2.loc.gov/diglib/ihas/html/ragtime/ragtime-home.html. On this Library of Congress site, probably the best site devoted to this musical form, the visitor can find essays about ragtime, sheet music, and audios.

"Scott Joplin: A Brief Biographical Sketch." http://www.edwardaberlin.com/work4.htm. Berlin is the major biographer of Joplin. This site contains a biography of Joplin that is based on extensive research.

Scott Joplin International Ragtime Foundation. http://www.scottjoplin.org/. Information about the foundation's activities, including plans for a museum dedicated to the composer in Sedalia, Missouri.

Multimedia Sources

Scott Joplin. Milburn, NJ: Meet the Musicians, 1999. VHS. Profiles Joplin as a man who broke down racial barriers with his music.

Scott Joplin. Universal, CA: Universal Pictures, 2001. VHS. Fictionalized account of Joplin's life starring Billy Dee Williams as the ragtime composer.

53. W. E. B. Du Bois Publishes *The Souls of Black Folk* (1903)

W. E. B. Du Bois ranks alongside Booker T. Washington and Frederick Douglass as one of the most influential African American men of the era before the civil rights movement of the 1960s. A cofounder of the National Association for the Advancement of Colored People (NAACP), his most influential work was *The Souls of Black Folk*.

Born in Massachusetts in 1868, Du Bois in 1895 became the first African American to earn a doctorate from Harvard University. A sociologist, Du Bois struggled to find a job despite his stellar credentials. He joined the faculty of historically black Atlanta University in 1897. When Sam Hose died at the hands of a lynch mob in 1899, Du Bois prepared a scholarly essay on the especially gruesome murder. Then, he passed a store displaying Hose's knuckles in a jar. Du Bois threw away his essay and began writing *The Souls of Black Folk*. The book, a passionate attack on the supposed benefits of accommodationism, directly challenged Booker T. Washington. Du Bois famously identified "the color line" as the central issue of the twentieth century.

In 1905, Du Bois helped form the Niagara Movement to challenge Washington's leadership. The movement focused on obtaining full political rights for African Americans to speed civil advancement. The movement proved short-lived, however. In 1909, Du Bois joined a mixed-race group of activists to create the National Association for the Advancement of Colored People. Du Bois edited the NAACP magazine, *The Crisis,* from 1910 to 1934. Increasingly focused on pan-Africanism, Du Bois became more militant and controversial. Atlanta University eventually dismissed him for his radical views in 1944. The NAACP threw him out in 1948 for criticizing American foreign policy, particularly his sympathy for the Soviet Union. Du Bois moved to Ghana in 1961 and died as a Ghanaian citizen in 1963.

TERM PAPER SUGGESTIONS

1. Du Bois argued that Booker T. Washington did not correctly value voting, belittled racism, and opposed the ambitions of bright African Americans to pursue advanced learning. Examine Du Bois's criticisms.

2. What sort of futures did W. E. B. Du Bois and Booker T. Washington envision for black America?

3. Discuss the Niagara Movement. How did Du Bois plan to secure full civil and political rights for African Americans?

4. A biographer of Du Bois has argued that he always had influence but not power. Examine Du Bois's life. Is this claim true?

5. Many African Americans, including Du Bois, had a positive view of the Soviet Union. Examine the links between African Americans and communism in the

first half of the twentieth century. Why were blacks like Du Bois drawn to communism?

ALTERNATIVE TERM PAPER SUGGESTIONS

1. Design an online biographical sketch of Du Bois with hyperlinks that explain *The Souls of Black Folk,* the Niagara Movement, and the NAACP.

2. Du Bois argued that the African American in the United States would never be viewed as an equal until Africa had been freed from the domination of whites. Design two posters persuading African Americans to take an interest in freeing Africa from imperialism.

SUGGESTED SOURCES

Primary Sources

Du Bois, W. E. B. *The Autobiography of W. E. B. Du Bois: A Soliloquy on Viewing My Life from the Last Decade of Its First Century.* New York: International Publishers, 1968. In his nineties, Du Bois looked back on his life.

Du Bois, W. E. B. *Color and Democracy: Colonies and Peace.* Millwood, NY: Kraus-Thomson, 1975. Originally published in 1945, this book reflects Du Bois's fight against imperialism in Africa.

Du Bois, W. E. B. *Dusk of Dawn: An Autobiography of a Concept of Race.* Millwood, NY: Kraus-Thomson, 1975. Originally published in 1940, this is a study of the notion of race.

Du Bois, W. E. B. *The Souls of Black Folk.* Mineola, NY: Dover, 1994. This collection of essays is Du Bois's most significant work.

Walden, Daniel, ed. *W. E. B. Du Bois: The Crisis Writings.* Greenwich, CT: Fawcett, 1972. Collects Du Bois's writings from when he served as the editor of this NAACP magazine.

Secondary Sources

Crouch, Stanley, and Playthell Benjamin. *Reconsidering the Souls of Black Folk: Thoughts on the Groundbreaking Classic Work of W. E. B. Du Bois.* Philadelphia: Running Press, 2002. Evaluates Du Bois's criticisms 100 years after the publication of his book.

DeMarco, Joseph P. *The Social Thought of W. E. B. Du Bois.* Lanham, MD: University Press of America, 1983. Analyzes Du Bois's views about race.

Lewis, David Levering. *W. E. B. Du Bois: Biography of a Race, 1868–1919.* New York: Henry Holt, 1993. Examines the path that Du Bois took from scholar to political activist.

Lewis, David Levering. *W. E. B. Du Bois: The Fight for Equality and the American Century, 1919–1963.* New York: Henry Holt, 2000. Superb study of Du Bois's struggle on behalf of blacks during the second half of his life.

World Wide Web

"An American Nightmare." www.nytimes.com/books/98/05/03/reviews/980503.03ayrest.html. Describes the Sam Hose lynching and Du Bois's reaction to it as part of a larger essay on segregation.

"A Biographical Sketch of W. E. B. Du Bois." http://www.duboislc.org/html/DuBoisBio.html. Very good introduction to Du Bois with a guide to further reading.

"NAACP—W. E. B. Du Bois." http://www.naacp.org/about/history/dubois/. Biographical sketch of the activist and scholar from the organization that he helped to found.

"A Timeless Legacy: Celebrating 100 Years of W. E. B. Du Bois's the Souls of Black Folk." http://findarticles.com/p/articles/mi_m0DXK/is_26_19/ai_98171169. Explains the legacy of Du Bois.

Multimedia Sources

Against the Odds: The Artists of the Harlem Renaissance. Arlington, VA: PBS Home Video, 2004. DVD. Looks at the way in which Du Bois helped shape this movement.

History of Black Achievement in America. New York: Ambrose Video, 2005. DVD. Programs 5 and 6 address Du Bois.

The Rise and Fall of Jim Crow. San Francisco: California Newsreel, 2004. DVD. Covers Du Bois's formation of the NAACP.

54. Jack Johnson Becomes the First Black Heavyweight Boxing Champion (1908)

In the twentieth century African Americans gained recognition as sports figures. Jack Johnson, in an enormously symbolic event, became the first black heavyweight champion of the world when he defeated Tommy Burns in Sydney, Australia, in 1908. With the victory he challenged the racial superiority of whites, prompting whites to frantically search for a "great white hope" who could defeat Johnson.

Johnson, the son of a former slave, learned to fight in Galveston, Texas. After winning a number of hometown and regional bouts, he won the unofficial black heavyweight title in 1903. Johnson then began traveling the country to defend his title. About 1905, he began to be viewed as a contender for the heavyweight championship of the world. An especially good defensive fighter, Johnson also began to gain a reputation for flamboyant dressing, taunting opponents in the ring, and dating white women. In 1908, Johnson knocked out Burns and sent shock waves around the world. Former heavyweight champion James J. Jeffries came out of retirement to beat Johnson for the sake of the white race. Johnson completely dominated the fight and retained his title. Whites responded with attacks upon blacks, with most of the disturbances occurring in the South.

To try to control Johnson and other blacks who might emulate him, white-dominated legislatures passed several laws. A 1912 federal law prohibited the interstate transportation of fight films, so that fewer people would see Johnson defeating white boxers. Ten states passed new laws on miscegenation, preventing blacks and whites from engaging in sexual intercourse. Johnson was arrested in 1912 for violating the Mann Act by transporting a woman across state lines for sexual purposes. The woman involved, his white secretary and girlfriend, refused to testify against him. Johnson left the United States, lost his title in 1915, and died after driving his car too fast in 1946.

TERM PAPER SUGGESTIONS

1. Compare and contrast Jack Johnson with Muhammad Ali.

2. Trace the history of African Americans and heavyweight boxing in the twentieth century.

3. Jack Johnson focused on his personal right to equality with whites, rather than advocating for the advancement of the status of all African Americans. Discuss whether Johnson should be viewed as hero, as many of his black contemporaries saw him, or just as an extraordinary athlete.

ALTERNATIVE TERM PAPER SUGGESTIONS

1. Create a Web site that pays tribute to Johnson's accomplishments as an athlete and as a man who challenged white racist views.

2. Create a Web site that provides a short history of the most influential black athlete of each decade since 1900, starting with Jack Johnson for the first decade of the twentieth century.

SUGGESTED SOURCES

Primary Source

Johnson, Jack. *In the Ring and Out.* London: Proteus, 1977. Johnson's autobiography appeared in 1927 and has been reprinted under various titles. The book is factually unreliable.

Secondary Sources

Batchelor, Denzil. *Jack Johnson and His Times.* London: Phoenix Sports Books, 1956. Batchelor, a British journalist who specialized in boxing, wrote the first study of Johnson.

Farr, Finis. *Black Champion: The Life and Times of Jack Johnson.* New York: Scribner, 1964. Solid biography of the boxer that sets him in the context of a very racist era.

Gilmore, Al-Tony. *Bad Nigger!: The National Impact of Jack Johnson.* Port Washington, NY: Kennikat Press, 1975. Captures the shock waves that Johnson sent through white communities and the pride that he inspired among blacks.

Kent, Graeme. *The Great White Hopes: The Quest to Defeat Jack Johnson.* Stroud, England: Sutton, 2005. Entertaining account of the desperate efforts of whites to find a white boxer who could defeat Johnson and prove the superiority of the white race.

Roberts, Randy. *Papa Jack: Jack Johnson and the Era of White Hopes.* New York: Free Press, 1983. This is the most authoritative biography of the boxer.

World Wide Web

"Jack Johnson." http://www.cyberboxingzone.com/boxing/jjohn.htm. This is the best Web site on the boxer, with video clips of many of his fights and details about his career.

"Jack Johnson." http://www.si.umich.edu/CHICO/Harlem/text/jajohnson.html. Balanced biography of the boxer.

"Johnson Boxed, Lived, on Own Terms." http://espn.go.com/sportscentury/features/00014275.html. Profiles Johnson's boxing career but does not provide much historical context.

"Profile of Boxer Jack Johnson." http://afroamhistory.about.com/od/jackjohnson/p/bio_johnson_j.htm. Short biography and one photograph of the boxer.

Multimedia Sources

Great White Hope. Hollywood, CA: 20th Century Fox, 1970. VHS. Fictionalized
    account of Johnson's life starring James Earl Jones and Jane Alexander.
Unforgivable Blackness: The Rise and Fall of Jack Johnson. Hollywood, CA: Para-
    mount PBS Home Video, 2005. DVD. This is a Ken Burns film and
    reflects the filmmaker's typical excellence.

55. Formation of the National Association for the Advancement of Colored People (NAACP) (1909)

The National Association for the Advancement of Colored People
(NAACP) is the leading civil rights organization in the history of
the United States. It has worked chiefly through the legal system to promote voting rights and attack segregation.

The NAACP formed on February 12, 1909 as an interracial organization
focused upon racial justice. Of the 60 people who called for the creation of
the new group, only 7 were black. W. E. B. Du Bois, Ida B. Wells-Barnett,
and Mary Church Terrell were among the founders. The NAACP's stated
goal was to secure for all people the rights guaranteed by the Thirteenth,
Fourteenth, and Fifteenth Amendments to the Constitution that promised
equal protection of the law and the right to vote. By 1919, the NAACP
had about 90,000 members and more than 300 local branches. In the
1920s, it attacked lynching. During the Great Depression of the 1930s, it
focused on economic justice. In the 1940s, the NAACP kept pushing for
an anti-lynching law and fought Jim Crow segregation. In the 1950s,
NAACP attorney Thurgood Marshall won the *Brown v. Board of Education*
case that ended the segregation of public schools. In the 1960s, the NAACP
focused on passing civil rights legislation. Along the way, NAACP officials
such as Harry T. Moore and Medgar Evers were killed by white racists for
advocating on behalf of blacks.

Since the end of the civil rights movement of the 1960s, the NAACP
has struggled to find a place. The current goals of the group focus on
improving educational and economic opportunities. Its membership and
significance have dropped in the past few decades, but it remains the leading organization for the advancement of African Americans.

TERM PAPER SUGGESTIONS

1. In 1910 the NAACP defeated an Oklahoma law in *Guinn v. United States* that prohibited blacks from voting by means of a grandfather clause. Discuss how the grandfather clause discriminated against African Americans.

2. Medgar Evers, a Mississippi field secretary for the NAACP, died for his activism. Evers's widow, Myrlie, would later head the NAACP. Discuss the life and death of Medgar Evers.

3. The NAACP worked through the legal system to improve life for African Americans. Discuss the merits of this strategy.

4. Compare and contrast the NAACP with another major civil rights organization of the 1960s, perhaps the Student Nonviolent Coordinating Committee.

5. Profile a leader of the NAACP, perhaps Mary Ovington or Medgar Evers.

ALTERNATIVE TERM PAPER SUGGESTIONS

1. Create a virtual field trip that takes viewers to locations related to the history of the NAACP, such as the city where Medgar Evers died and the city where Reverend Oliver Brown tried to send his daughter to a white public school.

2. Design a timeline of specific events involving the NAACP.

SUGGESTED SOURCES

Primary Sources

Evers-Williams, Myrlie. *The Autobiography of Medgar Evers: A Hero's Life and Legacy Revealed Through His Writings, Letters, and Speeches.* New York: Basic Civitas, 2006. A collection of writings by Evers with limited value.

NAACP, comp. *NAACP.* Washington, DC: NAACP and The Crisis Publishing, 2008. Essentially a coffee table history of the organization but a very good collection of NAACP materials.

Secondary Sources

Brown, Jennie. *Medgar Evers.* Los Angeles: Holloway House Publishing, 1994. Short biography of the NAACP leader.

Jonas, Gilbert. *Freedom's Sword: The NAACP and the Struggle Against Racism, 1909–1969.* New York: Routledge, 2007. This is the most comprehensive account of the NAACP's history.

Nossiter, Adam. *Of Long Memory: Mississippi and the Murder of Medgar Evers.* New York: Da Capo Press, 2002. Examines the significant changes in the attitudes of white Mississippians toward race since the 1963 murder of NAACP staffer Medgar Evers.

Sartain, Lee. *Invisible Activists: Women of the Louisiana NAACP and the Struggle for Civil Rights, 1915–1945.* Baton Rouge: Louisiana State University Press, 2007. This scholarly book shows how women served as the spine of the NAACP by raising funds and managing daily operations.

Tushnet, Mark V. *The NAACP's Legal Strategy Against Segregated Education, 1925–1950.* Charlotte: University of North Carolina Press, 2005. Discusses how the NAACP developed the strategy that led to the *Brown v. Board of Education* victory.

Wedin, Carolyn. *Inheritors of the Spirit: Mary White Ovington and the Founding of the NAACP.* New York: Wiley, 1999. Ovington, a white daughter of abolitionists, took a tour of the South in the wake of bloody race riots. Determined to improve life for African Americans, she spearheaded the founding of the NAACP.

World Wide Web

"Black History—NAACP." http://www.africanaonline.com/orga_naacp.htm. Excellent, balanced essay on the history of the NAACP from 1909 to the present.

"NAACP—Los Angeles Branch." http://www.naacp-losangeles.org/. Includes a history of the Los Angeles chapter as well as information on its educational and economic development projects.

"National Association for the Advancement of Colored People." http://afroamhistory.about.com/od/naacp/a/naacp.htm. Good balanced essay on the history and importance of the organization.

"The National Association for the Advancement of Colored People." http://www.naacp.org/. The organization's site includes its history as well as its current activities.

"Texas NAACP." http://www.texasnaacp.org/. This state chapter site includes the history of the Texas NAACP and its current projects.

Multimedia Source

Walk a Mile in My Shoes: The 90-Year Journey of the NAACP. Morris Plains, NJ: Lucerne Media, 2001. VHS. Award-winning history of the organization that highlights its role in anti-lynching activism and school integration.

56. Charles Davenport Publishes *Eugenics: The Science of Human Improvement by Better Breeding* (1910)

The eugenics movement, popular in the first decades of the twentieth century, sought to create a superior nation by limiting births by those deemed inferior. African Americans were among those deemed unfit to reproduce. More than 60,000 Americans—many of them black—were forcibly sterilized to prevent them from passing on supposedly defective genes. Charles Davenport was one of the American leaders of the eugenics movement.

British biologist Francis Galton coined the term "eugenics" in 1883 to describe the intelligence inherited through genes. According to eugenicists, the stock of genetically healthy individuals could be improved through selective breeding. Some eugenicists advocated removing purportedly unhealthy individuals—criminals, those with low IQs, and African Americans—from the gene pool by forced sterilization. Davenport, who earned a Ph.D. in zoology from Harvard University in 1892, studied the effects of selection on agricultural animals. In 1904, he became director of the Station for Experimental Evolution in Cold Spring Harbor, with the assignment of promoting and coordinating research on problems relating to heredity. Soon human genetics and its offshoot, eugenics, came to occupy most of Davenport's attention. In his 1910 *Eugenics,* Davenport defined eugenics as "the science of human improvement by better breeding." Davenport conducted research that linked genetics to alcoholism, pellagra (later shown to be due to a vitamin deficiency), criminality, feeblemindedness, bad temper, intelligence, and manic depression. His studies prompted state legislators to pass laws authorizing compulsory sterilization of those deemed to be genetically inferior. When the U.S. Supreme Court authorized forced sterilization in *Buck v. Bell* in 1927, the decision led to a spate of sterilizations across the nation.

The association of eugenics with Nazi race hygiene discredited the field. However, the 1994 publication of Richard J. Herrnstein and Charles Murray's *The Bell Curve: Intelligence and Class Structure in American Life* demonstrated that some scientists are still confusing personal prejudices with scientific evidence. The book argued that African Americans as a class were less intelligent than whites.

TERM PAPER SUGGESTIONS

1. Discuss the connection between eugenics and racism.
2. Examine the claims about African Americans made in *The Bell Curve*. Discuss whether these claims reflect good science or personal prejudices.
3. W. E. B. Du Bois supported the eugenics movement. Examine Du Bois's views on eugenics.
4. Examine the U.S. Supreme Court's decision in *Buck v. Bell* that ultimately led to the forced sterilization of thousands of African American women.

ALTERNATIVE TERM PAPER SUGGESTIONS

1. Create a Microsoft PowerPoint presentation that explains the eugenics movement.
2. There is increasing interest in genetic engineering to create better human beings. Write an op-ed essay that uses lessons learned from the eugenics movement to warn about genetic engineering.

SUGGESTED SOURCES

Primary Sources

Davenport, Charles. *Davenport's Dream: 21st Century Reflections on Heredity and Eugenics.* Cold Spring Harbor, NY: Cold Spring Harbor Laboratory Press, 2005. The vast majority of Davenport's writings are difficult to locate today. This book contains a reprint of Davenport's *Heredity in Relation to Eugenics* as well as a set of essays by academics who discuss Davenport's ideas.

Herrnstein, Richard J., and Charles Murray. *The Bell Curve: Intelligence and Class Structure in American Life.* New York: Free Press, 1996. Extremely controversial book about differences in intelligence.

Secondary Sources

Black, Edwin. *War Against the Weak: Eugenics and America's Campaign to Create a Master Race.* Oskkosh, WI: Dialog Press, 2003. Examines the eugenics movement of the late nineteenth and early twentieth centuries.

Brunius, Harry. *Better for All the World: The Secret History of Forced Sterilization and America's Quest for Racial Purity.* New York: Vintage, 2007. Analyzes how the American pursuit of moral and social purity led people to base national policy on pseudoscience. Brunius examines the thoughts of Charles Davenport.

Dorr, Gregory Michael. *Segregation's Science: Eugenics and Society in Virginia.* Charlottesville: University of Virginia Press, 2008. Traces the intersection of race and science, going all the way back to Thomas Jefferson.

English, Daylanne K. *Unnatural Selections: Eugenics in American Modernism and the Harlem Renaissance.* Charlotte: University of North Carolina Press, 2003. Discusses writings by W. E. B. Du Bois that expressed support for eugenics.

Kuhl, Stefan. *The Nazi Connection: Eugenics, American Racism, and German National Socialism.* New York: Oxford University Press, 2002. Argues that many of the assumptions underlying Nazi thought could be found among American scientists.

Larson, Edward J. *Sex, Race, and Science: Eugenics in the Deep South.* Baltimore, MD: Johns Hopkins University Press, 1996. Examines southern laws that sought to prevent the white race from being "tainted" by African American blood.

Lombardo, Paul A. *Three Generations, No Imbeciles: Eugenics, the Supreme Court, and Buck v. Bell.* Baltimore, MD: Johns Hopkins University Press, 2008. Supreme Court Justice Oliver Wendell Holmes stated his support of the forced sterilization of poor, white Carrie Buck, saying that "three generations of imbeciles" was enough. Lombardo discusses the case that gave legal support to the forced sterilization of poor, black women.

Nourse, Victoria F. *In Reckless Hands: Skinner v. Oklahoma and the Near-Triumph of American Eugenics.* New York: W.W. Norton, 2008. When prison authorities in Oklahoma attempted in 1936 to sterilize prisoner Jack Skinner, the case went all the way to the Supreme Court. This book examines the case in which the inmates ultimately triumphed.

Roberts, Dorothy. *Killing the Black Body: Race, Reproduction, and the Meaning of Liberty.* New York: Vintage, 1998. Discusses the history of attempts by U.S. policymakers to control black women's reproductive freedom.

Rosenberg, Charles E. *No Other Gods: On Science and American Social Thought.* Baltimore, MD: Johns Hopkins University Press, 1997. Examines the social history of science.

World Wide Web

"The Bell Curve and Eugenics." http://www.hartford-hwp.com/archives/45/026.html. Good discussion of *The Bell Curve.*

"Eugenics in Alabama." http://www.encyclopediaofalabama.org/face/Article.jsp?id=h-1367. Essay from the *Encyclopedia of Alabama* that discusses the sterilization of women of color in order to create a more perfect America.

"Fighting Fire with Fire: African Americans and Hereditarian Thinking, 1900–1942." http://www.wfu.edu/~caron/ssrs/Dorr.rtf. Gregory Dorr examines the eugenic beliefs of three African Americans: W. E. B. Du Bois, Thomas Wyatt Turner, and Marcus Garvey.

"Of Liberty and Justice for All: The American Eugenics Movement." http:// www.geocities.com/rationalargumentator/Eugenics.html. Excellent essay by Anna Kaluzny on the eugenics movement.

"Plaidder's Handy Guide to the Wonderful World of Eugenics." http:// www.plaidder.com/eugen.htm. An FAQ about genetics that is exceptionally useful as an introduction to the field despite its British focus.

Multimedia Source

Homo Sapiens 1900. New York: First Run Features, 2004. DVD. Explores the history of attempts to improve the human race through biological means, including sterilization and selective breeding.

57. Universal Negro Improvement Association (UNIA) Founded (1914)

Marcus Garvey founded and led the Universal Negro Improvement Association (UNIA), the largest organization dedicated to African American economic self-determination and racial pride. He laid the groundwork for the development of black pride that lay at the foundation of the civil rights movement. Both Jamaica's Rastafarian movement and the Nation of Islam were influenced by Garvey.

Garvey, born in St. Ann's Bay, Jamaica in 1887, founded the UNIA in Kingston, Jamaica in 1914. After achieving limited success, he moved to New York City in 1916 and established UNIA headquarters in Harlem. Garvey emphasized self-reliance, political self-determination, and the creation of a black nation on the continent of Africa. He became enormously popular among African Americans who appreciated his message that blacks should take control of their own destiny.

Chapters of the UNIA sprouted across the United States. Garvey responded to this support by creating the Negro Factories Corporation in 1918 to support the development of black-owned businesses. He also created the Black Star Steamship Line to provide a means for African Americans to go back to Africa. The company's three ships also shuttled goods and people between the United States, Africa, the Caribbean, and Central America. As a black-owned and black-run company, it became a symbol of racial pride. In 1921, the Black Star Line went into bankruptcy.

A year later, the U.S. government indicted Garvey on mail fraud charges related to the sale of Black Star stock. Sentenced to serve five years in the Atlanta federal penitentiary, Garvey was deported to Jamaica upon his release. To many African Americans, Garvey's conviction served as an example of the government's persecution of a strong black man.

TERM PAPER SUGGESTIONS

1. Both Marcus Garvey and Malcolm X advocated black pride. Compare and contrast the two leaders.
2. Discuss Garvey's "Back to Africa" movement.
3. Garvey cited Booker T. Washington as a major influence. Compare and contrast Garvey's UNIA with Washington's Tuskegee Institute.
4. Garvey told African Americans in a speech that "There shall be no solution to this race problem until you yourselves strike the blow for liberty." Discuss Garvey's philosophy of racial improvement.

ALTERNATIVE TERM PAPER SUGGESTIONS

1. Create a Web page with hyperlinks that explain Garvey's ideas and his relationship to other leaders and organizations in African American history.
2. Create a Web site that provides a short history of the major black political leaders of each decade since 1900, including Garvey for the 1920s.

SUGGESTED SOURCES

Primary Sources

Blaisdel, Bob, ed. *Selected Writings and Speeches of Marcus Garvey.* Mineola, NY: Dover Thrift, 2005. Collects Garvey's most famous writings, including "Declaration of the Rights of the Negro Peoples of the World" and "Africa for the Africans."

Garvey, Marcus, and Amy Jacques Garvey. *The Philosophy and Opinions of Marcus Garvey, Or, Africa for the Africans.* New York: Majority Press, 1986. First published in 1923, this book is a good introduction to Garvey's thinking on racial pride and was co-written with his wife.

Secondary Sources

Cronon, E. David. *Black Moses: The Story of Marcus Garvey and the Universal Negro Improvement Association.* Madison: University of Wisconsin Press, 1960. Outlines the major events of Garvey's life.

Grant, Colin. *Negro with a Hat: The Rise and Fall of Marcus Garvey.* New York: Oxford University Press, 2008. The definitive biography of Garvey.

World Wide Web

"American Experience—Marcus Garvey." http://www.pbs.org/wgbh/amex/ garvey/. Complements the PBS documentary on Garvey with images, a timeline, and biographical sketches.

"Marcus Garvey—The Official Site." http://www.marcusgarvey.com/. The premiere site on Garvey, with articles, poems, and a biographical sketch. The site includes Garvey's statement to the press following his arrest for mail fraud.

Multimedia Sources

Marcus Garvey: A Giant of Black Politics. New York: Screen Edge, 2008. DVD. Good biography of the UNIA founder.

Marcus Garvey: Look for Me in the Whirlwind. New York: PBS, 2002. DVD. Part of the American Experience series, this is a good introduction to the life of Garvey.

58. *The Birth of a Nation* Rejuvenates the Ku Klux Klan (1915)

The film *The Birth of a Nation* has remained very controversial in the decades since its 1915 debut for its interpretation of race relations in American history. Director D. W. Griffith created a blockbuster film, but he did so by portraying the Ku Klux Klan as heroic for its vigilante actions against blacks.

Griffith developed *The Birth of a Nation*'s script from a popular play and novel about the Civil War, *The Clansman,* by Thomas Dixon Jr. The story centers on two families, the southern Camerons and the northern Stonemans. Their friendship as the film begins symbolizes a united nation. The politics of the film become apparent as soon as the arrival of African slaves on American shores is introduced as the event that brought strife to the United States. Griffith blames the Civil War and its aftermath on blacks and politicians. As the fighting ends and Reconstruction begins, Griffith shows a South that is victimized by northern politicians. The blacks in the South are portrayed as evil, racially embittered, slovenly, and lustful toward white women. A Cameron son, angered by the death of his sister at the hands of a black would-be rapist, forms the Ku Klux Klan to protect whites.

The Birth of a Nation is generally regarded by film historians as the most important film of the early silent era, both artistically and politically. Over three hours, the film was the longest ever made in the United States up to that time. It was also the most technically dazzling, with creative camera movement and angles, close-ups, panning and tracking, crosscutting to simultaneously occurring events, montage editing, iris shots, split screen, fade-ins and fade-outs, and long shots. These techniques had been used before, but never to such great effect and never in such a way as to involve the audience so deeply. The film was a blockbuster, earning $18 million. So many people saw the movie that the film is credited with widening the film audience beyond the working class to include the middle and upper classes. Schoolchildren were taken to the movie to learn history.

Griffith, the son of a Confederate officer, told the history of the Civil War and Reconstruction as southern whites understood it in the early twentieth century. However, his story had little to do with reality. Blacks held majorities in only two state legislatures during Reconstruction and never had much genuine power. The myth of the black rapist was exploded by journalist Ida B. Wells in the 1890s as a means of justifying white violence against blacks. But Griffith's version of history, in which everything was fine until the North decided to meddle and the blacks got uppity, endured for decades. Subsequent movies on the subject followed the same line, although with less offensive racism. Not until the civil rights movement of the 1960s would American historians seriously challenge the view that Reconstruction was a disaster because it attempted to create a better world for blacks.

TERM PAPER SUGGESTIONS

1. Research the image of African Americans on film.
2. The National Association for the Advancement of Colored People launched the first boycott of a film in response to *The Birth of a Nation*. Examine the black response to the movie.
3. Examine the response of Americans to *The Birth of a Nation*.
4. The Second Ku Klux Klan began on Stone Mountain, Georgia as a response to this film. Trace the history of the version of the Klan that was strongest in the 1910s and 1920s.

ALTERNATIVE TERM PAPER SUGGESTIONS

1. Use and cite clips from some films and television shows that feature African American characters to create a two-minute iMovie. It should accurately depict negative images about blacks that damage race relations.

2. D. W. Griffith saw African American males as lazy, lustful, and criminal-minded. Review media representations of blacks in a set of newspapers or magazines to see if that image is still common today. Create a Microsoft PowerPoint presentation to present your findings.

3. Copies of *The Birth of a Nation* are readily available. See the film for yourself. Write an editorial that compares and contrasts the portrayal of African Americans with the portrayal of whites while urging a boycott of the film.

SUGGESTED SOURCES

Primary Source

The Birth of a Nation 1915. Edina, MN: Alpha Video, 2005. DVD. Reprint of the film.

Secondary Sources

Chadwick, Bruce. *The Reel Civil War: Mythmaking in American Film.* New York: Alfred A. Knopf, 2001. Contrasts the reality of the war with its image in movies.

Christensen, Terry. *Reel Politics: American Political Movies from Birth of a Nation to Platoon.* New York: Basil Blackwell, 1987. *The Birth of a Nation* became the first political movie. This books sets it in moviemaking context.

Cuniberti, John. *The Birth of a Nation: A Formal Shot-by-Shot Analysis Together with Microfiches.* New York: Research Publications, 1979. A detailed examination of Griffith's work that focuses more on the director's artistic achievements.

Hurwitz, Michael. *D. W. Griffith's Film, The Birth of a Nation: The Film That Transformed America.* New York: BookSurge, 2006. Discusses the impact of the film in an accessible fashion, but Stokes's book is better researched.

Snead, James. *White Screens, Black Images: Hollywood from the Dark Side.* New York: Routledge, 1994. Examines the historically negative view of African Americans in the movies.

Stokes, Melvyn. *D. W. Griffith's The Birth of a Nation: A History of the Most Controversial Motion Picture of All Time.* New York: Oxford University Press, 2008. A deeply researched work that examines the artistic merits and cultural impact of the film.

World Wide Web

"Birth of a Nation." http://video.google.com/videoplay?docid=-5639233 838609252948. Google has made the entire 180-minute film available to view for free.

"The Birth of a Nation (1915)." http://www.filmsite.org/birt.html. Detailed review, synopsis, and discussion of the film.

"Culture Shock: Theater, Film, and Video: D. W. Griffith's *The Birth of a Nation, 1915.*" http://www.pbs.org/wgbh/cultureshock/flashpoints/theater/ birthofanation_a.html. Briefly discusses public responses to Griffith's film from 1915 until 1999, when the Directors Guild of America decided to remove Griffith's name from its award for career achievement because of his history of promoting intolerable racial stereotypes.

"Trailer—The Birth of a Nation." http://www.youtube.com/watch?v=a9UPOkI-pR0A. Shows the original trailer for the film.

59. The Great Migration (1915–1920)

The Great Migration is the largest voluntary movement of African Americans in the history of the United States. In search of improved economic, social, and political opportunities, African Americans moved from the South to the cities of the North.

This massive movement of blacks was sparked by several events. Declining prices for cotton seriously hurt southern farmers. As prices were beginning to recover, the boll weevil, an agricultural pest, destroyed much of the cotton crop for several years in a row. Meanwhile, the start of World War I had slowed immigration to a crawl. Factory owners of the North needed workers yet could not find the immigrant laborers who had filled positions in the past. Factory owners went to the South to recruit African Americans at the same time that African Americans were desperate for a better life. In the South, black workers could make $0.50 to $2 a day. In the North, the same workers could make $2 to $5 a day. Between 1915 and 1920, about 500,000 to one million African Americans moved from the South to the North. The effect proved dramatic. Detroit had about 6,000 blacks prior to World War I, while Chicago had 10,000 black residents in 1910, and New York City had 100,000. By the end of the 1920s, Detroit had 120,000 blacks, Chicago had 240,000, and New York City had 330,000. The sudden influx of African Americans sometimes created racial tensions, as indicated by race riots in East St. Louis and

Chicago. By and large, through their migration African Americans found better wages, better schools, voting opportunities, and less racism.

TERM PAPER SUGGESTIONS

1. Examine how the boll weevil prompted many African Americans to abandon cotton farms in the South for the factories of the North.
2. Discuss the impact of World War I on African American migration.
3. African Americans relied upon other blacks for assistance in assimilating to life in the North. Research the help provided by black organizations.
4. Discuss the challenges faced by African Americans who moved to the North.

ALTERNATIVE TERM PAPER SUGGESTIONS

1. Assume that you are the first in your family to move from the rural South to a city in the North. Exchange four letters with a brother who is thinking about joining you.
2. Assume that you are a factory owner in Detroit, Chicago, or New York City who is desperate to get workers. Design a brochure and a poster to persuade African Americans to emigrate from the South to work in your company.

SUGGESTED SOURCES

Primary Source

"Chicago: Destination for the Great Migration." http://www.loc.gov/exhibits/african/afam011.html. A Library of Congress site that uses original letters and photographs to illuminate the migration.

Secondary Sources

Gregory, James N. *The Southern Diaspora: How the Great Migrations of Black and White Southerners Transformed America*. Charlotte: University of North Carolina Press, 2007. Compares and contrasts black and white migration from the South to the North.

Grossman, James R. *Land of Hope: Chicago, Black Southerners, and the Great Migration*. Chicago: University of Chicago Press, 1991. Detailed analysis of the migration of African Americans to Chicago and the aftermath of the mass movement.

Lemann, Nicolas. *The Promised Land: The Great Black Migration and How It Changed America*. New York: Vintage, 1992. Examines the post-1940 movement of blacks from the South to the North.

Reich, Steven A., ed. *Encyclopedia of the Great Black Migration.* Westport, CT: Greenwood Press, 2006. Gives a good overview of the migration.

World Wide Web

"American History 102: Civil War to the Present: Black Migration." http://us.history.wisc.edu/hist102/lectures/lecture09.html. Contains the text and links from a lecture by Stanley K. Schultz, professor of history at the University of Wisconsin.

"Great Migration." http://www.encyclopedia.chicagohistory.org/pages/545.html. Excellent essay on the Great Migration from the *Encyclopedia of Chicago.*

Multimedia Source

Goin' To Chicago: Great Migration. Los Angeles: California Newsreel, n.d. VHS. Includes archival footage to show how the movement of blacks to the North helped shape Chicago.

60. Race Riots (1919–1921)

Urban race riots that swept through northern cities in 1919 emphasized that poor race relations were not limited to the South. The violence pointed out racial divisions throughout the country.

Much of the racial anger involved increased competition between blacks and whites for jobs in northern cities. Whites also objected to African Americans living in previously white neighborhoods and taking scarce housing. The first major race riot erupted in East St. Louis, Illinois in 1917, when whites angry about losing work to blacks rioted for four days. The riot resulted in the deaths of over 100 African Americans. In the next few years, blacks died in street confrontations with whites. By 1919, the rise of the Ku Klux Klan combined with previously existing tensions to make it unsafe for African Americans to walk the streets in some areas. More than 200 people, including servicemen in uniform, died in racially-motivated attacks. Such violence peaked in the summer of 1919 and did not entirely disappear. One of the worst race riots occurred in Tulsa, Oklahoma in 1921. Oil drilling had attracted a large number of black workers to the city. When a police officer arrested a black man for allegedly assaulting a white woman, black veterans of World War I refused to be intimidated. They tried to protect the prisoner from a white lynch mob. The police arrested many African Americans, removed guns from many others, and refused to protect blacks from marauding white mobs. By the end of the riot, the black section of Tulsa lay in smoking ruins and about 50 blacks lay dead. Insurance companies refused compensation to about 1,000 black homeowners while President Warren G. Harding ignored appeals for help.

TERM PAPER SUGGESTIONS

1. The myth associated with riots is that blacks did something wrong, perhaps participate in the rape of a white woman, to bring down the wrath of whites. Discuss the motivations behind race riots.

2. Examine the Tulsa race riot of 1921. Did blacks passively respond to the threat posed by whites, or is this an example of black resistance to white violence?

3. The white leaders of Tulsa tried to erase any evidence of the race riot from history books. Discuss how history can be shaped by political and social factors, using the Tulsa race riot as an example.

4. The Oklahoma state commission appointed in 1997 to investigate the Tulsa race riot recommended that reparations be paid. Discuss the justifications for paying damages.

ALTERNATIVE TERM PAPER SUGGESTIONS

1. Create a Web site that lists the major race riots in the history of the United States. Using hypertext links, provide a short history of each riot.

2. Write an editorial for a newspaper that advocates or opposes paying reparations for the victims of race riots.

SUGGESTED SOURCES

Primary Source

Chicago Commission on Race Relations. *The Negro in Chicago: A Study of Race Relations and a Race Riot in 1919.* New York: Arno Press, 1968. This is a reprint of a 1922 book published as a part of an official effort to determine the causes of the unrest.

Secondary Sources

Brophy, Alfred L. *Reconstructing the Dreamland: The Tulsa Riot of 1921: Race, Reparations, and Reconciliation.* New York: Oxford University Press,

2003. Examines the riot and how Tulsa has struggled to acknowledge its violent racist past.

Carr, Pat M. *If We Must Die: A Novel of Tulsa's 1921 Greenwood Riot.* Fort Worth: Texas Christian University Press, 2002. Novel about a white teenage girl who shares the experiences of black friends during the race riot.

Hirsch, James S. *Riot and Remembrance: The Tulsa Race War and Its Legacy.* New York: Houghton Mifflin, 2002. Uses oral histories, court records, and government reports to examine the riot.

Madigan, Tim. *The Burning: Massacre, Destruction, and the Tulsa Race Riot of 1921.* New York: St. Martin's Griffin, 2003. Shows how the riot touched the lives of individuals by creating full portraits of black and white Tulsa citizens.

Whitaker, Robert. *On the Laps of Gods: The Red Summer of 1919 and the Struggle for Justice That Remade a Nation.* New York: Crown, 2008. Examines an Arkansas race riot, the Elaine Massacre, that left over 100 African Americans dead.

World Wide Web

"Final Report of the Oklahoma Commission to Study the Tulsa Race Riot of 1921." http://www.tulsareparations.org/FinalReport.htm. The commission recommended that the state of Oklahoma pay reparations for the Tulsa race riot. The report explains those findings.

"The Tulsa Race Riot of 1921." http://www.montgomerycollege.edu/departments/hpolscrv/VdeLaOliva.html. Short essay with photographs about the riot.

"The Tulsa Reparations Coalition." http://www.tulsareparations.org/. This group formed to push Oklahoma to pay damages.

Multimedia Source

In Search of History: The Night Tulsa Burned. New York: A&E Home Video, 1999. DVD. Uses the testimony of survivors and photographs to tell the story of the Greenwood section of Tulsa before and after the riot.

61. Brotherhood of Sleeping Car Porters (BSCP) Is Founded (1925)

The Brotherhood of Sleeping Car Porters (BSCP) became the first union for African Americans. A. Philip Randolph founded the organization in

1925 to gain better wages and hours for the porters of the Pullman Company. The group became a major advocate for civil rights.

The Pullman Company provided luxury train service to white passengers. It preferred to hire porters with jet-black skin to emphasize the distinctions between the black workers and the white patrons. The firm also preferred black workers because they could be paid less. The porters, many of whom possessed college educations, enjoyed a measure of status in African American communities because of their extensive travels and immaculate dress. On the job, the porters suffered demeaning treatment from both white customers and white management. As one notorious example, the men were permitted to sleep only in three-hour installments in the smoking room attached to the men's restroom.

Randolph began the BSCP with about 1,900 of the 10,000 porters. African Americans were slow to recognize the value of a union, while Pullman strongly opposed it. The BSCP negotiated its first contract with Pullman in 1937. Through its existence, the BSCP proved that African Americans could organize on their own behalf and get results. The BSCP disappeared when it merged with the Brotherhood of Railway and Airline Clerks in 1978. By that time, the era of luxury rail travel had long ago ended.

TERM PAPER SUGGESTIONS

1. African Americans were historically excluded from labor unions and, as a result, they deeply mistrusted unions. Discuss how A. Philip Randolph and the BSCP changed black attitudes toward unions.

2. Many of the porters possessed college educations, yet they shined shoes for a living. They viewed this work as a good job. Discuss the economic situation facing blacks in the early twentieth century that made black men regard a demeaning job far below their talents as a plum job.

3. Discuss the involvement of the BSCP in the civil rights movement.

4. Compare and contrast a predominantly white union, perhaps the American Federation of Labor or the Knights of Labor, with the BSCP.

ALTERNATIVE TERM PAPER SUGGESTIONS

1. Create a Web site that pays tribute to African American workers. Be sure to include the challenges that black workers have faced in each decade since the end of slavery.

2. Assume that you are a porter in 1925 when A. Philip Randolph is forming his union. Create a blog that discusses your situation at work, Randolph's promises, and your interest in joining his union.

SUGGESTED SOURCES

Primary Source

Grizzle, Stanley G. *My Name's Not George: The Story of the Brotherhood of Sleeping Car Porters: Personal Reminiscences of Stanley G. Grizzle.* New York: Umbrella Press, 1998. A rare account from a black working man of the early twentieth century. The porters so objected to being called George that they formed a society to protest the habit.

Secondary Sources

Bates, Beth Tompkins. *Pullman Porters and the Rise of Protest Politics in Black America, 1925–1945.* Chapel Hill: University of North Carolina Press, 2001. Sets the union in the context of the civil rights movement.

Harris, William H. *Keeping the Faith: A. Philip Randolph, Milton P. Webster, and the Brotherhood of Sleeping Car Porters, 1925–1937.* Urbana: University of Illinois Press, 1977. Excellent study of the early years of the union.

Tye, Larry. *Rising from the Rails: Pullman Porters and the Making of the Black Middle Class.* New York: Holt, 2005. A very readable history of both black labor history and American business history.

World Wide Web

"Brotherhood of Sleeping Car Porters." http://www.blackpast.org/?q=aah/brotherhood-sleeping-car-porters-1925-1978. Encyclopedia essay on the union.

"Brotherhood of Sleeping Car Porters." http://www.encyclopedia.chicagohistory.org/pages/174.html. An essay from the *Encyclopedia of Chicago* on the labor union.

"Brotherhood of Sleeping Car Porters." http://www.windsor-communities.com/african-labour-brotherhood.php. Excellent history of the labor union and the challenges facing African American porters, from a site devoted to African Canadian history.

"Choosing Servility to Staff America's Trains." http://www.aliciapatterson.org/APF2101/Tye/Tye.html. Contains an essay on the union and a number of photographs of porters at work.

"The Evolution of the Union." http://www.aphiliprandolphmuseum.com/evo_history4.html. This site, from the A. Philip Randolph Museum, discusses the creation of the Brotherhood of Sleeping Car Porters by the Pullman porters.

Multimedia Sources

Miles of Smiles, Years of Struggle. Los Angeles: California Newsreel, n.d. VHS. Chronicles the creation of the first black trade union and the harsh discrimination that the porters faced.

Rising from the Rails: The Story of the Pullman Porter. New York: MS Production Group, 2006. DVD and VHS. A documentary that complements Tye's book of the same name.

10,000 Black Men Named George. Los Angeles: Paramount, 2002. DVD. Fictionalized story of the porters that stars Andre Braugher and Charles S. Dutton.

62. Harlem Renaissance (1920s)

The Harlem Renaissance was a literary and cultural movement that celebrated African Americans.

The Harlem Renaissance passed through three stages. In the first, which ended about 1923, whites began to take an interest in black life and subjects. The white artists of this period included playwrights Ridgely Torrence, Emily Hapgood, and Eugene O'Neill, as well as the writer Thomas Stribling. In the second phase, from 1924 to 1926, blacks produced works about blacks rather than sitting passively as the subjects of white creations. The leaders of this period included James Weldon Johnson and Alain Locke. Influenced by Charles Spurgeon Johnson of the National Urban League and Walter White of the National Association for the Advancement of Colored People, these artists sought to present blacks in the best possible light as a way of winning acceptance by whites. In the final phase, younger African Americans rebelled against the conservatism of older leaders. They celebrated the black ghetto, the working class, and the rural South. These writers included Claude McKay, Langston Hughes, Wallace Thurman, and Zora Neale Hurston. The poet Hughes is the most enduring literary figure of the Harlem Renaissance. Like the other figures of the Harlem Renaissance, he would inspire the black arts movement of the 1960s. The Harlem Renaissance collapsed in the 1930s as the Great Depression sapped energy and money from the movement.

TERM PAPER SUGGESTIONS

1. Discuss how the Harlem Renaissance represented a black pride movement.
2. Compare and contrast two writers of the Harlem Renaissance.
3. Discuss the controversy among African Americans over whether a realistic portrayal of black life or the presentation of elite, light-skinned blacks would best serve the goals of the Harlem Renaissance.

ALTERNATIVE TERM PAPER SUGGESTIONS

1. Use an iPod to collect songs produced by black artists during the Harlem Renaissance. Use the songs to illustrate a discussion of Harlem Renaissance music.
2. Create a Web page that pays tribute to the Harlem Renaissance. Be sure to include a definition of the movement as well as information on the major figures of the movement.

SUGGESTED SOURCES

Primary Sources

"Guide to Harlem Renaissance Materials." http://www.loc.gov/rr/program/bib/harlem/harlem.html. This Library of Congress site contains original materials from the era, including sheet music, photographs, and life histories.

Lewis, David Levering, ed. *The Portable Harlem Renaissance Reader.* New York: Penguin, 1994. Collects some of the writings of major figures of the Renaissance.

Secondary Sources

Huggins, Nathan. *The Harlem Renaissance.* New York: Oxford University Press, 1971. A solid history of the significance of the movement.

Hutchinson, George. *The Harlem Renaissance in Black and White.* Cambridge, MA: Belknap Press, 1995. Examines interracial cooperation in the movement.

Lewis, David Levering. *When Harlem Was In Vogue.* New York: Penguin, 1997. Traces the history of Harlem from 1905 to the race riot of 1935.

Wall, Cheryl. *Women of the Harlem Renaissance.* Bloomington: Indiana University Press, 1995. Corrects the misconception that only men made major contributions to the movement.

World Wide Web

"Drop Me Off in Harlem." http://artsedge.kennedy-center.org/exploring/
harlem/. Discusses the themes and works of the Harlem Renaissance.

"Harlem: Mecca of the New Negro: A Hypermedia Edition of the March 1925
Survey Graphic Harlem Number." http://etext.lib.virginia.edu/harlem/.
Reprints essays about Harlem by writers of the Harlem Renaissance.

"Harlem Renaissance." http://www.42explore2.com/harlem.htm. This site,
aimed at students, contains links to over 150 sites providing biographies
of individuals connected to the Harlem Renaissance.

"Harlem Renaissance." http://www.pbs.org/newshour/forum/february98/
harlem_2-20.html. Discusses a San Francisco exhibit on the Harlem
Renaissance and includes materials that make it a mini virtual exhibit.

"Harlem Renaissance." http://www.pbs.org/wnet/ihas/icon/harlem.html. Brief
essay on the movement.

Multimedia Sources

Against the Odds: The Artists of the Harlem Renaissance. New York: PBS, 1993.
DVD. Focuses on the visual artists of the era.

Harlem Renaissance: The Music and Rhythms That Started a Cultural Sensation.
New York: Kultur Video, 2004. DVD. Focuses on the works of Nat King
Cole, Fats Waller, Cab Calloway, Dorothy Dandridge, and the Mills
Brothers.

63. Elijah Muhammad Joins the Nation of Islam (1931)

Elijah Muhammad turned the black separatist organization called the
Nation of Islam into one of the largest religious organizations in the
United States. By doing so, he became one of the most important African
Americans of the twentieth century.

Muhammad, born Elijah Poole in Georgia in 1897, witnessed the
lynching of a teenage acquaintance as a child. A white man later taunt-
ed him with the severed ears of a black man as Poole walked home.
Muhammad cited the horror of these instances as one of the reasons
why he turned to black separatism. Struggling to find work to support
his family, Muhammad left the South for Detroit in 1923. Introduced
to Islam by his father, Muhammad joined the Nation of Islam in 1931.

He became fully immersed in the movement and rejected his slave name of Poole. In 1933, when Nation of Islam founder Wallace D. Fard stepped aside, Muhammad took control of the organization. He focused on total economic independence from whites. As Muhammad gained strength, the U.S. government began to watch him. He served a jail sentence for draft evasion during World War II and became the subject of 20 years of FBI surveillance. However, by the 1970s, Muhammad's conservatism appealed to whites concerned about the increasing radicalism of the civil rights movement. Muhammad died in 1975 with his protégé Louis Farrakhan taking his place as the leader of the Nation of Islam.

TERM PAPER SUGGESTIONS

1. Both Marcus Garvey and Elijah Muhammad advocated black economic independence. Compare and contrast the two leaders.
2. Discuss the beliefs of Elijah Muhammad with respect to education.
3. Compare and contrast Elijah Muhammad with a Christian black leader, perhaps Martin Luther King Jr.
4. Religion has often served as a liberating source. Discuss how Islam liberated Elijah Muhammad.

ALTERNATIVE TERM PAPER SUGGESTIONS

1. Create a Microsoft PowerPoint presentation that explains the views of the Nation of Islam.
2. Create a Web page that introduces the major black religious denominations, including the Nation of Islam, the African Methodist Episcopal Church, and the African Methodist Episcopal Zion Church.

SUGGESTED SOURCES

Primary Source

Muhammad, Elijah. *Message to the Blackman in America*. Chicago: Secretarius Memps, 2006. Explains Muhammad's philosophy for racial uplift.

Secondary Sources

Clegg, Claude Andrew, III. *An Original Man: The Life and Times of Elijah Muhammad*. New York: St. Martin's Press, 1997. A balanced biography of the controversial religious leader.

Evanzz, Karl. *The Messenger: The Rise and Fall of Elijah Muhammad.* New York: Pantheon Books, 1999. Solid biography with an appendix that contains selected declassified government documents on Muhammad and key figures in the Nation of Islam.

Gardell, Mattias. *In the Name of Elijah Muhammad: Louis Farrakhan and the Nation of Islam.* Durham, NC: Duke University Press, 1996. Discusses Farrakhan's controversial leadership of the Black Muslims.

Pitre, Abul. *The Educational Philosophy of Elijah Muhammad: Education for a New World.* Lanham, MD: University Press of America, 2007. Examines Muhammad's beliefs about education.

Walker, Dennis. *Islam and the Search for African-American Nationhood: Elijah Muhammad, Louis Farrakhan, and the Nation of Islam.* Atlanta: Clarity Press, 2005. Examines the rise of the Black Muslims, Muhammad's ideology, and Farrakhan's leadership.

World Wide Web

"Elijah Muhammad." http://foia.fbi.gov/foiaindex/muhammad.htm. Contains 28 pages of FBI files on the Nation of Islam leader.

"Elijah Muhammad." http://www.africawithin.com/bios/elijah_muhammad.htm. Brief biography of the leader.

"Elijah Muhammad Speaks." http://www.youtube.com/watch?v=2vr9Y5U GDLg. A YouTube video of a short speech by Muhammad.

"An Historical Look at the Honorable Elijah Muhammad." http://www.noi.org/ elijah_muhammad_history.htm. The Nation of Islam's biography of its leader.

Multimedia Source

Black Americans of Achievement: Elijah Muhammad. Bala Cynwyd, PA: Schlesinger Video Productions, 1994. VHS. A short documentary aimed at secondary school students.

64. The Scottsboro Boys Case (1931)

The Scottsboro Boys were a group of nine African American youths who became an international cause célèbre when they were charged with raping two white women in Alabama. On the basis of extremely flimsy evidence, the defendants received what critics described as a "legal lynching."

The case began on March 25, 1931 with a brawl between black and white hobos riding a freight train. When the white youths lost the fight, they complained, and a posse stopped the train to arrest the black youths. The posse also discovered two white women wearing men's clothing, a common Great Depression strategy to avoid sexual assault in an era when many rode the rails to save on transportation costs. The nine boys and two women were taken to Scottsboro, the county seat of Jackson County, Alabama. A medical examination of the women revealed sexual activity within the past twelve hours but no signs of sexual assault. The boys— Clarence Norris, Olen Montgomery, Haywood Patterson, Ozie Powell, Willie Roberson, Charlie Weems, Eugene Williams, and brothers Andrew and Leroy Wright—were jailed. At 20, Weems was the oldest, with Leroy Wright as the youngest at 13. Under pressure from a lynch mob and a local prosecutor, the women charged rape. A subsequent investigation revealed that they were prostitutes with a history of arrests. Nevertheless, they became symbols of white southern womanhood. The sheriff moved the boys to protect them from being lynched. At the trial, the nine youths did not receive adequate legal counsel. The all-white jury found eight of the boys guilty, and the judge sentenced the eight to death. The jurors agreed about the guilt of Leroy Wright, but 11 wanted death while the 12th juror refused, thereby resulting in a mistrial.

Communists came to the aid of the boys and made the case into an international one. Communist-led protests took place in northern cities as well as London, Paris, and Moscow. As a result of the publicity, the Scottsboro Boys came to be seen as the victims of a miscarriage of justice. After a series of trials, the state of Alabama dropped charges against the four youngest defendants—Leroy Wright, Montgomery, Roberson, and Williams. The others received prison sentences of varying lengths with the last released in 1950. In 1976, Alabama Governor George Wallace pardoned all of the Scottsboro Boys. By that time, only Norris survived.

TERM PAPER SUGGESTIONS

1. The vigorous Communist support of the Scottsboro Boys prompted many African Americans to view the party in a positive light. Examine the relationship of African Americans and the Communist Party.

2. In *Norris v. Alabama,* the U.S. Supreme Court ruled that the exclusion of African Americans from jury service deprived black defendants of equal

protection under the law, as guaranteed by the Fourteenth Amendment. Discuss this court case.

3. Discuss the public response to the Scottsboro case.

4. Discuss why the Communist Party elected to become involved in the Scottsboro case.

ALTERNATIVE TERM PAPER SUGGESTIONS

1. There is resistance among some Americans to serving on juries. Create a Web page that uses the Scottsboro case and the history of all-white jury trials to encourage African Americans to welcome jury service.

2. Compare and contrast accounts of the case from the *New York Times* and a black newspaper. An African American newspaper account can be found at http://www.afro.com/history/scott/young.html while the *New York Times* can be accessed through http://www.law.umkc.edu/faculty/projects/FTrials/scottsboro/Newspapr.htm.

SUGGESTED SOURCES

Primary Sources

Norris, Clarence, and Sybil D. Washington. *The Last of the Scottsboro Boys.* New York: G.P. Putnam's Sons, 1979. Norris, the last survivor of the case, collaborated on his autobiography.

Patterson, Haywood, and Earl Conrad. *Scottsboro Boy.* Garden City, NY: Doubleday, 1950. Patterson became the first defendant to tell his story.

Secondary Sources

Carter, Dan T. *Scottsboro: A Tragedy of the American South.* Baton Rouge: Louisiana State University Press, 1979. Probably the best book on the case, by a noted historian of the American South.

Goodman, James. *Stories of Scottsboro.* New York: Pantheon Books, 1994. Good discussion of the case.

Horne, Gerald. *Powell v. Alabama: The Scottsboro Boys and American Justice.* New York: Franklin Watts, 1997. Examines one of the U.S. Supreme Court cases that grew out of the case.

World Wide Web

"American Experience: Scottsboro, An American Tragedy." http://www.pbs.org/wgbh/amex/scottsboro/. Linked to the PBS documentary, this site includes a timeline, map of the route that the freight train took, and biographies.

"The Case of the Scottsboro Boys." http://www.writing.upenn.edu/~afilreis/88/ scottsboro.html. Examines the Communist view of the case and the involvement of members of the Communist Party.

"Famous American Trials: The Scottsboro Boys." http://www.law.umkc.edu/ faculty/projects/ftrials/scottsboro/scottsb.htm. Explains the trial with chronology, biographies, and letters.

"The Greatest Trials of All Time: The Scottsboro Boys." http://www.courttv.com/ archive/greatesttrials/scottsboro/trials.html. Excellent CourtTV site that includes interviews with historians and video clips.

"The Trials of the Scottsboro Boys." http://www.law.umkc.edu/faculty/projects/ FTrials/scottsboro/SB_acct.html. Detailed essay on the case.

Multimedia Source

Scottsboro: An American Tragedy. New York: PBS, 2000. DVD. Part of the American Experience series, this is a superb account of the case.

65. Mississippi Health Project Begins (1934)

The Mississippi Health Project attempted to address the notoriously poor health of African Americans in the South. Plagued by poverty and racism, southern blacks had trouble accessing even basic health care. As a result, African Americans suffered poorer health and higher death rates than whites in the South.

Midwives provided the great majority of medical care for African Americans in the antebellum years. Best known for assisting women through childbirth, these older women also provided a range of medical services, especially herbal remedies. As medicine advanced in the late nineteenth and early twentieth centuries, African American midwives faded away. Blacks in the rural South lost access to many older forms of medical care at the same time that they could not obtain new forms of care. Hospitals often did not admit blacks. Few black physicians were available, and plantation owners did not see the value in providing health care to the farm workers. In response, black women activists from the North traveled to the South to assist poor blacks in rural areas.

The Alpha Kappa Alpha sorority, a member of the National Council of Negro Women founded by Mary McLeod Bethune, founded the

Mississippi Health Project. This Great Depression program, under the leadership of Dorothy Ferebee, a physician, began with the aim of immunizing children throughout the Mississippi Delta and incidentally providing help to anyone who came to a clinic. The women working with the project found that illnesses resulting from poor nutrition, especially pellagra, were commonplace. By providing basic medical care and nutritional advice, the program ultimately bettered the lives of 15,000 black Mississippians. The Mississippi Health Project ended in 1941 as a casualty of gasoline rationing during World War II.

TERM PAPER SUGGESTIONS

1. Racism affected more than a person's political and economic opportunities. It also killed. Discuss the health care provided to African Americans in the South in the Jim Crow years.
2. Discuss the difficulties faced by black physicians in the South.
3. Examine one of the nutritional diseases, perhaps pellagra, common to poor blacks in the rural South.
4. Charles Drew, an African American surgeon and physician, revolutionized the medical profession by determining the science necessary to preserve blood. He created blood banks. Trace the history of his life.

ALTERNATIVE TERM PAPER SUGGESTIONS

1. Assume that you have been asked to help persuade people in a black community to participate in a Red Cross blood drive. Create a Microsoft PowerPoint presentation about the life and times of Charles Drew to point out the contributions that blacks have made to medicine as well as the importance of donating blood.
2. The Web sites on African American health issues are not aimed at high school students. Create a Web site that will alert your peers to the history of African American health care.

SUGGESTED SOURCES

Primary Sources

Carnegie, Mary Elizabeth. *The Path We Tread: Blacks in Nursing, 1854–1990.* New York: National League for Nursing Press, 1991. Carnegie, who fought for African American nurses to be regarded as the equals of their white colleagues, shows the trials and tribulations of black nurses.

Conner, Douglas L., and John F. Marszalek. *A Black Physician's Story: Bringing Hope in Mississippi.* Jackson: University Press of Mississippi, 1985. Of all the places to be a black physician, it is difficult to think of a state more challenging than Mississippi in the Jim Crow era. This is the autobiography of a pioneering physician.

Hine, Darlene Clark, ed. *Black Women in the Nursing Profession: A Documentary History.* New York: Garland, 1985. Hine, one of the foremost historians of African American history, gathered documents exploring the challenges faced by nurses trying to integrate the nursing profession and provide quality care for patients.

Secondary Sources

Beardsley, Edward H. *A History of Neglect: Health Care for Blacks and Mill Workers in the Twentieth-Century South.* Knoxville: University of Tennessee Press, 1987. Shows how poverty and racism killed workers in the New South.

Gamble, Vanessa N. *Germs Have No Color Lines: Blacks and American Medicine, 1900–1940.* New York: Garland, 1989. Good history of African American health care.

Holt, Thomas C. *A Special Mission: The Story of Freedmen's Hospital, 1862–1962.* Washington DC: Howard University Press, 1975. Traces the history of the first hospital dedicated to the treatment of black patients.

Jones, James H. *Bad Blood: The Tuskegee Syphilis Experiment.* New York: Maxwell McMillan International, 1993. In this experiment, African American men were refused treatment for syphilis so that scientists employed by the federal government could monitor the effects of the disease. The episode is now viewed as one of the major human rights abuses of twentieth-century United States and a disgrace to the medical profession.

Lichello, Robert. *Pioneer in Blood Plasma: Dr. Charles Richard Drew.* New York: J. Messner, 1968. Good biography of the man who created blood banks.

Mitchem, Stephanie Y. *African American Folk Healing.* New York: New York University Press, 2007. Discusses folk healing practices, such as curing a nosebleed by holding a silver quarter on the back of the neck, that have become woven into the health care practices of many modern African American families.

Savitt, Todd Lee. *Medicine and Slavery: The Diseases and Health Care of Blacks in Antebellum Virginia.* Urbana: University of Illinois Press, 1978. One of the very few studies of black health care during the era of slavery.

Smith, Susan L. *Sick and Tired of Being Sick and Tired: Black Women's Health Activism in America, 1890–1950.* Philadelphia: University of

Pennsylvania Press, 1995. Superb discussion of why black women mobilized to improve African American health care.

World Wide Web

"African American Health Care Statistics." http://www.blackhealthcare.com/BHC/HealthStatistics/healthstatistics1.asp. Provides facts to support the claim that a significant gap remains between the state of health of black America and white America.

"Charles Drew—The Blood Bank." http://inventors.about.com/library/inventors/bldrew.htm. Provides a brief biography of Drew.

"Kellogg African American Health Care Project." http://www.med.umich.edu/haahc/. Uses documents and oral histories, accessible through the site, to document the black health care experience in Michigan from the early twentieth century through the present.

Ward, Tom. "Medical Missionaries of the Delta: Dr. Dorothy Ferebee and the Mississippi Health Project, 1935–41." *Journal of Mississippi History* 63.3 (Fall 2001): 194. Available through JSTOR, this is a good discussion of the shock that northern African American women experienced when they attempted to better the health of rural blacks in Mississippi.

66. Boxer Joe Louis Defeats Primo Carnera (1935)

Black heavyweight boxer Joe Louis fought three major bouts in the 1930s that promised to either prove the superiority of whites or the strength of African Americans. In the first match, against Italy's Primo Carnera, Louis seemed to be fighting to avenge the invasion of Ethiopia by Italy. In the second and third bouts, against Germany's Max Schmeling, Louis challenged Aryan superiority and became the hero of most Americans.

Joe Louis, the grandson of slaves, was born in Alabama in 1914 as Joseph Louis Barrow. The family later moved to Detroit, where Louis began his boxing career. In April 1934, he became the American Athletic Union light heavyweight champion. He turned professional that July and won all 12 of his fights in 1934. On June 25, 1935 at Yankee Stadium, Louis scored an impressive six-round knockout over the former heavyweight champion, Primo Carnera. The fight, promoted as Africa versus Italy, attracted an enormous amount of attention in an era when boxing rivaled only baseball as the sport of choice for Americans. Louis, nicknamed the

"Brown Bomber," became a hero to black Americans for his skills and toughness.

On June 18, 1936 in New York City, Louis faced former heavyweight champion Max Schmeling of Germany. A darling of Adolf Hitler and the Nazi regime, Schmeling represented Aryan superiority. The Germans stated that Louis was the representative of an inferior race. Black and white Americans united across racial lines to urge Louis to knock out the German. Instead, Louis suffered his first professional defeat when Schmeling knocked him to the canvas with a right hand in the 12th round. Louis became heavyweight champion of the world in 1937 with a victory over fellow American Jim Braddock. He defended the title against Schmeling on June 22, 1938 in a bout billed as the "fight of the century." Louis knocked out Schmeling in the first round in a blow against Nazi racial superiority. Louis fought until 1951, compiling a record of 65 wins and 3 losses.

TERM PAPER SUGGESTIONS

1. Compare and contrast boxers Joe Louis and Jack Johnson or Muhammad Ali.
2. Examine the social and political significance of the fight between either Carnera and Louis or Louis and Schmeling.
3. Examine the black athlete as a civil rights icon.

ALTERNATIVE TERM PAPER SUGGESTIONS

1. Assume that you have been hired by Joe Louis's manager to promote his fight against Carnera or Schmeling. Draw up a publicity campaign to sell tickets. The campaign should include several posters.
2. Prepare a biography of Louis that includes songs and images from the World War II era.

SUGGESTED SOURCES

Primary Sources

Louis, Joe. *My Life*. New York: Ecco Press, 1997. Candid autobiography of the Brown Bomber that discusses Louis's womanizing, business failures, and other personal issues.

Von Der Lippe, George, trans. *Max Schmeling: An Autobiography*. Santa Monica, CA: Bonus Books, 1998. Schmeling is notorious for not always being factual about his life, but this is nevertheless an interesting biography of a man who had a Jewish manager and offered financial support to a broke Louis in his later years.

Secondary Sources

Bak, Richard. *Joe Louis: The Great Black Hope.* New York: Da Capo Press, 1998. Discusses both Louis's life and what makes a hero in the eyes of the African American community.

Erenberg, Lewis. *The Greatest Fight of Our Generation: Louis vs. Schmeling.* New York: Oxford University Press, 1998. Examines the 1938 fight that remains one of the most memorable events in boxing history.

Margolick, David. *Beyond Glory: Joe Louis vs. Max Schmeling and a World on the Brink.* New York: Vintage, 2006. Argues that Louis united Americans behind a common cause and undermined the Aryan notion of racial superiority.

World Wide Web

"Joe Louis." http://www.ibhof.com/jlouis.htm. A brief biography of the boxer from the International Boxing Hall of Fame.

"Joe Louis—The Brown Bomber." http://www.boxrec.com/list_bouts.php? human_id=9027&cat=boxer. Provides Louis's career boxing record.

Multimedia Sources

History Undercover—Louis vs Schmeling: The Real Story. New York: A&E Home Video, 2006. DVD. Good coverage of the fight of the century.

Joe Louis: America's Hero . . . Betrayed. New York: HBO Home Video, 2008. DVD. Excellent documentary of the boxer and the racial challenges that he faced.

Joe Louis: An American Hero. New York: Rounder Select, 2001. CD. A collection of songs including Lil Johnson's "Winner Joe (The Knock-Out King)" and Memphis Minnie's "He's in the Ring (Doin' the Same Old Thing)."

67. Mary McLeod Bethune Joins the New Deal (1936)

Mary McLeod Bethune, possibly the most influential black woman of the twentieth century, became a force for the advancement of African Americans by serving in the administration of President Franklin D. Roosevelt and by founding historically black Bethune-Cookman College.

Born in South Carolina to former slaves, Bethune overcame the handicaps of poverty and a dark, heavily African appearance. Planning to become a missionary in Africa, she attended the school of famed evangelist Dwight Moody to prepare. Upon graduation, she was rejected for a posting because no African American missionaries were needed in Africa. Bethune then decided to become an educator and became the first black woman to found an institute of higher learning when she opened her college in Daytona Beach, Florida in 1904. The largest organization of black women at this time, the National Association of Colored Women (NACW), promoted intensive social service at the local level to boost the quality of African American home life and educate the mothers of the race. Bethune served as its head from 1924 to 1928. Deciding that the NACW did not focus enough on political activities, she founded the National Council of Negro Women (NCNW) in 1935 to lobby the government.

A close friend of Eleanor Roosevelt, Bethune headed the Division of Negro Affairs of the National Youth Administration from 1935 to 1943. She became the first black woman to hold a high government position. This position enabled her to channel funds to black education. Unable herself to set New Deal policies, Bethune persuaded powerful whites to follow her recommendations.

TERM PAPER SUGGESTIONS

1. When Mary McLeod Bethune accepted President Roosevelt's invitation to direct the Division of Negro Affairs, she envisioned dozens of black women following in her footsteps by taking government positions of high trust and strategic importance. Profile some of the women who followed Bethune and made her vision come true.

2. Bethune, a very fashionable woman, wore long capes, colorful jewelry, and a cane that she carried for "swank." She often said, "Look at me, I am black, I am beautiful." Examine the use of fashion by African Americans to make a political point.

3. Review the treatment of African Americans in the New Deal.

4. Profile the members of the so-called Black Cabinet of President Franklin D. Roosevelt.

   Originally a Republican, Bethune became a loyal Democrat. Discuss why so many African Americans abandoned the Party of Lincoln for the Party of Franklin Roosevelt.

ALTERNATIVE TERM PAPER SUGGESTIONS

1. Mary McLeod Bethune experienced discrimination as an African American, as a woman, and as a black person with a very dark complexion. Create a Microsoft PowerPoint presentation that discusses the history of discrimination within the black community over shades of color.

2. Assume that you are a newspaper reporter for a black publication. The election of 1936 is approaching. Write an editorial urging African Americans to abandon their historic support for Republican candidates and vote for President Franklin D. Roosevelt.

SUGGESTED SOURCES

Primary Source

McCluskey, Audrey Thomas, and Elaine M. Smith, eds. *Mary McLeod Bethune: Building a Better World.* Bloomington: Indiana University Press, 2001. Contains many of Bethune's letters, essays, and other papers.

Secondary Sources

Birnbaum, Jonathan, and Clarence Taylor, eds. *Civil Rights Since 1787.* New York: New York University Press, 2000. An essay by Darlene Clark Hine and Kathleen Thompson examines Bethune and the Black Cabinet.

Brown, Nikki. *Private Politics and Public Voices: Black Women's Activism from World War I to the New Deal.* Bloomington: Indiana University Press, 2006. A chapter covers the involvement of black women with the Democratic Party.

Damhorst, Mary Lynn, Kimberly A. Miller-Spillman, and Susan O. Michelman. *The Meanings of Dress.* New York: Fairchild, 2005. Essays cover dress as nonverbal communication as well as continuing struggles in the black community over the issues of complexion.

Franklin, John Hope, and Alfred A. Moss Jr. *From Slavery to Freedom: A History of African Americans.* New York: Alfred A. Knopf, 1994. Discusses the Black Cabinet.

Hanson, Joyce A. *Mary McLeod Bethune and Black Women's Political Activism.* Columbia: University of Missouri Press, 2003. A superb account of Bethune's leadership of the National Association of Colored Women and the National Council of Negro Women.

King, John T., and Marcet H. King. *Mary McLeod Bethune: A Woman of Vision and Determination.* Lake Junaluska, NC: Commission on Archives and History, United Methodist Church, 1977. Solid biography of Bethune.

Sitkoff, Harvard. *A New Deal for Blacks: The Emergence of Civil Rights as a National Issue.* New York: Oxford University Press, 1978. Excellent discussion of African American history in the 1930s.

Weiss, Nancy J. *Farewell to the Party of Lincoln: Black Politics in the Age of FDR.* Princeton, NJ: Princeton University Press, 1983. Examines the switch that many African Americans made in the 1930s from the Republican to the Democratic Party.

World Wide Web

"Mary McLeod Bethune." http://www.africawithin.com/bios/mary_bethune.htm. Contains a short essay on Bethune, a copy of her last will and testament, and a photo gallery.

"Mary McLeod Bethune." http://www.floridamemory.com/onlineclassroom/ MaryBethune/. Contains interviews with Bethune, photographs of her, and drafts of Daniel Mortimer Williams's uncompleted biography.

"Mary McLeod Bethune." http://www.lkwdpl.org/WIHOHIO/beth-mar.htm. This Women in History site profiles Bethune and includes links, such as one to sound files in the New York Public Library Schomburg Center for Research in Black Culture in which Bethune speaks of the power of education.

"Mary McLeod Bethune." http://www.ncnw.org/about/bethune.htm. The National Council of Negro Women provides this biography of its founder.

"Mary McLeod Bethune Council House Historic Site." http://www.nps.gov/ mamc/. A National Park Service site that introduces the Washington, D.C. townhouse that served as Bethune's home and the headquarters of the National Council of Negro Women.

Multimedia Sources

Black Americans of Achievement: Mary McLeod Bethune. Bala Cynwyd, PA: Schlessinger Video, n.d. VHS. Short biography aimed at grade school students.

Mary McLeod Bethune: The Spirit of a Champion. History on Video, 2008. DVD. Sixty-minute biography of the educator and activist.

68. March on Washington's Double V Campaign (1941)

The "Double V" campaign aimed to achieve two victories, or "v"s, by defeating racism at home and fascism abroad. It resulted in gains in the military and the defense industry for African Americans as the United States mobilized to fight World War II.

The *Pittsburgh Courier,* the most widely circulated African American newspaper of the 1940s, initiated the Double V campaign to protest ongoing discrimination against African Americans. To many Americans, it seemed profoundly odd that the United States was fighting to bring democracy to Europe but could not extend it to blacks at home. The black press throughout the country supported the *Courier*'s efforts. Blacks were soon creating Double V songs, and women adopted Double V hairstyles.

A. Philip Randolph picked up the campaign. The head of the Brotherhood of Sleeping Car Porters, Randolph sought equal opportunities and equal pay for blacks who worked in factories or served in the military. He organized the March on Washington Movement to embarrass President Franklin D. Roosevelt into removing the barriers confronting black workers. He threatened to have at least 25,000 African Americans march through the nation's capital on July 1, 1941. On June 25, 1941, Roosevelt stopped this potential public relations nightmare by agreeing to Randolph's demands. He issued Executive Order 8802, which outlawed racial discrimination in defense industries and established the Fair Employment Practices Committee to investigate complaints lodged by black workers.

TERM PAPER SUGGESTIONS

1. Examine the history of the Double V campaign. Why did it succeed?
2. Discuss the challenges faced by African Americans who remained on the home front during World War II.
3. Discuss the strategy employed by A. Philip Randolph. Was it in the best interests of African Americans to threaten to embarrass the United States on the eve of war?

ALTERNATIVE TERM PAPER SUGGESTIONS

1. Assume that you are a black worker in an aircraft factory in 1941. Write a series of letters to a brother or sister in which you describe your economic plight and your support of the Double V campaign.
2. A. Philip Randolph has asked you to create a Web page promoting the Double V campaign.
3. Create a blog about the efforts to win the Double V campaign.

SUGGESTED SOURCES

Primary Source

"Double V Campaign." http://www.nasm.si.edu/blackwings/hdetail/detailbw
.cfm?bwID=BW0034. Consists entirely of a photocopy of a 1942
Pittsburgh Courier article on the Double V campaign.

Secondary Sources

Harris, William V. *The Harder We Run: Black Workers Since the Civil War.* New
York: Oxford University Press, 1982. Discusses the quest of the black
worker for equality.

Pfeffer, Paula F. A. *Philip Randolph: Pioneer of the Civil Rights Movement.* Baton
Rouge: Louisiana State University Press, 1990. Discusses Randolph's
involvement with the Double V campaign.

World Wide Web

"History Now: The Double V Campaign." http://www.historynow.org/
12_2007/historian5.html. Discusses the Double V campaign during
World War II.

"The Pittsburgh Courier." http://www.nasm.si.edu/blackwings/hdetail/
detailbw.cfm?bwID=BW0034. Brief history of a newspaper that was
once the most widely circulated African American paper.

"The Pittsburgh Courier During World War II." http://www.yurasko.net/vv/
index.html. Reprints college student William Yurasko's research paper
on the famed black newspaper.

69. Tuskegee Airmen Silence Skeptics with Victories in Italy (1944)

The Tuskegee Airmen successfully challenged the common white belief
that African Americans lacked the intelligence and courage to serve as
pilots. The airmen's combat success weakened the War Department's general policy of banning black men from combat units.

At the start of World War II, African Americans who wanted to serve
their country in the military faced considerable racism. Black recruits
were typically assigned menial tasks and were segregated from white
troops. Secretary of War Henry L. Stimson insisted that blacks lacked
the capacity to serve as leaders. Under pressure to integrate African

Americans into the army and in need of more men to fight, the War Department opened a segregated training facility for pilots on the grounds of Booker T. Washington's Tuskegee Institute. The school possessed an airfield and had a proven civilian pilot training program.

The 992 men trained at Tuskegee became pilots, navigators, and bombardiers, with 450 of them serving overseas in Europe. About 150 died in training or on combat flights. Known as the "Red-Tailed Angels" for the distinctive bright red paint on the tails of their planes, the Tuskegee Airmen did not lose a single bomber that they were escorting to enemy fire in more than 200 combat missions. This record stood unmatched by any other fighter group. The Tuskegee Airmen served in the 332nd Fighter Group. This group, the 332nd, consisted of four fighter squadrons: the 99th, the 100th, the 301st, and the 302nd. The 99th won two Presidential Unit Citations for outstanding tactical air support and aerial combat. The 332nd won a Presidential Unit Citation for a bomber escort mission to Berlin, Germany in March 1945, during which it destroyed three German ME-262 fighters and damaged five additional fighters without losing any U.S. aircraft. In total, the Tuskegee Airmen destroyed or damaged over 409 German aircraft, 950 ground units, and sank a battleship destroyer.

TERM PAPER SUGGESTIONS

1. Examine the struggles of African Americans to become pilots during World War II.
2. Discuss the impact of the Tuskegee Airmen on the fight to win equal treatment for African Americans.
3. Black airmen faced racism at home and overseas. Discuss the combat experiences of the Tuskegee Airmen.
4. A number of prominent black men, such as Nation of Islam leader Elijah Muhammad and writer Bayard Rustin, refused to be inducted into the military. Discuss whether resisting military service or welcoming military service represented the best strategy for achieving racial gains.

ALTERNATIVE TERM PAPER SUGGESTIONS

1. Interview an African American who served in the military during the Vietnam War. Compare and contrast his or her experiences with those of the Tuskegee Airmen.
2. Create a Web site that pays tribute to one of the Tuskegee Airmen.

SUGGESTED SOURCES

Secondary Sources

Francis, Charles E., and Adolph Caso. *The Tuskegee Airmen: The Men Who Changed a Nation.* Boston: Branden, 1997. First published in 1955, this classic history of the airmen has been updated and expanded by Caso.

Hardesty, Von. *Black Wings: Courageous Stories of African Americans in Aviation and Space History.* New York: HarperCollins, 2008. Includes a chapter on the Tuskegee Airmen and sets them within the context of black achievement in the air.

Homan, Lynn M., and Thomas Reilly. *Black Knights: The Story of the Tuskegee Airmen.* Gretna, LA: Pelican, 2001. Good account of the challenges faced by the men and their accomplishments in the air.

Scott, Lawrence P., and William M. Womack Sr. *Double V: The Civil Rights Struggle of the Tuskegee Airmen.* East Lansing: Michigan State University Press, 1998. Sets the achievements of the airmen in the context of the civil rights movement.

World Wide Web

"Honor Thy Father: A Tuskegee Airman." http://www.josephgomer.com/. A tribute to Joseph Gomer by his daughter, this site includes photographs and an extensive biography of the pilot. Phyllis Gomer Douglass's essay describes her father's experiences with racism during World War II.

"Tuskegee Airmen." http://www.nationalmuseum.af.mil/factsheets/factsheet.asp?id=1356. The National Museum of the U.S. Air Force has provided an essay that explains the significance of the Tuskegee Airmen and notes that the air force became the first branch of the military to erase the color line.

"The Tuskegee Airmen and Eleanor Roosevelt." http://www.fdrlibrary.marist.edu/tuskegee.html. This Franklin D. Roosevelt Presidential Library site explains First Lady Eleanor Roosevelt's support of the Tuskegee Airmen. It includes photocopied letters by Roosevelt to one of the airmen, Cecil Peterson.

"Tuskegee Airmen Facts." http://www.tuskegee.edu/Global/story.asp?S=1127695A. A Tuskegee University site that provides a good introduction to the training program and the achievements of the airmen.

"Tuskegee Airmen, Inc." http://www.tuskegeeairmen.org/. This Web site of Tuskegee Airmen is "dedicated to honoring the accomplishments of African Americans who participated in air crew, ground crew and operations support training in the Army Air Corps during WW II."

"Tuskegee Airmen National Historic Site." http://www.nps.gov/tuai. Introduces the visitor to the Alabama park where the airmen trained and provides a virtual museum exhibit.

"The Tuskegee Airmen: The Sky Was the Limit." http://www.afroam.org/history/tusk/tuskmain.html. Essay that introduces the airmen, with links to related documents such as the War Department's 1940 Statement of Policy on segregation of the armed forces.

Multimedia Sources

America's Black Warriors: Two Wars to Win. New York: A&E Television Networks, 2004. DVD and VHS. Originally shown on The History Channel in 1998, this documentary features numerous African-American World War II veterans who discuss the prejudice they encountered and the battles they fought.

Black Aviators: Flying Free. New York: A&E Television Networks, 2001. VHS. Uses first-person recollections, photos, and film footage to describe the world of the black aviators who broke down racial barriers.

The Tuskegee Airmen. Alexandria, VA: PBS Home Video, 2003. VHS. Introduces surviving airmen and looks back at their accomplishments.

70. *Morgan v. Virginia* Rules That Segregation on Interstate Buses Is Illegal (1946)

During World War II, civil rights organizations rapidly expanded. This increase in both membership and activities culminated in several wartime and early postwar victories, including *Morgan v. Virginia* in 1946.

The legal case began with Irene Morgan (later Irene Morgan Kirkaldy), a black "Rosie the Riveter" who worked in a plant that made bombers for use in World War II. On a muggy day in July 1944, Morgan boarded a Greyhound bus in Gloucester County, Virginia to return to her home and two children in Baltimore. When all the seats in the bus filled with passengers, the bus driver asked Morgan to give up her seat to a white person. She refused. She had paid her money for the seat. A sheriff's deputy, called by the bus driver, put his hand on Morgan to intimidate her to move. Morgan kicked the deputy, clawed him, and tried to tear his clothes. She refused to bite him only because she thought that he looked dirty. Arrested in

Saluda, Virginia, Morgan pled guilty and paid a $100 fine for resisting arrest. She refused to pay a $10 fine for violating a Virginia law that required segregated seating in public transportation. The National Association for the Advancement of Colored People represented Morgan as she appealed.

By a vote of six to one on June 3, 1946, the Supreme Court ruled that the Virginia law violated the "commerce clause" in the Constitution. Justice Stanley F. Reed, writing for the majority, stated that seating arrangements in interstate transportation required a uniform rule to promote and protect national travel. The Court declared that Morgans's right of equal protection under the law had been violated. With this decision, the Court undermined the *Plessy v. Ferguson* ruling of 1896 and moved closer to ending segregation throughout the nation.

TERM PAPER SUGGESTIONS

1. Both Morgan and Rosa Parks refused to give up their seats on a bus. Compare and contrast *Morgan v. Virginia* with the Montgomery Bus Boycott.

2. Rosa Parks is one of the best-known Americans of the twentieth century. Few people walking down the street can identify Irene Morgan. Explore why Parks is remembered but Morgan has been forgotten.

3. Irene Morgan has been described as the first of the Freedom Riders. What were the Freedom Rides? Examine the history of this type of civil rights protest.

4. Discuss the right of equal protection as defined by the Supreme Court.

ALTERNATIVE TERM PAPER SUGGESTIONS

1. Many of the pivotal figures in the civil rights movement have not received their proper due. Pay tribute to Irene Morgan by creating a Web site that explains her contributions to freedom.

2. Assume that you have been asked to gain public support for a historical marker to be placed in Saluda, Virginia or Morgan's hometown of Gloucester, Virginia about the *Morgan v. Virginia* case. Create a Microsoft PowerPoint presentation to explain the significance of the decision.

SUGGESTED SOURCES

Primary Source

Green, Robert P., Jr. *Equal Protection and the African-American Constitutional Experience: A Documentary History.* Westport, CT: Greenwood Press, 2000. Contains a copy of the *Morgan v. Virginia* decision.

Secondary Sources

Arsenault, Raymond. *Freedom Riders: 1961 and the Struggle for Racial Justice.* New York: Oxford University Press, 2007. Arsenault sets the 1961 Freedom Rides in historical context and gives Morgan her due as a civil rights pioneer.

Barron, Jerome A., and C. Thomas Dienes. *Constitutional Law.* St. Paul, MN: Thomson/West, 2005. Introduction to constitutional law with a focus on equal protection.

Conant, Michael. *The Constitution and Economic Regulation: Objective Theory and Critical Commentary.* New Brunswick, NJ: Transaction, 2008. Includes a chapter on the rights of persons and businesses under the Equal Protection Clause.

Hoffer, Peter Charles, Williamjames Hull Hoffer, and N. E. H. Hull. *The Supreme Court: An Essential History.* Lawrence: University Press of Kansas, 2007. Perhaps the best summary of the intellectual, social, cultural, economic, and political events that have influenced the decision-making of the U.S. Supreme Court.

Lee, Francis Graham. *Equal Protection: Rights and Liberties Under the Law.* Santa Barbara, CA: ABC-CLIO, 2003. A reference book that provides information on key people, cases, and events.

Tsesis, Alexander. *We Shall Overcome: A History of Civil Rights and the Law.* New Haven, CT: Yale University Press, 2008. Traces civil rights legislation over the past two centuries.

Williams, Juan. *Thurgood Marshall: American Revolutionary.* Pittsburgh: Three Rivers Press, 2000. Marshall, as an NAACP attorney, represented Irene Morgan before the Supreme Court. This is a comprehensive biography of the famed attorney and Supreme Court justice.

World Wide Web

"The Freedom Rider a Nation Nearly Forgot: Woman Who Defied Segregation Finally Gets Her Due." http://www.washingtonpost.com/ac2/wp-dyn ?pagename=article&node=&contentId=A3740-2000Jul29. This *Washington Post* article discusses how history has largely forgotten Irene Morgan.

"Irene Morgan." http://h0bbes.wordpress.com/2006/11/06/irene-morgan/. This Seventh-Day Adventist Web site notes Morgan's membership in the denomination but focuses on her court case. It includes a link to Bayard Rustin's song "You Don't Have to Ride Jim Crow Here," about Morgan's refusal to tolerate Jim Crow laws.

"Irene Morgan Kirkaldy, Rights Pioneer, 90, Dies." http://www.nytimes.com/ 2007/08/13/us/13kirkaldy.html. The *New York Times* obituary for Morgan discusses the court case that brought her fame.

Multimedia Source

You Don't Have to Ride Jim Crow! New Hampshire Public Television, 1995. VHS. This documentary includes an interview with Morgan about her refusal to give up her seat on the bus.

71. President Harry S. Truman Desegregates the U.S. Military (1948)

On July 26, 1948, President Harry S. Truman issued the order to integrate the U.S. armed services. His decision created a military where advancement was based only on merit. The military then served as a model of desegregation for the civilian community.

World War II and the onset of the Cold War transformed the battle for African American civil rights. In the Cold War, the United States could not afford to alienate hearts and minds in Europe, Asia, Africa, and Latin America. Soviets used the poor treatment of African Americans in the South in propaganda that presented the Soviet Union as the true protector of the downtrodden. By 1948, Truman recognized that the United States could not present itself as the beacon of liberty while denying equality to the young men and women who served the flag around the world. He decided to integrate the armed forces.

Yet Truman's actions were unexpected. Truman had demonstrated little interest in African Americans throughout his lackluster career in Congress. However, when black activists presented President Truman with evidence of the brutality shown to blacks in the South, he took immediate action.

Stunned at the extent of the abuse, Truman immediately appointed the Committee on Civil Rights to recommend preventive measures. The move proved risky, as Truman alienated many southern Democrat voters by promoting civil rights. The committee recommended both the creation of a civil rights commission to investigate abuses and the denial of federal aid to any state that mandated segregated schools and public facilities. Truman went a step further on July 26, 1948 with Executive Order 9981.

This order to desegregate the armed forces sat unimplemented until the Korean War. In January 1950, army regulations were issued that directed efficient employment of manpower without regard to race.

In March 1950, the army abolished quotas that restricted the recruiting of black soldiers. As a result, enlistment of black men increased well beyond the requirements of segregated units. Commanders then began assigning black soldiers wherever they were needed and expressed satisfaction with the results. Fears of hostility and tension between blacks and whites proved unfounded. Officers stated that the only color recognized by the army was army green. As the Department of the Army realized, a segregated army made no sense militarily. Given the tensions of the Cold War and the need for economical use of manpower in the modern armed forces, it was foolish to make policy decisions based on the social standards of some white Americans. For national security reasons, segregated units had to be made obsolete.

TERM PAPER SUGGESTIONS

1. Examine the process of integrating the armed forces, which actually began under President Franklin D. Roosevelt.
2. Explore why Truman elected to integrate the military despite the political risks. He very narrowly won reelection in 1948, with backlash against his civil rights program nearly costing him the election.
3. Did an executive order rather than a law passed by Congress serve as the best method of integrating the military? Explain.
4. The Cold War between the Soviet Union and the United States had an impact upon civil rights. Examine the impact of the Cold War on civil rights in the 1948 to 1953 period.

ALTERNATIVE TERM PAPER SUGGESTIONS

1. Assume that you are an advisor to President Truman. You have been asked to give a presentation to the president about the pros and cons of integrating the U.S. armed services. Prepare a Microsoft PowerPoint presentation.
2. Assume that you are a young black man in the newly-integrated U.S. Army. Create a blog that describes your experiences.

SUGGESTED SOURCES

Primary Sources

"Executive Order 9981." http://www.trumanlibrary.org/9981.htm. Provides the original document as well as a text version of the order.

Giangreco, D. M., and Kathryn Moore. *Dear Harry: Truman's Mailroom, 1945–1953*. New York: Stackpole, 1999. Thousands of messages sent to President Truman by private citizens and famous figures about such topics as integration.

Secondary Sources

Dalfiume, Richard M. *Desegregation of the U.S. Armed Forces: Fighting on Two Fronts, 1939–1953*. Columbia: University of Missouri Press, 1969. Examines pressures for integration, the first steps toward integration, and the difficulties of enacting Truman's order.

MacGregor, Morris J., Jr. *The Integration of the Armed Forces, 1940–1965*. Washington, DC: U.S. Army Center of Military History, Government Printing Office, 1989. Covers the pressure to integrate during World War II until the general acceptance of blacks in the military.

McCullough, David. *Truman*. New York: Simon and Schuster, 1992. An award-winning and best-selling biography that makes the late president come vividly to life.

World Wide Web

"Biography of Harry S. Truman." http://www.whitehouse.gov/history/presidents/ht33.html. The White House Historical Society biography of Truman.

"Harry S. Truman Library and Museum." http://www.trumanlibrary.org/. Includes a biography of Truman and featured essays with quizzes on subjects of interest during his presidency.

Multimedia Sources

Truman. Hollywood, CA: HBO Home Video, 2000. DVD. Gary Sinise stars in this fictional account of the trials and tribulations of the president.

Truman. Hollywood, CA: PBS Paramount, 2006. DVD. Part of PBS's American Experience series, this is a stellar biography of the president.

72. Jackie Robinson Breaks the Color Bar in Baseball (1947)

Baseball has historically been described as America's pastime, yet African Americans were long excluded from the highest level of the game. Blacks could play in the Negro Leagues but not in Minor League Baseball or

Major League Baseball (MLB). When Jackie Robinson broke MLB's color line in 1947, he opened the floodgates, as a host of other black players jumped from the Negro Leagues to the Major Leagues.

MLB never formally banned blacks from playing. The prohibition was just a matter of custom, albeit a firmly entrenched one. Since the early days of the Negro Leagues, sportswriters for African American newspapers had condemned MLB for keeping black ballplayers out of their game. Most of the black players in the Negro Leagues also barnstormed around the nation, playing exhibition games. Often they faced white-only teams of Major Leaguers and defeated them.

By the 1930s, the attacks on segregated baseball had grown very strong, but Major League Commissioner Kennesaw Mountain Landis wanted blacks to remain in their own league. When flamboyant showman Bill Veeck announced his intention to break the color line by hiring the best talent available, including black players, to staff the Philadelphia Phillies, Landis blocked Veeck from purchasing the Phillies. Despite shortages of white players during World War II, no blacks were invited to the majors. When Landis died in 1944, Happy Chandler succeeded him. A former U.S. senator from Kentucky, Chandler did not appear to be a pathbreaker for integration. However, Chandler argued that if blacks could fight against the Nazis and the Japanese, then they could fight for a major league team. Branch Rickey, seeking to improve his woeful team, then signed Jackie Robinson.

Robinson became the first African American to play MLB when he joined the Brooklyn Dodgers in 1947, after serving an apprenticeship in the Negro Leagues with the Kansas City Monarchs. Some Negro league players thought that Robinson was the wrong man to break the color barrier because he was not a good enough player. They worried that he would fail, thereby giving credence to the notion that blacks were not good enough to compete against whites. However, in 10 seasons, Robinson batted .311. An infielder who played both first and second base, Robinson was named to the all-star team six times, played on six pennant winners, and formed part of Brooklyn's only World Series squad. He achieved all of these triumphs while white, racist players waited for him on the base paths with sharpened spikes, pitchers threw at his head to test him, and racial insults flew at him from opposing fans and players. Hate mail excoriating the Dodgers for hiring Robinson, plus letters attacking him personally, piled up in the team offices. While Robinson never publicly reacted to the hatred, the stress gave him stomach pains for the duration of his career and may have shortened his life. In the next years, teams rushed to sign stars from the Negro Leagues. The Boston Red Sox became the last team to integrate in 1959.

TERM PAPER SUGGESTIONS

1. Trace the history of the Negro Leagues, perhaps focusing on one of the teams.
2. Provide a biography of a player who either spent time in the Negro Leagues or who became one of the first African Americans to play MLB.
3. Interview an African American who came of age in the 1980s or earlier about the disappearance of blacks in present-day baseball.
4. The Civil Rights Game, an exhibition played each year in Memphis, Tennessee, where civil rights leader Martin Luther King Jr. was assassinated, is just one way in which MLB is attempting to revive the interest of blacks in playing baseball. In 1992, it began Reviving Baseball in Inner Cities (RBI), with blacks forming nearly half of the youths who participate in the program. Trace the history of the efforts to attract blacks back to baseball. Are these programs successful at increasing interest?

ALTERNATIVE TERM PAPER SUGGESTIONS

1. Create a Microsoft PowerPoint presentation about the history of blacks in baseball.
2. Prepare a podcast about Jackie Robinson's debut with the Brooklyn Dodgers. Make sure that you include a brief history of blacks in baseball and a description of how Robinson has been received by other players and fans.
3. Create a Web site devoted to African Americans in baseball. See examples of Web sites dedicated to Jackie Robinson.

SUGGESTED SOURCES

Primary Source

Robinson, Jackie, and Alfred Duckett. *I Never Had It Made: An Autobiography of Jackie Robinson.* New York: Harper Perennial, 2003. Robinson's account of breaking baseball's color line.

Secondary Sources

Freedman, Lew. *African American Pioneers of Baseball: A Biographical Encyclopedia.* Westport, CT: Greenwood Press, 2007. Provides short biographies of the first blacks to play the national pastime.

Lamb, Chris. *Blackout: The Untold Story of Jackie Robinson's First Spring Training.* Lincoln: University of Nebraska Press, 2004. Describes the challenges that Robinson faced as he participated in spring training in the segregated state of Florida.

Linge, Mary Kay. *Jackie Robinson: A Biography.* Westport, CT: Greenwood Press, 2007. For high school students and up.

Rielly, Edward J., ed. *Baseball and American Culture: Across the Diamond.* New York: Haworth Press, 2003. Shows how baseball and American society interact, with chapters devoted to the desegregation of spring training, the popularization of the Negro Leagues, and blacks in baseball in the nineteenth century.

Tygiel, Jules. *Baseball's Great Experiment: Jackie Robinson and His Legacy.* New York: Oxford University Press, 1997. Good examination of Robinson's achievement and his impact on baseball.

World Wide Web

"Baseball and Jackie Robinson." http://memory.loc.gov/ammem/collections/robinson/. This Library of Congress site includes a timeline and photographs of early baseball players, as well as other materials related to baseball between the 1860s and the 1960s.

"Jackie Robinson Biography." http://www.biography.com/search/article.do ?id=9460813. Includes videos about Robinson.

"The Jackie Robinson Foundation." http://www.jackierobinson.org/. Founded as a memorial to Jackie Robinson, this foundation is dedicated to promoting his memory and supporting higher education for minority youths.

"National Baseball Hall of Fame." http://web.baseballhalloffame.org/index.jsp. This site includes brief biographies of Hall of Fame inductees, among them players from the Negro Leagues. (Negro league stars were first inducted in 1971.) The Research Library includes three useful sources: 1) the Abner Library Catalog has entries on books that address the Negro Leagues; 2) under Selective Bibliographies there are 44 book titles and 147 journal articles dealing with Jackie Robinson; and 3) Archival Finding Aids and Inventories, Wendell Smith Papers. Smith, a newspaper reporter for the African American *Pittsburgh Courier,* campaigned for the desegregation of baseball.

"Negro Baseball Leagues." http://www.blackbaseball.com/. With content provided by the director of research at the Negro Leagues Baseball Museum, this is the best source for information about the Negro Leagues.

"Negro Leagues Baseball Museum." http://www.nlbm.com. The Negro Leagues Baseball Museum opened in Kansas City, Missouri in 1991. This site provides a listing of the leagues and a listing of teams by region.

"The Official Site of Jackie Robinson." http://www.jackierobinson.com/. Along with a biography of Robinson, this site includes statistics, photos, quotes, wallpapers, and screensavers.

Multimedia Sources

Baseball: A Film by Ken Burns. New York: PBS, 1994. 10 DVDs. This massive documentary catalogs the history of baseball from the 1840s to 1994. It includes a segment on the debut of Jackie Robinson.

When It Was a Game. New York: HBO Home Video, 2001. 3 DVDs. This documentary discusses the inclusion of African American baseball players.

73. *Brown v. Board of Education* (1954)

The 1954 *Brown v. Board of Education* decision is one of the most significant in American history. It overturned the "separate but equal" doctrine established in 1896 that made racial segregation legal in public facilities. *Brown* integrated the public schools.

Despite the requirement that schools be equal, black schools did not have the facilities or textbooks available at white schools. The National Association for the Advancement of Colored People (NAACP) had long protested such treatment with limited success. NAACP attorney Thurgood Marshall argued in both *McLaurin v. Oklahoma* and *Sweatt v. Painter* that segregation itself was inherently unequal and that it denied African Americans protections guaranteed by the Fourteenth Amendment. In 1949, five groups of plaintiffs approached the NAACP to challenge unequal elementary schools. The cases were grouped together as *Brown* and went before the U.S. Supreme Court.

The *Brown* opinion, read on May 17, 1954 by Chief Justice Earl Warren, stated that segregation might generate a feeling of inferiority in black children that would last a lifetime. The Court ruled that segregation had no valid purpose, had been imposed to give blacks lower status, and violated the Constitution. A separate 1955 decision, known as *Brown II,* set guidelines for desegregation but established only a "with all deliberate speed" timetable. Southerners resisted the decision violently, shut down public schools, and took as much time as they could to integrate. Florida schools only integrated in 1970, as one example of all deliberate speed.

TERM PAPER SUGGESTIONS

1. On the 50th anniversary of the *Brown* decision, many black scholars were debating whether desegregating public schools had actually benefited African American students. Discuss the significance of the *Brown* decision. Was the Court correct that black students would benefit from integration?

2. Discuss southern white resistance to the *Brown* decision.

3. The *Brown* decision overturned *Plessy v. Ferguson*. Compare and contrast the two Supreme Court decisions.

4. Discuss the implementation of the *Brown* decision. Why did the Supreme Court refuse to order immediate integration?

ALTERNATIVE TERM PAPER SUGGESTIONS

1. Create a Microsoft PowerPoint presentation that identifies the many legal decisions and events over the decades that led to the desegregation of public schools.

2. Create a Microsoft PowerPoint presentation that examines the *Brown* decision and resistance to it.

SUGGESTED SOURCES

Primary Sources

Martin, Waldo E. *Brown v. Board: A Brief History with Documents*. Boston: Bedford St. Martins, 1998. Collects original documents and commentaries essential to understanding the landmark Supreme Court decision.

"National Archives: Teaching with Documents: *Brown v. Board of Education*." http://www.archives.gov/education/lessons/brown-v-board/. Contains a link to the original Supreme Court decision.

Secondary Sources

Bartley, Numan V. *The Rise of Massive Resistance: Race and Politics in the South During the 1950s*. Baton Rouge: Louisiana State University Press, 1969. Describes *Brown*'s impact and attacks upon it by such groups as the White Citizens' Councils.

Branch, Taylor. *Parting the Waters: America in the King Years, 1954–1963*. New York: Simon and Schuster, 1988. A remarkable and exhaustive study of

Martin Luther King's early life and the major events of mid-twentieth-century America.

Cottrell, Robert J., Raymond T. Diamond, and Leland B. Ware. *Brown v. Board of Education: Caste, Culture, and the Constitution.* Lawrence: University Press of Kansas, 2003. Focuses on the decision, including its cultural impact and the effect on the Supreme Court.

Dudziak, Mary. *Cold War Civil Rights: Race and the Image of American Democracy.* Princeton, NJ: Princeton University Press, 2002. Enormously influential book that explains the federal government's support of civil rights as part of an effort to counter Communist propaganda during the Cold War.

Kluger, Richard. *Simple Justice: The History of Brown v. Board of Education and Black America's Struggle for Equality.* New York: Knopf, 1975. The definitive study of the *Brown* decision.

McMillen, Neil R. *The Citizens' Councils: Organized Resistance to the Second Reconstruction, 1954–64.* Chicago: University of Illinois Press, 1971. Examines how whites organized in the South in opposition to the *Brown* decision.

Patterson, James T. *Brown v. Board of Education: A Civil Rights Milestone and Its Troubled Legacy.* New York: Oxford University Press, 2001. An examination of the case with an appendix that details four decades of desegregation.

Sitkoff, Harvard. *The Struggle for Black Equality, 1954–1980.* New York: Hill and Wang, 1981. Probably the best short history of the civil rights movement.

Wilkinson, J. Harvie. *From Brown to Bakke: The Supreme Court and School Integration: 1954–1978.* Examines key court cases and the legal aspects of integration.

World Wide Web

"*Brown v. Board of Education* (1954)." http://www.landmarkcases.org/brown/home.html. Provides a history of the case, key biographies, full text of the majority opinion, and an essay that discusses whether the promise of *Brown* has been achieved.

"*Brown v. Board of Education* (II)." http://www.oyez.org/cases/1950-1959/1954/1954_1/. This site addresses the means by which the decision should be implemented. It provides the written opinion of the U.S. Supreme Court as well as photos of the justices.

"History of *Brown v. Board.*" http://public.findlaw.com/civil-rights/race-discrimination/brown-vs-boe-history(1).html. Provides a very detailed history of the Supreme Court decision.

Multimedia Source

Eyes on the Prize: America's Civil Rights Years. Blackside, 1986. VHS. The first two episodes of this series focus on *Brown v. Board* and its immediate aftermath.

74. Lynching of Emmett Till (1955)

The brutal murder of 14-year-old Emmett Till in August 1955 by white racists in Mississippi became a rallying point for the civil rights movement. Public outrage over the case prompted Congress to include a provision for the federal investigation of civil rights violations in the Civil Rights Act of 1957.

Mamie Till of Chicago sent her only child, Emmett Louis Till, to visit relatives in the Mississippi Delta in August 1955. As a northerner, Till did not understand the racial mores of the South. He bragged to some other black southern boys that he had a white girlfriend in Chicago. The skeptical friends dared Till to enter a grocery store and ask the white clerk for a date. Till reportedly squeezed Carol Bryant's hand and whistled at her before the other boys rushed him away. Bryant reported the encounter to her husband. On August 28, 1955, Roy Bryant and his half-brother J. W. Milam abducted Till from his great-uncle's home in the middle of the night. Three days later, Till's naked, beaten, and decomposed body was pulled from the Tallahatchie River. The boy had been shot through the head. Mamie Till put Emmett in an open casket so all the world could see what had happened to her boy. All the world did look, including *Ebony* magazine, which put a photo of Till in his casket on its cover. A generation of African Americans would remember seeing that cover. In a trial that received heavy press coverage, Bryant and Milam were acquitted by an all-white jury despite the fact that they admitted abducting Till. The men celebrated their victory by granting an interview in which they proudly recounted their murder of Till.

TERM PAPER SUGGESTIONS

1. Mamie Till put the following statement on her son's tombstone: "A little nobody who shook up the world." Discuss the significance of the Emmett Till case.

2. Compare and contrast Till's murder with another of the shocking killings of the civil rights era, the shooting of activist Medgar Evers in 1963. Be sure to include a discussion of the prosecution of Evers's killer and the interest in bringing Till's killers to justice.

3. Describe what life was like for African American teenagers growing up in the South in the age of Jim Crow segregation.

4. Emmett Till was oneof many victims of lynching. Ida B. Wells fought against lynching in the late nineteenth century but could not get support from the white community. Discuss why Till's murder in 1955 provoked such wide-spread horror.

ALTERNATIVE TERM PAPER SUGGESTIONS

1. Mamie Till viewed her son's murder and the public response to it as part of a larger stream of history. Create an annotated timeline to graphically prove Till's belief.

2. Conduct a Web search for "Emmett Till." Discuss how Till has been represented on the Web.

SUGGESTED SOURCES

Primary Sources

Metress, Christopher. *The Lynching of Emmett Till: A Documentary Narrative.* Charlottesville: University of Virginia Press, 2002. Collects more than 100 documents, including news accounts, memoirs, poems, and fictional accounts, that illuminate the Till case.

Till-Mobley, Mamie, and Christopher Benson. *The Story of the Hate Crime That Changed America.* New York: One World/Ballantine, 2004. The first half of this book focuses on the murder of Emmett Till, with the second half addressing Till-Mobley's search for meaning in life. It is an inspiring book.

Secondary Sources

Crowe, Chris. *Mississippi Trial, 1955.* New York: Puffin, 2003. This novel shows the point of view and ethical dilemmas facing a white teenager in the South who interacts with the Till case.

Whitfield, Stephen J. *A Death in the Delta: The Story of Emmett Till.* Baltimore, MD: Johns Hopkins University Press, 1991. Well-written account that focuses on the impact of the case upon such civil rights activists as Malcolm X and Toni Morrison.

World Wide Web

"Emmett Till: A Series of Four Lessons." http://www.facinghistory.org/resources/units/emmett-till-a-series-four-lessons?gclid=CPf48JKbgZYCFRg6awodsQaYFA. This site, which emphasizes moral choices, complements the documentary film *The Murder of Emmett Till*. Activities on the site provide a vehicle for discussing the film and placing the event in historical context.

"History of Lynching in the United States." http://www.umass.edu/complit/aclanet/ACLAText/USLynch.html. Lists information related to lynching, including justifications and numbers.

"Killers' Confessions." http://afroamhistory.about.com/od/emmetttill/a/emmetttill.htm. After being acquitted, the killers of Till spoke to a reporter from *Look* magazine. Double jeopardy prevented the district attorney from trying the men a second time, but the Justice Department contemplated prosecuting one of the women—the only survivor of the case—in the twenty-first century for violating Till's civil rights.

"The Murder of Emmett Till." http://afroamhistory.about.com/od/emmetttill/a/emmetttill.htm. Good essay on the case with links to related sites, such as the confession of Till's killers, and a timeline.

"Primary Sources: Reactions in Writing." http://www.pbs.org/wgbh/amex/till/filmmore/ps_reactions.html. Reprints correspondence from ordinary citizens, the FBI, and the Justice Department about the case.

"Race: The Power of an Illusion." http://www.pbs.org/race/000_General/000_00-Home.htm. This is the online companion to California Newsreel's film of the same name. It examines the concept of race in a thought-provoking manner.

Multimedia Sources

Eyes on the Prize. New York: PBS and Blackside, 1990. VHS and DVD. This landmark series of 14 episodes covers all the major events of the civil rights movement, including Till's lynching.

Free at Last: Civil Rights Heroes. New York: Image Entertainment, 2005. DVD. A better title would be "Civil Rights Martyrs," since this video covers the individuals, including Emmett Till, who gave their lives for the civil rights movement.

The Murder of Emmett Till. New York: PBS, 2003. DVD. Typically excellent episode of the American Experience series.

Understanding the Civil Rights Movement. New York: Educational Video Network, 2004. DVD. Explains the events that led to the civil rights movement.

The Untold Story of Emmett Louis Till. Velocity/Thinkfilm, 2004. DVD. Uses
  archival photos and footage to tell Till's story and the nation's shocked
  reaction to the blithe unconcern that the white citizens of a small town
  in Mississippi displayed to the brutal murder of a black boy. The film
  does a wonderful job of capturing the 1950s South.

75. Rosa Parks Is Arrested (1955)

Racial segregation was the rule during the 1950s in the southern states,
where the great majority of black Americans lived. No Jim Crow law
angered black people in Montgomery, Alabama more than bus segregation. There were about 50,000 African Americans in the city, and blacks
made up 66 percent of bus riders. More blacks rode the bus than whites
because fewer blacks could afford a car. To ride a bus, a black person
would step through the first door, pay, exit back out the door, and enter
the bus from the second door. Once through the second door, blacks
were expected to take a seat at the back of the bus, then gradually fill
up the seats until meeting the white section. If a white person entered a
full bus, an African American was expected to surrender his or her seat,
since Montgomery had a local ordinance that required blacks to give up
their seat on public transportation to a white when asked.

  Rosa Parks was a quiet, churchgoing, married woman who worked as
a seamstress in a downtown department store. As secretary for the local
National Association for the Advancement of Colored People, Parks also
knew that the civil rights organization sought a test case to challenge
bus segregation in Montgomery. She got on a bus on December 1,
1955. She did not intend to get arrested and, contrary to popular belief,
she was also not especially physically tired, although she had just ended
a long workday during the busy Christmas season. At the next stop,
some whites entered and filled up every seat. One white man remained
standing and the bus driver, James Blake, asked Parks to give up her
seat. Believing that black compliance with segregation had only led to
worse treatment, Parks was tired of giving in. She refused to move
and was arrested.

  In the early morning hours after Parks's arrest, black community leaders blanketed African American sections of Montgomery with leaflets urging support of a one-day bus boycott as a protest. This one-day boycott

proved so successful that the leaders decided to continue the protest in an attempt to obtain substantial change. For months, blacks formed car-pools, hitchhiked, or simply walked. The boycott was almost completely effective. It put economic pressure not only on the bus company but on many Montgomery merchants as well, because the boycotters found it difficult to get to downtown stores and shopped instead in their own neighborhoods. Still, the white town fathers held out against the boycott. A federal district court overturned the "separate but equal" doctrine established by the Supreme Court in the 1896 *Plessy v. Ferguson* case, and, in November 1956, the Supreme Court let the lower court decision stand without review. The next day, blacks boarded the buses in Montgomery.

TERM PAPER SUGGESTIONS

1. What is nonviolent direct action? Explain the concept behind the strategy. How did the strategy work in the Montgomery Bus Boycott?

2. Using the Montgomery Bus Boycott as an example, explain the role that economic pressure played in the civil rights movement.

3. Discuss how the indignities of segregation gave birth to the civil rights movement. What was life like for blacks under the Jim Crow system?

4. Research what happened to Rosa Parks after the Montgomery Bus Boycott ended. Many blacks were hesitant to resist segregation because of the high costs of resistance. Would you have made the same choice as Parks in light of the price that you would pay?

5. How did the Montgomery Bus Boycott differ from previous civil rights challenges?
   What is the legacy of the Montgomery Bus Boycott? How did it change the lives of blacks in Montgomery and across the nation?

ALTERNATIVE TERM PAPER SUGGESTIONS

1. Assume that you are a supporter of the Montgomery Bus Boycott. Design a Web page to draw attention to your cause and to attract further support.

2. Assume that you are a participant in the Montgomery Bus Boycott. Write a blog that describes why you are boycotting, the difficulties of protesting, and what you expect to achieve.

SUGGESTED SOURCES

Primary Sources

"Act of Courage, The Arrest Records of Rosa Parks." The National Archives. http://www.archives.gov/education/lessons/rosa-parks/. Provides a diagram of the seat in the bus taken by Parks as well as her fingerprint card and arrest record.

Parks, Rosa, and Jim Haskins. *Rosa Parks: My Story.* New York: Dial Books, 1992. Parks's autobiography.

Secondary Sources

Brinkley, Douglas. *Rosa Parks.* New York: Viking, 2000. A superb, concise history of Parks.

Kohl, Herbert R. *She Would Not Be Moved: How We Tell the Story of Rosa Parks and the Montgomery Bus Boycott.* New York: New Press, 2005. Examines how children's books have misrepresented Rosa Parks's behavior as being motivated by tiredness instead of courage and determination, thereby doing a disservice to the black community.

Parks, Rosa, and Gregory Reed. *Quiet Strength: The Faith, the Hope, and the Heart of a Woman Who Changed a Nation.* Grand Rapids, MI: Zondervan Publishing House, 1994. Emphasizes Parks's religious beliefs.

Williams, Donnie. *The Thunder of Angels: The Montgomery Bus Boycott and the People Who Broke the Back of Jim Crow.* Chicago: Lawrence Hill Books, 2006. Stories of the Montgomery Bus Boycott typically focus on Parks. This book examines the many other people, such as E. D. Nixon and Virginia Durr, who helped to make the boycott a success.

Williams, Juan. *Eyes on the Prize: America's Civil Rights Years, 1954–1965.* New York: Viking Penguin, 1987. This is a companion book to the film series of the same name, with a section devoted to Rosa Parks.

World Wide Web

"A Guide to Materials for Rosa Parks." http://www.loc.gov/rr/program/bib/rosaparks/rosaparks.html. Links to the African American collection of the Library of Congress as well as numerous Web sites, an online catalog of photographic images, and lesson plans.

"Rosa Parks Library and Museum." http://montgomery.troy.edu/rosaparks/museum/. Links to the Montgomery, Alabama museum dedicated to Parks and to the history of the bus boycott.

"Rosa Parks Profile—Academy of Achievement." http://www.achievement.org/autodoc/page/par0bio-1. Provides a biography of Parks.

Multimedia Source

The Rosa Parks Story. Xenon, 2003. DVD. A fictional account of Parks's refusal to give up her seat, with Angela Bassett portraying the civil rights activist.

76. Crisis at Little Rock (1957)

The crisis at Little Rock's Central High School in 1957 grew out of the *Brown* decision desegregating public schools. Arkansas Governor Orval Faubus challenged federal authority over the schools by defying a court order to integrate the all-white school.

On a September day in 1957, nine Little Rock teenagers walked to their first day at school. Melba Pattillo, Ernest Green, Gloria Ray, Carlotta Walls, Terrence Roberts, Jefferson Thomas, Minnijean Brown, Thelma Mothershed, and Elizabeth Eckford were preparing to integrate Central High School, one of the top public schools in the nation. They were met by soldiers from the Arkansas National Guard who blocked their way. Governor Faubus, a racial moderate who saw his political career collapsing, had decided to play the race card to boost his reelection chances. He had ordered out the National Guard. The students turned back. Eckford, separated from the rest, faced an angry mob that screamed abuse and threatened to lynch her. A black photographer on the scene, Alex Wilson, refused the mob's orders to "run, nigger, run." When President Dwight D. Eisenhower saw the photographs of Wilson being beaten and the mob chasing Eckford, he took immediate action. He nationalized the Arkansas National Guard, sent the 101st Airborne Division to the state, and ordered the troops to escort the children to school. The soldiers remained for months, even though calm returned to Little Rock within days. Eisenhower became the first president since Reconstruction to protect the civil rights of African Americans through the use of military force.

TERM PAPER SUGGESTIONS

1. Examine the crisis in Little Rock. Why did whites strongly oppose integration, and why did blacks take the risk of attending an all-white school?

2. Compare and contrast the Little Rock crisis with the *Brown* decision.

3. Discuss the actions of someone involved with the Little Rock crisis. Why did Eisenhower, Faubus, Daisy Bates, or one of the Little Rock Nine become

involved with integrating Central High School? What happened after integration?

ALTERNATIVE TERM PAPER SUGGESTIONS

1. Hazel Bryan, a white teenager who is famously pictured in a photograph screaming racial insults at Elizabeth Eckford, later apologized for her actions. Assume that you can send a letter back through time to the teenage Bryan in 1957. Describe how her efforts to stop Eckford are misguided.

2. Find a black person who attended a segregated school or a person of any race who attended a newly integrated school. Interview the individual to discover the challenges that she or he faced in school and whether she or he believes that integration has been beneficial.

SUGGESTED SOURCES

Primary Sources

Bates, Daisy. *The Long Shadow of Little Rock: A Memoir.* Little Rock: University of Arkansas Press, 2007. Upon its original publication in 1962, this book was banned throughout the South. Bates served as the president of the Arkansas branch of the National Association for the Advancement of Colored People (NAACP) and played a critical role in arranging for the integration of Central High.

Beals, Melba Pattillo. *Warriors Don't Cry.* New York: Simon Pulse, 2007. Aimed at teenagers, this book by one of the Little Rock Nine recounts the drama of 1957. Beals relies on her diary and notes made by her mother.

Secondary Sources

Counts, Will. *A Life Is More Than a Moment: The Desegregation of Little Rock's Central High.* Bloomington: Indiana University Press, 2007. A graduate of Central High School and a news photographer with the Little Rock *Arkansas Democrat,* Counts obtained the most dramatic photographs of the crisis. This book contains fascinating updates on Hazel Bryan and Elizabeth Eckford.

Jacoway, Elizabeth. *Turn Away Thy Son: Little Rock, the Crisis That Shocked the Nation.* New York: Free Press, 2007. The focus of this book is Faubus, a man trying to save his political career against opponents using segregationist rhetoric to win voters.

World Wide Web

"Central High's 50th State." http://www.arkansas.com/central-high/
?siteid=19&bannerid=924&source=google&gclid=CMX3tMv0gZYCF
SAUagodNmiJEg. This site, created by the state of Arkansas, contains
links to photographs, a timeline, and the Central High School Museum.
"Little Rock National Historic Site." http://www.nps.gov/nr/travel/civilrights/ar1.
htm. Not an especially informative site, it focuses on Central High School.

Multimedia Sources

Crisis at Central High. New York: HBO Home Video, 1994. VHS. Originally
shown in 1981, this film focuses on its white star, played by Joanne
Woodward, instead of the characters of the black students.
Ernest Green Story. Orlando: Buena Vista Home Video, 1993. VHS. Green,
played by Morris Chestnut, graduated from Central High School after
helping to integrate it.
Little Rock Central High: 50 Years Later. HBO Home Video, 2007. DVD. Documentary that examines the crisis and its repercussions.

77. North Carolina A&T Students Initiate a Sit-In Protest (1960)

On February 1, 1960, four black college students from North Carolina
A&T College sat down at a whites-only lunch counter at a Woolworth's
department store in Greensboro, North Carolina. By doing so, they set
off a series of protests in which students occupied segregated restaurants
to protest segregationist policies.

Many public places in the South were segregated according to race.
Many restaurants did not serve African Americans in order to appease
whites who did not want blacks to receive equal treatment. The custom
made it difficult for blacks who were traveling to find meals on the road,
and it emphasized that African Americans were second-class citizens.
Anger at such indignities prompted college students to fight back. In
Greensboro, Joseph McNeil, Franklin McCain, Ezell Blair Jr., and David
Richmand attended the largest historically black college in the state. They
knew that they risked life and limb by daring to integrate the lunch
counter. They also knew that the Woolworth's restaurant lost money
when they remained in their seats until the business closed for the day,

since those seats could not be filled by paying customers. The four first-year students then returned for the next five days to occupy the lunch counter. They were joined by an ever-larger group of angry whites who protested the presence of the students by screaming insults, pouring condiments on their heads, and generally conducting themselves in a disorderly fashion. Unable to make money, the store eventually shut its doors.

Sit-ins had been conducted successfully before Greensboro, but the Greensboro protest drew considerable media attention. Other students heard about it and copied it. Black or racially-integrated groups of students would sit down in white-only spaces and refuse to move until they were served or forcibly removed. Other civil rights activists would march with signs outside of the restaurants to publicize the protests inside. By the end of 1960, about 70,000 African American students had participated in some form in sit-ins throughout the South.

TERM PAPER SUGGESTIONS

1. Compare and contrast the Greensboro and Nashville sit-ins.
2. Trace the history of the Greensboro sit-in.
3. Southerners typically responded to events such as the Greensboro sit-ins by stating that they must be the work of "outside agitators." Examine the participants in sit-ins. What were their motives? Were they outsiders?
4. The success of sit-ins sparked wade-ins (integrating beaches), jail-ins (refusing to bail out of jail), and other protests that focused on taking over public spaces. Discuss the effectiveness of this protest tactic.
5. Compare and contrast a nonviolent sit-in with a violent protest, perhaps a riot.

ALTERNATIVE TERM PAPER SUGGESTIONS

1. Create a graphic novel about the Greensboro sit-in, perhaps by using "Comic Life" software from the Plasq.com Company.
2. Assume that you are asked to participate in a sit-in to protest a wrong. Write a letter to recruit friends to join you. Be sure to discuss the effectiveness of sit-ins as a protest strategy.

SUGGESTED SOURCES

Primary Sources

Chafe, William. *Remembering Jim Crow: African Americans Tell About Life in the Segregated South.* New York: New Press, 2001. This book does not address the sit-in movement, but it describes exactly what it felt like to be black in the South in 1960.

Proudfoot, Merrill. *Diary of A Sit-in.* Urbana: University of Illinois Press, 1990. Proudfoot participated in a 1960 sit-in.

Secondary Sources

Chafe, William H. *Civilities and Civil Rights: Greensboro, North Carolina and the Black Struggle for Freedom.* New York: Oxford University Press, 1990. Exceptionally readable account of the civil rights struggle in a city of the Deep South.

Crow, Jeffrey J., Paul D. Escott, and Flora J. Hatley. *A History of African Americans in North Carolina.* Raleigh: Office of Archives and History, North Carolina Department of Cultural Resources, 2002. Exhaustive state study that includes chapters on black life in the age of Jim Crow and the civil rights movement of the 1960s. It can easily double as a reference book, though a readable one.

Laue, James H. *Direct Action and Desegregation, 1960–1962: Toward a Theory of the Rationalization of Protest.* Brooklyn, NY: Carlson, 1989. Aimed at advanced scholars, this is a sociological study of civil rights protests.

Lewis, John, and Michael D'Orso. *Walking with the Wind: A Memoir of the Movement.* New York: Harvest Books, 1999. Lewis, one of the busiest civil rights activists of the 1960s, writes of his participation in sit-ins and other civil rights activities.

Oppenheimer, Martin. *The Sit-In Movement of 1960.* Brooklyn, NY: Carlson, 1989. Good study of the spread of the protests across the South.

Waskow, Arthur I. *From Race Riot to Sit-in, 1919 and the 1960s: A Study in the Connections between Conflict and Violence.* Gloucester, MA: Peter Smith, 1966. Interesting comparison of the success of nonviolent and violent protest methods.

Wolff, Miles. *Lunch at the 5 & 10.* Chicago: Ivan R. Dee, 1990. First published in 1970, this is the story of the Greensboro sit-in, with an afterword that updates on the lives of the four students who took seats. All suffered various forms of persecution for participating in the protest.

World Wide Web

"The Autobiography of Martin Luther King, Jr." http://www.stanford.edu/ group/King/publications/autobiography/chp_14.htm. The King Center has provided excerpts from King's autobiography that show his reaction to and support of the sit-ins by college students.

"Greensboro Sit-Ins: Launch of a Civil Rights Movement." http://www
.sitins.com/index.shtml. This is an absolutely fabulous site with an introduction by James Farmer, links to the original newspaper accounts of the
protests, a timeline, and description of key players. Audio clips from participants add light to the decision to protest.

"Lunch Counter Sit-Ins." http://afroamhistory.about.com/od/sitins/a/sitins.htm.
Includes an essay on sit-ins, links to related topics, and links to related
Web pages.

"Nashville Sit-Ins (1959–1961)." http://www.tnstate.edu/library/digital/
nash.htm. Detailed discussion of the 1960 Nashville sit-in, as well as
the sit-ins that preceded the 1960 Greensboro one that is typically identified as the start of this wave of the civil rights movement.

"Sit-In: A Tactical Analysis." http://www.campusactivism.org/uploads/
sit-in-tactical-analysis.pdf. Created by CampusActivism.com, this site
discusses the merits of sit-ins as a current protest tactic.

"Sit-Ins." http://www.watson.org/~lisa/blackhistory/civilrights-55-65/
sit-ins.html. Focuses on the first years of the sit-ins, 1960 and 1961, as
the protest form gained support.

"Turbulent Times: Sit-In Campaign." http://library.thinkquest.org/C004391F/
sit-in_campaign.htm. Brief essay on sit-ins that includes suggestions
given to demonstrators.

Multimedia Source

February One. Los Angeles: California Newsreel, 2004. DVD. Tells the story of
the Greensboro sit-in through firsthand accounts and archival footage.

78. Student Nonviolent Coordinating Committee (SNCC) Is Formed (1960)

The Student Nonviolent Coordinating Committee (SNCC; pronounced
"snick") is one of the major civil rights organizations of the 1960s.
Through leaders such as Ella Baker, Stokely Carmichael, Ruby Doris
Smith Robinson, and Julian Bond, it worked to end segregation in the
South through such protests as sit-ins, Freedom Rides, and voter registra-
tion drives.

When the Greensboro college students held a sit-in and other students
throughout the South quickly copied them, Baker concluded that the
existing, fairly conservative civil rights organizations were not meeting

the needs of youths impatient for change. Baker, executive director of the Southern Christian Leadership Conference (SCLC), held a meeting for student activists on April 15, 1960 at historically black Shaw University in Raleigh, North Carolina. The students, both black and white, formed SNCC with Marion Barry as its first chairman.

SNCC began chiefly as a channel for students to communicate about sit-ins. When protesters were hauled off to jail for requesting to purchase a cup of coffee, SNCC capitalized on the resulting nationwide publicity by organizing a "jail-no-bail" campaign that filled southern jails. When the sit-in campaign wound down in 1961, SNCC divided over tactics. Some members wanted to focus on demonstrations that would get publicity for the movement, while others wanted to focus on getting direct power by registering blacks to vote. SNCC joined the Freedom Rides organized by the Congress of Racial Equality (CORE) to integrate buses that crossed state lines. With the success of this protest, SNCC focused on voter education projects. SNCC members tolerated years of violent abuse before helping to win passage of the 1965 Voting Rights Act. At this point, weariness at the pace of change prompted some members, including Stokely Carmichael, to argue that the time had come for blacks to seize power rather than seek compromise with whites. Many of SNCC's white members and supporters no longer felt welcome and drifted away. Carmichael expelled the remaining white staff and denounced SNCC's white donors. For all essential purposes, SNCC died, though it did not disappear entirely until the early 1970s.

TERM PAPER SUGGESTIONS

1. Women active in the civil rights movement often have received less than their due for their contributions to the fight for freedom. Explore the activities of women in SNCC.

2. Compare and contrast Rosa Parks with Ella Baker.

3. Stokely Carmichael, later known as Kwame Ture, attracted considerable controversy throughout his life for his support of Black Power and hostility toward women's rights. Discuss his life story.

4. Compare and contrast SNCC with one of the other major civil rights organizations of the era, perhaps the NAACP, the SCLC, or CORE.

5. Examine Carmichael's strategy of pushing whites out of the civil rights movement to create a movement by blacks for blacks.

ALTERNATIVE TERM PAPER SUGGESTIONS

1. Find someone old enough to have lived through the civil rights era and to remember it clearly. Interview this person about his or her memories of the civil rights movement and report your findings. You might want to post a video of the interview, with your interviewee's explicit permission, on YouTube.

2. The archives of several newspapers including the *New York Times* can be accessed through databases. Examine the portrayal of SNCC in a newspaper from 1962 to 1970.

SUGGESTED SOURCES

Primary Sources

Carson, Clayborne. *The Student Voice, 1960–1965: Periodical of the Student Nonviolent Coordinating Committee.* Westport, CT: Greenwood Press, 1990. Reprints the magazine of SNCC and includes an index.

Carson, Clayborne, et al., eds. *The Eyes on the Prize Civil Rights Reader: Documents, Speeches, and Firsthand Accounts from the Black Freedom Struggle.* New York: Penguin, 1991. Produced in conjunction with the broadcast of the PBS *Eyes on the Prize* television series, this is a collection of over 100 court decisions, speeches, interviews, and other documents on the civil rights movement from 1954 to 1990.

Grant, Joanne. *Ella Baker: Freedom Bound.* New York: John Wiley, 1998. Baker served as an organizer with both the National Association for the Advancement of Colored People (NAACP) and SNCC. One of those individuals who worked tirelessly outside of the spotlight, she has never really received the credit that she is due for promoting civil rights.

Lewis, John, and Michael D'Orso. *Walking with the Wind: A Memoir of the Movement.* New York: Harvest Books, 1999. Lewis, who became chair of SNCC, participated in lunch counter sit-ins, Freedom Rides, and voter registration drives, among other activities. His autobiography is the story of the civil rights movement of the 1960s.

Secondary Sources

Halberstam, David. *The Children.* New York: Ballantine, 1999. One of the best American writers of the twentieth century, Halberstam creates a vivid portrait of young African Americans, including future SNCC leaders Marion Barry and John Lewis, who attended a nonviolent workshop in 1959 and then proceeded to play major roles in the significant events of the civil rights movement. Halberstam covers the founding of SNCC as well as conflicts within the movement over class, gender, and skin color.

Murphree, Vanessa. *The Selling of Civil Rights: The Student Nonviolent Coordinating Committee and the Use of Public Relations.* New York: Routledge, 2006. Provides an overview of SNCC's use of publicity to promote its mission and build a grassroots movement.

Zinn, Howard. *SNCC: Student Nonviolent Coordinating Committee: The New Abolitionists.* Boston: Beacon Press, 1968. One of the earliest studies of SNCC, it covers the activism of the group but not the divisions that ultimately killed it.

World Wide Web

"SNCC, 1960–1966." http://www.ibiblio.org/sncc/. This site covers the SNCC from its birth to 1966, when John Lewis was replaced by Stokely Carmichael as chairman and the organization changed its philosophy. The site covers sit-ins, Freedom Rides, and voter registration. It includes brief biographies of key figures and an audio interview with Julian Bond, who worked on SNCC voter registration drives in the Deep South.

"SNCC: What We Did—Student Nonviolent Coordinating Committee— Monthly Review, Oct, 2000 by Julian Bond." http://findarticles.com/p/ articles/mi_m1132/is_5_52/ai_66937932. Provides the full text of Bond's article on SNCC. Bond helped begin the sit-in movement in Atlanta in 1960 after hearing about the Greensboro sit-ins, and he later served as SNCC's communications director.

"Student Nonviolent Coordinating Committee." http://liberationcom munity.stanford.edu/clayarticles/black_women_3.htm. Examines the role of African American women in the formation of SNCC and in its activities.

"Student Nonviolent Coordinating Committee." http://www.pbs.org/wgbh/ amex/eyesontheprize/profiles/49_sncc.html. Complements the PBS series *Eyes on the Prize* with an essay on SNCC.

Multimedia Sources

Eyes on the Prize. New York: PBS and Blackside, 1990. VHS and DVD. This landmark series of 14 episodes covers all the major events of the civil rights movement from 1954 to 1985.

Understanding the Civil Rights Movement. New York: Educational Video Network, 2004. DVD. Explains the events that led to the civil rights movement.

79. Martin Luther King's "I Have a Dream" Speech (1963)

Civil rights leader Martin Luther King Jr. helped revolutionize race relations. He was the most eloquent and popular voice of the African American civil rights movement from the time of the Montgomery Bus Boycott in 1956 to his murder in 1968. No one else had King's ability to arouse his listeners to indignation against injustice, to persuade them to march and demonstrate at the risk of beatings, and to inspire faith in the triumph of love over hate.

King expressed a philosophy that suited the civil rights movement of the late 1950s and early 1960s. He rejected the idea that progress could come through negotiations or favors or the use of courts. He urged direct action by masses of people. Although he recognized that marches and demonstrations would likely result in white-directed violence, King insisted that the protesters be nonviolent. He had been heavily influenced by Henry David Thoreau's willingness to disobey the law to support a moral principle and Mohandas Gandhi's idea that the force of truth, acted out in massive disobedience, could win against the force of arms.

On June 11, 1963, President John F. Kennedy announced his intention to present Congress with a comprehensive civil rights bill. The legislation was intended to ban segregation in all public facilities, to promote black employment, and to end the disfranchisement of black would-be voters. In a dramatic expression of public support for the bill, King led the March on Washington for Jobs and Freedom. On August 28, King addressed an audience of more than 250,000 from the steps of the Lincoln Memorial. His "I Have a Dream" speech has been called the most powerful and important address delivered by a civil rights leader in the twentieth century. In it, he referenced the traditional symbols of American identity: patriotism, religious conviction, the Declaration of Independence, and the Constitution. The Civil Rights Act passed in 1964, after Kennedy's assassination.

TERM PAPER SUGGESTIONS

1. Martin Luther King Jr. based his philosophy of nonviolence on the teachings of Indian civil rights leader Mohandas K. Gandhi. Explain Gandhi's philosophy of nonviolence.

2. Henry David Thoreau, a nineteenth-century American philosopher, heavily influenced King. Research Thoreau. Explain his philosophy of civil disobedience.

3. Malcolm X and others have argued that it makes no sense to respond to violence with nonviolence. What are the benefits of a nonviolent approach and of a violent approach to civil rights activism? What are the drawbacks of each approach? Which approach would you choose if you were a 1960s civil rights activist?

4. King argued that injustice anywhere threatened justice everywhere. What do you think he meant by this? Do you agree or disagree with him? Give examples from history to support your argument.

5. King referenced the Declaration of Independence and the Constitution in his "I Have a Dream" speech. Read the Declaration of Independence and the Constitution. How do the two documents support the African American freedom movement?

6. A number of Martin Luther King's speeches and papers can be found on the Web at the King Research and Education Institute, at http://www.stanford.edu/group/King/mlkpapers/. Examine one of King's speeches from the 1950s, one from the early 1960s and the "I've Been to the Mountaintop" speech that King made just before his 1968 murder. Do King's goals change over time? What does he seek in each time period?

ALTERNATIVE TERM PAPER SUGGESTIONS

1. You are trying to drum up support for the Civil Rights Act introduced by President John F. Kennedy. Design a Web page to argue for the bill. Why is it needed?

2. Discuss how the ordinary American, who was perhaps not involved in civil rights protests, viewed Martin Luther King and responded to his murder. Interview someone who clearly remembers living through the 1960s and listening to King. Report on your findings.

SUGGESTED SOURCES

Primary Sources

Carson, Clayborne, ed. *The Autobiography of Martin Luther King, Jr.* New York: IPM in Association with Warner Books, 1998. Written with the cooperation of the King family, this is the best biography of King.

"I Have a Dream." www.youtube.com/watch?v=PbUtL_0vAJk. Provides the full 17-minute speech on video.

"I Have a Dream: U.S. Constitution Online." http://www.usconstitution.net/dream.html. Provides an introduction to the speech and the full text of the speech.

King, Coretta Scott. *My Life with Martin Luther King, Jr.* New York: Holt, Rinehart and Winston, 1969. King's life as seen through the eyes of his wife.

Martin Luther King, Jr. Encyclopedia. http://www.stanford.edu/group/King/liberation_curriculum/encyclopedia/. Contains short essays on topics such as Malcolm X, Alpha Phi Alpha Fraternity, and King National Holiday that have significance to the life of King.

The Martin Luther King, Jr. Research and Education Institute. www.kinginstitute.info. The largest online archive of King-related documents, including photocopies and scans of papers owned by other institutions.

Secondary Sources

Branch, Taylor. *Parting the Waters: America in the King Years, 1954–63.* New York: Simon and Schuster. 1988. A Pulitzer Prize-winning history of the civil rights movement.

Hansen, Drew D. *The Dream: Martin Luther King, Jr. and the Speech That Inspired a Nation.* New York: Ecco, 2003. Focuses on the "I Have a Dream" speech.

Oates, Stephen. *Let the Trumpet Sound: The Life of Martin Luther King, Jr.* New York: New American Library, 1985. A solid and readable biography of King.

Williams, Juan. *Eyes on the Prize: America's Civil Rights Years, 1954–1965.* New York: Viking Penguin, 1987. Pairs with the PBS television series *Eyes on the Prize.*

World Wide Web

The King Center. http://www.thekingcenter.org/. A memorial established by the King family to honor the work and legacy of Martin Luther King Jr. that includes a King chronology.

Multimedia Sources

Biography: Martin Luther King, Jr.: The Man and the Dream. New York: A&E, 2004. DVD. Part of the acclaimed A&E television biographical series.

Martin Luther King: I Have a Dream. MPI Home Video, 1986. DVD. Provides the speech in its entirety.

80. Birmingham Church Bombing (1963)

On September 15, 1963, a bomb planted by Ku Klux Klan member Robert "Dynamite Bob" Chambliss exploded in the basement of the Sixteenth Street Baptist Church in Birmingham, Alabama. The attack killed four black girls and horrified the nation.

The church, the center for the civil rights movement in Birmingham, had regularly attracted speakers such as Martin Luther King Jr. and Ralph Abernathy. It had served as the headquarters of a number of desegregation protests, such as the May 1963 Southern Christian Leadership Conference's rally. The September bombing fell on the church's annual Youth Sunday. Eleven-year-old Denise McNair had joined Cynthia Wesley, Carole Robertson, and Addie Mae Collins, all 14, to serve as ushers. The girls were getting ready in a restroom when the bomb exploded and buried them in rubble. Twenty others, many of them children, were injured by the blast.

The murders underscored the viciousness of the southern way of life. At a joint funeral for three of the girls that attracted 80,000 mourners, Martin Luther King Jr. delivered the eulogy. Many who heard his speech were divided between seeking peace and seeking revenge. Police arrested Chambliss shortly after the bombing but let him go. In 1977, Alabama Attorney General Bill Baxley reopened the case, convicted Chambliss, and sent him to prison for life. Herman Frank Cash, another prime suspect, died in 1994 before a case could be established against him. On May 17, 2000, Thomas Blanton Jr. and Bobby Frank Cherry were charged with the murder of the four girls. Both men received life in prison.

TERM PAPER SUGGESTIONS

1. Immediately following the bombing, a white supremacist stated that only whites could be regarded as innocent children and that the four dead girls were worth nothing since they were only blacks. Examine the impact of these four girls on the civil rights movement. How important were they?

2. Examine the civil rights history of Birmingham. Why did the KKK bomb the church? Why did Chambliss and the others believe that they could kill with impunity?

3. After national passions about civil rights had cooled, state and federal governments began to prosecute violent white supremacists who had escaped the reach of the law. Examine several of these prosecutions.

4. Black churches traditionally served as centers of civil rights activism. Explore this connection.

ALTERNATIVE TERM PAPER SUGGESTIONS

1. Martin Luther King Jr. urged nonviolence as the best strategy for winning civil rights. As they viewed the photographs of the four dead girls, many civil rights activists were sorely tempted to retaliate with violence. Create a podcast in which you urge activists to follow the path of nonviolence. You might want to quote King's eulogy found at http://www.africanamericans.com/MLKjrEulogy.htm.

2. A number of locations that became famous during the civil rights movement, such as the Sixteenth Street Baptist Church, are now being used as tourist attractions. Create a Web site that identifies buildings significant to civil rights in your community.

SUGGESTED SOURCES

Primary Source

Cobbs, Elizabeth, and Smith, Petric J. *Long Time Coming: An Insider's Story of the Birmingham Church Bombing That Rocked the World.* Birmingham, AL: Crane Hill, 1994. Elizabeth Cobb, the niece of Robert Chambliss, writes of growing up as the member of a Klan family. Cobb's testimony helped convict Chambliss.

Secondary Sources

Fallin, Wilson, Jr. *The African American Church in Birmingham, Alabama 1815–1963: A Shelter in the Storm.* New York: Garland, 1997. The author surprisingly does not even mention the bombing, but he does include an excellent chapter on the Birmingham black churches and the civil rights movement.

Hamlin, Christopher M. *Behind the Stained Glass: A History of Sixteenth Street Baptist Church.* Birmingham, AL: Crane Hill, 1998. Interesting study of a landmark historic site.

Lewis, John, and Michael D'Orso. *Walking with the Wind: A Memoir of the Movement.* New York: Harvest Books, 1999. Lewis, who served as chair of the Student Nonviolent Coordinating Committee, writes of his reaction to the church bombing.

Sikora, Frank. *Until Justice Rolls Down: The Birmingham Church Bombing Case.* Tuscaloosa: University of Alabama Press, 1991. The best study in print of the bombing, this is a readable account based on a wealth of primary sources.

World Wide Web

"Birmingham Public Library Digital Collections." http://www.bplonline.org/ resources/Digital_Project/SixteenthStBaptistBomb.asp. Includes photographs, newspaper clippings, and a reading list.

"The 1963 Birmingham Church Bombing." http://www.4littlegirls.com/. Provides a history of investigations into the bombings.

"The Sixteenth Street Baptist Church Bombing." http://afroamhistory .about.com/od/16thstreetbaptistchurch/a/16streetbombing.htm. Extensive essay on the bombing from the date of the attack in 1963 to the conviction of the last killer in 2002.

"16th Street Baptist Church Bombing: Forty Years Later, Birmingham Still Struggles with Violent Past." http://www.npr.org/templates/story/ story.php?storyId=1431932. NPR's *All Things Considered* reported on the anniversary of the murders on September 15, 2003. The site contains links to other NPR stories about the bombing, all of which relate to the trials of the bombers.

"We Shall Overcome—16th Street Baptist Church." http://www.nps.gov/nr/ travel/civilrights/al11.htm. This site, devoted to historic places of the civil rights movement, offers a short summary of the bombing and directions to visit the 16th Street Baptist Church.

Multimedia Sources

A Call to Conscience: The Landmark Speeches of Dr. Martin Luther King, Jr. New York: Intellectual Properties Management, 2001. Audiocassette. Contains King's eulogy for the bombing victims.

4 Little Girls. Los Angeles: HBO Home Video, 1998. VHS. Although documentaries generally are best used only as supplements to books on the same topic, this powerful Spike Lee film stands alone as a study of the bombing. It features interviews with the friends and families of the dead girls as well as archival photographs. This film packs a considerable emotional punch, much like the bombing did in 1963.

Free at Last: Civil Rights Heroes. New York: Image Entertainment, 2005. DVD. A better title would be "Civil Rights Martyrs," since this video covers the individuals, including the Birmingham Four, who gave their lives for the civil rights movement.

81. Civil Rights Act (1964)

The Civil Rights Act of 1964 culminated the long fight of African Americans for equality by withholding federal funds from segregated public programs and outlawing discrimination in public accommodations. It became the most far-reaching civil rights legislation since the Reconstruction era.

The Civil Rights Act had its roots in the Cold War. In June 1963, President John F. Kennedy proposed the legislation. A man far more interested in foreign policy than domestic concerns, Kennedy worried about the image the United States presented to the world. As the whole world watched, Birmingham, Alabama police used attack dogs and high pressure hoses on civil rights protesters. Reverend Martin Luther King Jr.'s arrest for requesting some democracy in the South received widespread coverage in Europe, Asia, Africa, and Latin America. The Soviet Union jumped on the discrepancy between the words of the United States and its actions in order to win hearts and minds throughout the world. To win the Cold War, Kennedy needed to address civil rights.

By 1963, civil rights had also become a moral issue for many whites. As Kennedy watched segregationists in the South assault blacks and stand in the doors of schoolhouses, he became ashamed. Kennedy went on national television to issue a moving appeal for justice. He stated that the United States would not be fully free until all of its citizens were free. He introduced the Civil Rights Act to make that freedom possible. In the wake of Kennedy's assassination, President Lyndon B. Johnson pushed the bill through Congress as a tribute to the slain leader.

TERM PAPER SUGGESTIONS

1. Examine the Civil Rights Act in the context of the Cold War.

2. Senator Barry Goldwater of Arizona, a Republican nominee for president in 1964, criticized the Civil Rights Act for damaging the property rights of business owners. Examine this complaint. Discuss whether the government should have the right to interfere with private businesses and, if so, under what circumstances.

3. When Lyndon B. Johnson signed the Civil Rights Act, he declared that he had just lost the South for the Democratic Party for a generation. Examine this claim. Was Johnson right?

4. Johnson, a native of Texas, argued that the question of race obsessed the South and prevented it from attending to its economic and educational problems. Discuss this claim.

5. Upon passage of the bill, Senator Edward Everett Dirksen stated that no army could withstand the strength of an idea whose time had come. Why did the Civil Rights Act pass in 1964? Examine the events that led to its passage.

6. Examine the significance of the Civil Rights Act. Did it succeed in substantially bettering the lives of blacks?

ALTERNATIVE TERM PAPER SUGGESTIONS

1. Martin Luther King Jr. wrote his "I Have a Dream" speech to encourage the passage of the Civil Rights Act. Write a speech of your own that encourages Congress to approve the bill.

2. Assume that you are a civil rights activist in the 1960s. Create a blog to describe your reactions to Kennedy's introduction of the Civil Rights Act, fears over Lyndon Johnson's attitudes toward civil rights, and passage of the legislation.

SUGGESTED SOURCES

Primary Sources

Carson, Clayborne, et al., eds. *The Eyes on the Prize Civil Rights Reader: Documents, Speeches, and Firsthand Accounts from the Black Freedom Struggle.* New York: Penguin, 1991. Complements the PBS video series by including primary sources about the civil rights movement, such as references to the Civil Rights Act.

"The Civil Rights Act of 1964." http://www.archives.gov/education/lessons/ civil-rights-act/. A National Archives site that provides a detailed essay about the act and a copy of the legislation.

Loevy, Robert D. *The Civil Rights Act of 1964: The Passage of the Law That Ended Racial Segregation.* Albany: State University of New York, 1997. This is a series of first-person accounts of the battle over the passage of the Civil Rights Act, given by Senator Hubert Humphrey, civil rights lobbyist Joseph L. Rauh Jr., and legislative aide John G. Stewart, among others.

Mayer, Robert H. *At Issue in History—The Civil Rights Act of 1964.* New York: Greenhaven Press, 2004. Collects primary and secondary sources about the history of the landmark legislation, the debate that surrounded it, and its legacy.

"Our Documents—Civil Rights Act of 1964." http://www.ourdocuments .gov/doc.php?flash=false&doc=97. Contains a photocopy of the legislation.

Secondary Sources

Dierenfield, Bruce J. *The Civil Rights Movement.* New York: Longman, 2008. Excellent synthesis of the entire civil rights movement with a focus on the 1960s.

Dudziak, Mary. *Cold War Civil Rights: Race and the Image of American Democracy.* Princeton, NJ: Princeton University Press, 2002. Enormously influential book that explains the federal government's support of civil rights as part of an effort to counter Communist propaganda during the Cold War.

Grofman, Bernard, ed. *Legacies of the 1964 Civil Rights Act.* Charlottesville: University of Virginia Press, 2000. Collects essays by historians, political scientists, sociologists, statisticians, and legal scholars about the impact of the landmark legislation.

Halpern, Stephen C. *On the Limits of the Law: The Ironic Legacy of Title VI of the 1964 Civil Rights Act.* Baltimore, MD: Johns Hopkins University Press, 1995. Challenges the wisdom of pursuing social reform through federal courts.

Lawson, Steven F., and Charles Payne. *Debating the Civil Rights Movement, 1945–1968.* Lanham, MD: Rowman and Littlefield, 2006. Designed for university courses in American history, this is the best short history of the civil rights movement.

World Wide Web

"1964 Civil Rights Act." http://www.spartacus.schoolnet.co.uk/USAcivil64. htm. Short essay on the legislative history of the act.

Multimedia Sources

Eyes on the Prize. New York: PBS and Blackside, 1990. VHS and DVD. This landmark series of 14 episodes covers all the major events of the civil rights movement from 1954 to 1985.

Understanding the Civil Rights Movement. New York: Educational Video Network, 2004. DVD. Explains the events that led to the civil rights movement.

82. Economic Opportunity Act (1964)

The Economic Opportunity Act of 1964, part of President Lyndon B. Johnson's Great Society, aimed to end poverty within a generation. It struck at the causes of poverty as well as its consequences. Johnson described it as "a hand up, not a hand out."

The consequences of racism mean that African Americans suffer from higher rates of poverty than whites. While Johnson's programs were color-blind, many of the beneficiaries were African American. The Economic Opportunity Act resulted in the creation of the Job Corps, Head Start, and Volunteers in Service to America (VISTA). The Job Corps, aimed at young adults, taught the skills necessary to find and keep a job. Head Start attempted to root out poverty by providing preschool children with the tools necessary to succeed in grade school. VISTA volunteers fought poverty in low-income communities by teaching literacy, improving health services, and bettering housing. All helped African Americans. The legislation created a legal services program for the poor that mediated disputes between tenants and landlords, husbands and wives, accused criminals and police. The legislation also distributed funds to programs that were already in existence, specifically work training programs within the Department of Labor as well as work-study, training, community work, and adult education programs within the Department of Health, Education, and Welfare.

The whole thrust of the Office of Economic Opportunity (OEO), the agency created to administer the War on Poverty, was to give as much autonomy as possible to grassroots efforts to eradicate poverty. Instead of the federal government trying to make decisions for various localities, the people who lived and worked in these areas would decide what was best for them. The program became the most controversial creation of the Johnson administration. Critics charged that the War on Poverty exceeded the proper role of government and stifled private efforts. They attacked its programs for being wasteful, mismanaged, counterproductive, and a cause of social and racial turmoil. President Richard Nixon eliminated many of the programs but some, such as Head Start, remain in existence.

TERM PAPER SUGGESTIONS

1. Examine President Lyndon B. Johnson's War on Poverty.
2. Trace the history of Head Start. Despite changes in presidential administrations, the program remains in existence. Why is it viewed as a success?

3. There has been a long-standing debate in American history over whether it is the proper place of government to become involved in social programs like Head Start and the Job Corps. Discuss whether the government has a responsibility to do more than conduct foreign policy, run the military, and distribute the mail.

4. The 1960s were an era of optimism. Johnson believed that, with his civil rights and antipoverty programs, he would create a Great Society. Evaluate Johnson's successes in creating a more perfect America.

ALTERNATIVE TERM PAPER SUGGESTIONS

1. Create a Web site that explains Johnson's War on Poverty. Why did he decide to address this problem, and what measures did he take?

2. Create a Web site that challenges the notion that most welfare goes to African Americans who do not deserve it.

SUGGESTED SOURCES

Primary Sources

"The Economic Opportunity Act of 1964." http://www2.volstate.edu/geades/FinalDocs/1960s/eoa.htm. Contains the full text of the legislation.

Gillette, Michael L. *Launching the War on Poverty: An Oral History.* New York: Twayne, 1996. Contains interviews with people who led the war.

Secondary Sources

Gilens, Martin. *Why Americans Hate Welfare: Race, Media, and the Politics of Antipoverty Policy.* Chicago: University of Chicago Press, 2000. Argues that most Americans will support aid to the deserving poor but mark African Americans as the undeserving poor who are lazy and do not actively seek employment.

Jansson, Bruce S. *The Reluctant Welfare State: A History of American Social Welfare Policies.* Pacific Grove, CA: Brooks/Cole, 1993. A solid history of efforts to help the poor.

Mills, Kay. *Something Better for My Children: The History and People of Head Start.* New York: Penguin, 1998. One of the very few books to examine a program that emerged from the Economic Opportunity Act.

Quadagno, Jill. *The Color of Welfare: How Racism Undermined the War on Poverty.* New York: Oxford University Press, 1996. Quadagno, a sociologist, argues that views about race must be considered when designing public policy programs and that Johnson failed by not doing so.

World Wide Web

"Lyndon B. Johnson's War on Poverty." http://www.npr.org/templates/story/
story.php?storyId=1589660. An NPR report on the 40th anniversary of
Johnson's attack on poverty that includes an audio link to Johnson's
speech on the topic.

"Modern History Sourcebook: President Lyndon B. Johnson: The War on Poverty, March 1964." http://www.fordham.edu/halsall/mod/1964johnson-
warpoverty.html. Reprints the text of Johnson's 1964 speech announcing
a War on Poverty.

Multimedia Source

America's War on Poverty: In This Affluent Society. New York: PBS, 1995. VHS.
Describes President Lyndon B. Johnson's determination that no one
should be poor in the richest country on Earth.

83. The Moynihan Report (1965)

Officially known as "The Negro Family: The Case for National Action,"
the Moynihan Report is named after Daniel Patrick Moynihan, an
assistant secretary of labor in the administration of President Lyndon
B. Johnson. The report linked African American poverty to the collapse
of the black family. By doing so, the report changed the debate about
poverty among African Americans, but it also became one of the most
hotly contested government papers ever issued.

The Moynihan Report grew out of Johnson's War on Poverty. While
considerable research existed about the nature of white poverty, few studies had been conducted on black poverty. Without knowledge of the
causes of black poverty, Johnson could not effectively address it. Moynihan, a trained sociologist who had grown up poor in the Hell's Kitchen
section of Manhattan, agreed to examine the black family.

Moynihan found that black poverty was rising even as black unemployment rates were dropping. Looking for a cause, he turned to the African
American family. Moynihan linked the problems of blacks in inner
cities—including drug abuse, high crime rates, and skyrocketing unemployment—to female-headed households. In doing so, Moynihan simply
provided the most famous example of policymakers who identify the
troubles of many present-day African American families as having roots

in a slave system that denied slaves the right to marry and severely curtailed men's authority over their children. He did not recommend specific solutions.

While the report initially received a positive response, attacks began within a few months of its publication. Moynihan was faulted for "blaming the victim" and justifying governmental disregard for the poor. Feminists charged that Moynihan had classified families headed by women as inherently pathological. In response to the Moynihan Report, researchers attempted to prove that the black family under slavery was healthy and stable. They identified these characteristics with a nuclear family headed by a strong male. Other historians began to call into question the sexist and ethnocentric assumptions that involved defending the black family by portraying it as copying white, middle-class norms.

TERM PAPER SUGGESTIONS

1. Trace the history of Lyndon Johnson's efforts to help the black poor.
2. Examine the life of Daniel Patrick Moynihan, especially his efforts to aid African Americans.
3. Evaluate the Moynihan Report today. Have his conclusions withstood the test of time? Does the black family still suffer from the problems identified in the Moynihan Report?

ALTERNATIVE TERM PAPER SUGGESTIONS

1. Create a Microsoft PowerPoint presentation that presents and critiques the major findings of the Moynihan Report.
2. Create a Web site that introduces and explores the Moynihan Report.

SUGGESTED SOURCES

Primary Sources

Moynihan, Daniel Patrick. *Family and Nation.* New York: Harcourt, 1987. Moynihan argues for a national family policy in these lectures. He points out that the family disintegration that once chiefly concerned minority families has become a general feature of American life.

Moynihan, Daniel Patrick. *Miles to Go: A Personal History of Social Policy.* Boston: Harvard University Press, 1997. This is Moynihan's evaluation of the reception of the Moynihan Report. He criticizes presidential administrations—Republican and Democratic—for failing to adequately assist the poor.

Moynihan, Daniel Patrick, et al., eds. *The Future of the Family.* New York: Russell Sage Foundation, 2006. Examines the state of the American family and addresses the ways in which public policy affects the family. The book is especially useful because it presents three vastly dissimilar recommendations—each representing a different segment of the political spectrum—for how family policy should adapt to reduced family income and lower parental involvement with children.

"The Negro Family: The Case for National Action." http://www.dol.gov/oasam/programs/history/webid-meynihan.htm. Reprints the report minus charts and graphics.

Secondary Sources

Hodgson, Godfrey. *The Gentleman from New York: Daniel Patrick Moynihan—A Biography.* Boston: Houghton Mifflin, 2000. Written by a close friend of Moynihan, the book takes an uncritical look at his life as a politician and policymaker.

Katzmann, Robert A. *Daniel Patrick Moynihan: The Intellectual in Public Life.* Baltimore, MD: Johns Hopkins University Press, 2004. This is a "Festschrift," a book created to pay tribute to a scholar. It discusses Moynihan's work as a politician and researcher on ethnicity, but it is celebratory in nature.

World Wide Web

"The Black Family: 40 Years of Lies." http://www.city-journal.org/html/15_3_black_family.html. In this *City Journal* essay, Kay S. Hymowitz argues that Moynihan was right and his recommendations would have helped the black family.

"Smart Library: The Moynihan Report." http://www.children.smartlibrary.org/newinterface/segment.cfm?segment=1806&table_of_contents=1503. Summarizes the report and includes charts from 1960 about U.S. unemployment by race and the percentage of children in broken homes by race.

84. Voting Rights Act (1965)

While the Civil Rights Act prohibited discrimination based upon race, it did not give any real power to African Americans. The Voting Rights Act of 1965 corrected that problem. With the vote, African Americans could control the police agencies and government offices that had long oppressed the black race. Black officials could also be elected to positions of significant power, such as police chief, mayor, and governor.

Shortly after taking office, President Lyndon B. Johnson began to address civil rights, much to the surprise of civil rights activists who had not expected much from a native southerner. The president from Texas used skills honed during his many years in Congress to promote the Twenty-Fourth Amendment to the Constitution in 1964, which outlawed poll taxes. The amendment, although a step in the right direction, still did not give equal voting rights to African Americans. Accordingly, Johnson submitted a bill to Congress that would enable blacks to play a prominent role in political life. The Voting Rights Act became law on August 6, 1965. It stopped the notoriously abusive treatment of would-be black voters by southerners by permitting the federal government to oversee voter registration practices. No longer would southern registrars be allowed to create bizarre tests for blacks attempting to cast a ballot. In areas with historically low African American voter turnout, the law supposed discrimination and permitted federal oversight.

TERM PAPER SUGGESTIONS

1. Discuss the long struggle for blacks to receive the right to vote.

2. Discuss the significance of the Voting Rights Act.

3. Compare and contrast the two major pieces of civil rights legislation of the 1960s, the Civil Rights Act and the Voting Rights Act.

4. The Civil Rights Act has received far more public attention than the Voting Rights Act. Discuss which piece of legislation has proven to be more critical for the betterment of African Americans.

5. Examine the many strategies, including the poll tax, that were used to prevent African Americans from voting.

ALTERNATIVE TERM PAPER SUGGESTIONS

1. Create an interactive map that shows whether African Americans have taken full advantage of the Voting Rights Act. List the percentages of African Americans who cast ballots in each state in recent presidential elections. Discuss the reasons for less than 100 percent participation.

2. Investigate the impact of the Voting Rights Act on the 2008 presidential election. Create an interactive map that matches voting districts with votes cast

for Barack Obama. Discuss whether Obama could have won without the black vote.

SUGGESTED SOURCES

Primary Sources

"The Avalon Project—Voting Rights Act of 1965." http://www.yale.edu/ lawweb/avalon/statutes/voting_rights_1965.htm. This is a Yale University Law School site that reprints the entire text of the legislation.
"Our Documents—Voting Rights Act of 1965." http://www.ourdocuments.gov/ doc.php?flash=false&doc=100. Provides a photocopy of the legislation.

Secondary Sources

Aretha, David. *Selma and the Voting Right Act.* New York: Morgan Reynolds, 2007. This book, aimed at young adults, examines voting rights in the belly of the southern beast.
Blum, Edward. *The Unintended Consequences of Section 5 of the Voting Rights Act.* New York: AEI Press, 2007. Discusses how the legislation has led to gerrymandering that benefits incumbent politicians.
Epstein, David L. *The Future of the Voting Rights Act.* New York: Russell Sage Foundation, 2006. Discusses whether Section 5 of the legislation should be terminated. Section 5 requires areas with a history of discriminatory practices to get permission from the federal government before implementing any change that affects voting.
Laney, Garrine P. *The Voting Rights Act of 1965: Historical Background and Current Issues.* New York: Novinka Books, 2004. Brief introduction to the legislation.
Morgan, Ruth P. *Governance by Decree: The Impact of the Voting Rights Act in Dallas.* Lawrence: University Press of Kansas, 2004. Examines racial politics in a major southern city and the impact of the landmark legislation.

World Wide Web

"National Commission on the Voting Rights Act." http://www.votingrigh tsact.org/. The commission held hearings across the country in 2005 on discrimination in voting and the impact of the Voting Rights Act. The commission's final report can be found in full on this site.
"Protect Voting Rights: Renew the Voting Rights Act." http://www .renewthevra.org/. The Voting Rights Act came up for renewal in 2006. This site discusses that process.

"Voting Rights Act." http://www.spartacus.schoolnet.co.uk/USAvoting65.htm. Brief essay on the legislation.

"Voting Rights Act of 1965." http://www.usdoj.gov/crt/voting/intro/intro _b.htm. The United States Department of Justice, Civil Rights Division, Voting Section has provided this introduction to federal voting rights laws.

Multimedia Source

Eyes on the Prize. New York: PBS and Blackside, 1990. VHS and DVD. This landmark series of 14 episodes covers all the major events of the civil rights movement from 1954 to 1985.

85. Watts Riot in Los Angeles (1965)

The Watts Riot in August 1965 left 34 dead, 1,000 injured, 4,000 arrested, and the civil rights movement on the defensive. The image of rage-filled African Americans replaced the image of nonthreatening protestors in the South. White backlash created by Watts led directly to Ronald Reagan's election as governor of California in 1966 and helped propel a conservative era in national politics.

The riot began with the arrest of a 21-year-old African American man, Marquette Frye, in the Los Angeles South Central neighborhood of Watts. A crowd of onlookers began to harass the police officer making the arrest. A second officer who arrived on the scene struck bystanders with his baton. News of the police brutality swept through the neighborhood and prompted a violent response that may have been fueled by an oppressive heat wave and overcrowding. Residents of Watts began looting and burning stores. In the six days of rioting, more than $200 million in property was destroyed. About 35,000 African Americans are estimated to have participated in the riot. The uprising stopped when 16,000 California National Guard members, county deputies, and Los Angeles police managed to quell it.

TERM PAPER SUGGESTIONS

1. Discuss whether the Watts Riot prompted a conservative political backlash.
2. Compare and contrast the Los Angeles riots of 1965 and 1992.

3. Trace the history of the Watts Riot. What prompted the riot, and what was the impact of it?

4. Examine whether the Watts Riot demonstrates that the Civil Rights Act and Voting Rights Act only benefitted the middle class.

5. W. E. B. Du Bois stated that the problem of the color line would define the twentieth century. Discuss whether the Watts Riot indicates that the class line became the defining issue of the last three decades of the century.

ALTERNATIVE TERM PAPER SUGGESTIONS

1. The Watts Riot went on for six days. Create six blog entries that describe an individual's reaction to the turmoil.

2. Assume that the California Historical Society is considering placing a historical monument to the Watts Riot. Create a Microsoft PowerPoint presentation designed to garner public support for the monument by explaining the significance of the riot to African American history.

SUGGESTED SOURCES

Primary Source

Burby, Liza N. *The Watts Riot.* New York: Lucent, 1997. Contains documents and photographs pertaining to the uprising.

Secondary Sources

Abu-Lughod, Janet L. *Race, Space, and Riots in Chicago, New York, and Los Angeles.* New York: Oxford University Press, 2007. An urban sociologist discusses how space, political regimes, and economic conditions shape the ways in which riots unfold.

Conot, Robert E. *Rivers of Blood, Years of Darkness: The Unforgettable Classic Account of the Watts Riot.* New York: William Morrow, 1968. A dramatic account of the riot that suffers a bit from its age.

Horne, Gerald. *Fire This Time: The Watts Uprising and The 1960s.* New York: Da Capo Press, 1997. Comprehensive study of the riot, its causes, and its aftermath.

Sears, David O. *The Politics of Violence: The New Urban Blacks and the Watts Riot.* Lanham, MD: University Press of America, 1981. Discusses the riot as a response to changes taking place within the cities.

World Wide Web

"Los Angeles Watts Riot of 1965." http://www.africanamericans.com/WattsRiots.htm. Brief discussion of the causes and impact of the riot.

"Watts Riot." http://video.google.com/videosearch?source=ig&hl=en&rlz=&q
=WATTS+RIOT&um=1&ie=UTF-8&sa=X&oi=video_result_group
&resnum=8&ct=title#. A YouTube clip of a scene from the riot.

"Watts Riot—40 Years Later." http://www.latimes.com/news/local/la-me-watts
11aug11,0,4693415,full.story?coll=la-home-headlines. In this *Los
Angeles Times* article, nine people who were in the midst of the riot
describe how it changed their lives and the city.

86. Black Panther Party Is Founded (1966)

Huey Newton and Bobby Seale founded the Black Panther Party (BPP) in
Oakland, California in October 1966. The organization promoted
African American self-defense and sought to restructure American society
to make it more politically, economically, and socially equal.

The BPP is the best-known part of the militant wing of the civil rights
movement. Influenced by the Black Power movement, the BPP stressed racial
dignity and self-reliance. Originally named the Black Panther Party for Self-
Defense, the group set up patrols in black neighborhoods to monitor police
activities and protect the residents from police brutality. Controversially, the
BPP stated that African Americans had the right to use violence in self-
defense. In May 1967, the group attracted quite a bit of media attention when
members wearing the distinctive black berets and black leather jackets of the
BPP marched with guns to the state capitol in California to protest a bill that
would outlaw the carrying of loaded weapons in public.

As racial tensions increased in the United States, the Federal Bureau of
Investigation (FBI) launched a program called COINTELPRO to disrupt
black militant organizations such as the BPP. Leaders of the BPP included
Eldridge Cleaver, Fred Hampton, and Assata Shakur. Hampton died in a
police raid in Chicago in 1970. Cleaver, Newton, and Shakur fled to
Cuba to escape prosecution. Seale left the BPP in 1974. Many other Panther leaders were killed, jailed, or in exile by 1975.

TERM PAPER SUGGESTIONS

1. The Black Panther Party collapsed because some members, such as Bobby
   Seale and Huey Newton, wanted to focus on community service projects like
   free medical clinics and food pantries. Other members, such as Eldridge
   Cleaver, emphasized a black revolution. Discuss this disagreement.

2. Discuss the Ten Point Program, available at http://www.blackpanther.org/, of the BPP. What were the organization's major goals and why?

3. Profile one of the leaders of the BPP.

4. Compare and contrast Huey Newton or Bobby Seale with Malcolm X or Martin Luther King Jr.

ALTERNATIVE TERM PAPER SUGGESTIONS

1. Create a rap song on an iPod that explains the significance of the Black Panthers.

2. Using photos and a song from the 1960s, create a music video on your iPod that illustrates the history of the Black Panther Party.

SUGGESTED SOURCES

Primary Sources

"Black Panther Newspaper Collection." http://www.etext.org/Politics/MIM/ bpp/. Contains original writings of the BPP from its first three years of existence (1966–1969), when it shocked the United States and prompted the FBI to try to shut it down.

"Black Panther Party Research Project." http://www.stanford.edu/group/ blackpanthers. Provides primary and secondary sources about the BPP.

"The Black Panthers." http://www.blackpanther.org/. Created by a foundation dedicated to furthering the social activism of the BPP, this site includes a copy of the BPP's Ten Point Program, the party's community service history, and information on the Black Panthers' Speaker's Bureau.

Foner, Philip S. *The Black Panthers Speak*. Philadelphia: Lippincott, 1970. One of the best sources on the Black Panthers, this collection contains cartoons, flyers, and essays by such BPP members as Huey Newton and Bobby Seale.

Heath, G. Louis, ed. *The Black Panther Leaders Speak: Huey P. Newton, Bobby Seale, Eldridge Cleaver, and Company Speak Out through the Black Panther Party's Official Newspaper*. Metuchen, NJ: Scarecrow Press, 1976. Reprints essays by the leaders of the BPP.

Seale, Bobby. *A Lonely Rage: The Autobiography of Bobby Seale*. New York: Times Books, 1978. The story of one of the founders of the BPP.

Secondary Sources

Cleaver, Kathleen, and George Katsiaficas. *Liberation, Imagination, and the Black Panther Party: A New Look at the Panthers and Their Legacy*. New York: Routledge, 2001. Kathleen Cleaver, the ex-wife of Eldridge Cleaver, belonged to the BPP in its heyday. The essays in this collection discuss the FBI's attack on the Black Panthers as well as the group's international impact.

Freed, Donald. *The Agony in New Haven: The Trial of Bobby Seale, Ericka Huggins, and the Black Panther Party.* New York: Simon and Schuster, 1973. Entertaining account of the trial and the racial tensions that accompanied it.

Jeffries, Judson L., ed. *Black Power in the Belly of the Beast.* Urbana: University of Illinois, 2006. Essays examine the history of the BPP and its legacy as well as the Deacons for Defense, a group that inspired the BPP.

Jones, Charles E., ed. *The Black Panther Party (Reconsidered).* Baltimore, MD: Black Classic Press, 1998. A mix of essays by historians of the BPP and members of the party.

World Wide Web

"Black Panther Party." http://www.marxists.org/history/usa/workers/black-panthers/. This is a Marxist history of the Black Panther Party, with original documents.

"Black Panther Party Photo Tour." http://www.bobbyseale.com/phototour/. History of the party through a series of photographs.

"Freedom of Information—Black Panther Party." http://foia.fbi.gov/foiaindex/bpanther.htm. Contains 2,895 pages of the FBI's records on the Winston-Salem, North Carolina chapter of the BPP.

"It's About Time: Black Panther Legacy and Alumni." http://www.itsabouttimebpp.com/home/home.html. Exceptional site with considerable information about women of the BPP and Assata Shakur. The audio and video links are extensive.

Multimedia Source

The Huey P. Newton Story. Luna Ray Films, 2001. DVD. This is director Spike Lee's examination of the Black Panther Party leader. It is typical of Lee's exceptional films.

87. Blacks Serve in the Military during the Vietnam War (1960s)

American involvement with the Southeast Asian country Vietnam had gradually escalated since the end of World War II. When Lyndon B. Johnson became president in 1963, he inherited an American commitment to prevent a Communist takeover in Vietnam. Following an apparent attack by North Vietnamese vessels upon U.S. warships in the Gulf of Tonkin, Johnson received authorization from Congress to take any steps necessary to prevent further aggression. In March 1965, the first U.S. combat troops arrived in Vietnam.

While 75 percent of draft-age men served during World War II, 59 percent of draft-age men in the Vietnam era received deferments, exemptions, or disqualifications that kept them out of the military. Approximately 12 percent of draft-age men were African American, yet black men were drafted at rates that exceeded that number for much of the war. Blacks were less likely than whites to receive a college exemption, for example. The general economic inequality between blacks and whites combined with discriminatory implementation of draft laws to make black men bear a special burden. Since draft laws favored middle-class white males, African American men were drafted at disproportionately high rates.

Young blacks who joined the military were promised generous benefits, marketable skills, and the opportunity for personal growth. In contrast to these promises, African American servicemen were frequently assigned to low-status jobs in the armed forces that corresponded to those that they had held in the civilian world. Racial inequality remained largely unchanged. Overrepresented in the infantry, black men also suffered high casualty rates. Yet, despite the risks of war, many black men enjoyed military service. High unemployment and racial discrimination in civilian society contrasted with higher incomes and greater prestige in the military.

On January 17, 1973, the United States, North and South Vietnam, and Communist guerrillas known as the Viet Cong signed a peace agreement. By this time, sharp divisions had emerged in the United States over the war, and Johnson had left the White House, largely because of his failure to win the war. On March 29, 1973, the last American combat troops left Vietnam. Within a few months, the war between North and South Vietnam resumed, and the military superiority of the North became evident. In 1975, North Vietnam invaded the South. When Congress refused to offer assistance, the South Vietnamese government collapsed and all of Vietnam became Communist.

The longest war in American history left a bitter legacy. More than 58,000 Americans died, 300,000 were wounded, and 2,500 were declared missing. Of the wounded, more than 100,000 returned missing one or more limbs, and over 150,000 combat veterans suffered post-traumatic stress and drug or alcohol addiction. Most veterans readjusted well to civilian life, but they had to carry the stigma of having served in an unpopular war that the United States lost.

TERM PAPER SUGGESTIONS

1. Compare and contrast African American involvement in World War II and Vietnam.
2. Boxer Muhammad Ali refused to be drafted to serve in the Vietnam War and, as a result, lost his heavyweight boxing title. Research Ali's case.
3. Toward the end of his life, Martin Luther King Jr. spoke out against the Vietnam War. Research King's opposition to the war.
4. General Colin Powell, a former national security adviser and secretary of state as well as a Vietnam veteran, credits the military with making him into a success. His experiences in Vietnam later shaped his views about when and how U.S. forces should be used in conflicts in other countries. Research Powell's life.

ALTERNATIVE TERM PAPER SUGGESTIONS

1. Assume that you are living in 1968 and a close African American friend has just received notice that he has been drafted. Write a letter in which you advise him to resist the draft or to join the military.
2. In 1970, the rock band Creedence Clearwater Revival released the hit song "Fortunate Son." The song, largely biographical of lead singer John Fogarty, is highly critical of the people who urge the country to go to war but then use their political connections to avoid fighting in the war. Write a song about the treatment that black men received during Vietnam.
3. Interview a person who lived during the Vietnam era about his or her recollections of the African American response to the war. After obtaining the interviewee's written permission, post the video on YouTube.
4. Create a YouTube video about African American participation in the Vietnam War.

SUGGESTED SOURCES

Primary Sources

McMahon, Robert J. *Major Problems of the Vietnam War.* Boston: Houghton Mifflin, 2003. Includes accounts by soldiers and policymakers.

Terry, Wallace. *Bloods: An Oral History of the Vietnam War by Black Veterans.* New York: Random House, 1984. A fascinating collection of interviews about serving in the war.

Secondary Sources

Astor, Gerald. *The Right to Fight: A History of African Americans in the Military.* New York: Da Capo Press, 1999. Covers blacks in combat from the Revolutionary War to the present, but the focus is on the period between the 1898 Spanish American War and the Korean War of 1950–1953.

Buckley, Gail Lumet. *American Patriots: The Story of Blacks in the Military from the Revolution to Desert Storm.* New York: Random House, 2002. This is a 608-page popular account of blacks in the armed services that relies heavily upon interviews to cover soldiers in the more recent wars.

DeGroot, Gerard J. *A Noble Cause?: America and the Vietnam War.* Harlow, England: Longman, 2000. A good general history of the Vietnam War.

Edgerton, Robert B. *Hidden Heroism: Black Soldiers in American Wars.* New York: Basic Books, 2002. Focuses on the racist myth that blacks are unwilling and unable to fight by exploring black heroism and the over-representation of blacks in the current military.

Graham, Herman, III. *The Brothers' Vietnam War: Black Power, Manhood, and the Military Experience.* Gainesville: University Press of Florida, 2003. A scholarly account of African Americans in the Vietnam War that includes quite a bit of coverage of the home front and blacks in the navy.

Herring, George C. *America's Longest War: The United States and Vietnam, 1950–1975.* New York: Random House, 1986. Written by a well-respected military historian, this is probably the most widely-read history of the Vietnam War.

Nalty, Bernard C. *Strength for the Fight: A History of Black Americans in the Military.* New York: Free Press, 1986. A very analytical examination of the history of race relations in the U.S. armed forces.

Tucker, Spencer C., ed. *Encyclopedia of the Vietnam War: A Political, Social, and Military History.* Santa Barbara, CA: ABC-CLIO, 1998. This is the only encyclopedia devoted to the Vietnam War as well as the most comprehensive reference work to address the conflict.

Westheider, James E. *Fighting on Two Fronts: African Americans and the Vietnam War.* New York: New York University Press, 1997. A good scholarly account of the difficulties facing black soldiers in a racist era.

Wright, Kai. *Soldiers of Freedom: An Illustrated History of African Americans in the Armed Forces.* New York: Black Dog and Leventhal, 2002. Covers 1775 to 2001 using military photos that are chiefly drawn from the National Archives and the Library of Congress.

World Wide Web

"AfricanAmericans.Com—Military Participation: The Vietnam War." http://
www.africanamericans.com/MilitaryVietnamWar.htm. A balanced
account of blacks in Vietnam that does not repeat some of the myths
associated with the war.

"African Americans in the Vietnam War." http://www.english.uiuc.edu/maps/
poets/s_z/stevens/africanamer.htm. Reprints two essays from Spencer
Tucker's *Encyclopedia of the Vietnam War.*

"Spartacus Educational." http://www.spartacus.schoolnet.co.uk/VNprotest.htm.
Includes a history of the Vietnam War with links to primary sources
about the war.

"Vietnam War Statistics." http://www.mrfa.org/vnstats.htm. The Mobile River-
ine Force Association, an organization of Vietnam War veterans, has
gathered a wonderful collection of statistics about all aspects of the war.
The association home page, at www.mrfa.org, contains information for
veterans interested in filing medical claims, a guide to things to do when
a veteran dies, and information about some charitable projects for
veterans.

Multimedia Sources

Vietnam: A Retrospective. Washington, DC: National Archives, 2007. 6 DVDs.
Videos produced by the U.S. government during the war.

The Vietnam War. New York: The History Channel, 2008. 2 DVDs. A general
account of the war that includes black veterans.

88. *Loving v. Virginia* (1967)

Segregation of African Americans did not just involve restaurants
and schools. In many states throughout the nation, blacks and whites
were prohibited from marrying one another. Virginia had a ban on interracial marriages that dated to 1691. In that state, violators of the ban
faced a prison term of one to five years. Nevertheless, Mildred Jeter, a
black woman, and Richard Loving, a white man employed as a brick-
layer, married in Washington, D.C. in 1958. The subsequent events
would end with the legalization of interracial marriages in the United
States.

Jeter and Loving had grown up together in the small Virginia town of
Sparta. They did not know another black-white couple at the time that

they decided to tie the knot. No one from their families objected to the match. However, an anonymous enemy notified authorities about the marriage. On July 15, 1958, three Caroline County, Virginia lawmen entered the home of the Lovings at two in the morning and dragged them out of bed and to jail. The couple were convicted of the crime of their marriage. In lieu of a prison term, they accepted exile from the state for 25 years. In 1964, Mildred Loving asked Attorney General Robert Kennedy if the Civil Rights Act would permit her and her husband to return home. Kennedy said that it would not. In 1965, the Lovings launched a protest of the ban. They lost in the Virginia Supreme Court but appealed. The subsequent June 12, 1967 U.S. Supreme Court decision in *Loving v. Virginia* legalized interracial marriage.

In 1960, there were 51,000 black and white couples. By 2000, this number had reached 450,000, only a fraction of total marriages in the United States. The marriage of Richard and Mildred Loving had ended by this time, however. In 1975, a drunk driver had broadsided the couple's car and killed Richard. Loving was survived by his three children with Mildred.

While American attitudes toward mixed marriages improved over the decades, many white and black Americans continued to oppose a close relative marrying a person of the other race. In 2000, 86 percent of African Americans surveyed by Harvard University declared that they would welcome a white person into their families, but only 55 percent of white families responded in kind.

The gradually more open attitudes toward interracial marriage can be credited in part to *Loving v. Virginia.* The U.S. Supreme Court decision that overturned the Virginia mixed marriage ban also overturned similar bans in 16 other states. Meanwhile, 14 states had already repealed their laws by 1967. Some states continued to keep their bans on the books, but these laws were legally unenforceable in the wake of the court decision. In 2000, Alabama became the last state to remove its anti-miscegenation law from the books.

TERM PAPER SUGGESTIONS

1. Virginia's law banning marriage between blacks and whites hinged on the notion of race. Many scholars have argued that race is simply something constructed by society and that it has no scientific basis. Research the idea of race and analyze it from a historical perspective.

2. The *Loving* decision had the potential to have an enormous impact upon the lives of ordinary Americans. Explore the impact of this decision upon people living today.

3. In its decision, the Supreme Court stated that it had consistently opposed racial distinctions as being offensive to a free people. Read about the cases cited by the Supreme Court, *Hirabayashi, McLaughlin,* and *Korematsu.* How do these cases compare and contrast with *Loving?*

4. The Equal Protection Clause has often been cited in defense of civil rights. Discuss the Equal Protection Clause.

ALTERNATIVE TERM PAPER SUGGESTIONS

1. Assume that you are the attorney defending the Lovings. Prepare a Microsoft PowerPoint presentation to the U.S. Supreme Court arguing for the overturning of the Virginia law.

2. Create a YouTube video showing the impact of the *Loving* decision, perhaps exploring what it is like to grow up in an interracial family.

SUGGESTED SOURCES

Primary Sources

Loving v. Virginia. http://www.law.umkc.edu/faculty/projects/ftrials/conlaw/ loving.html. Reprints the June 12, 1967 U.S. Supreme Court decision.

"The Oyez Project, *Loving v. Virginia,* 388 U.S. 1 (1967)." http://www.oyez.org/ cases/1960-1969/1966/1966_395/. Contains oral and written arguments presented to the Supreme Court.

Secondary Sources

"The Crime of Being Married." *Life* 60 (March 18, 1966): 85–91. A very early account of the legal difficulties of the Lovings, written prior to the Supreme Court decision.

Lewis, Earl, and Heidi Ardizzone. *Love on Trial: An American Scandal in Black and White.* New York: W.W. Norton, 2002. Examines the notorious Rhinelander case of 1924, in which Leonard Rhinelander sought the annulment of his marriage to Alice, the child of a white mother and mixed-race father, on the grounds that she was not white. The trial included a debate over whether Alice was "white," "colored," or "Negro," and it contributed to a legal hardening of racial lines in America.

Moran, Rachel F. *Interracial Intimacy: The Regulation of Race and Romance.* Chicago: University of Chicago Press, 2003. Argues that even without a solid biological definition of race, laws about mixed marriages have been put in place to prevent the loss of white privilege.

Newbeck, Phyl. *Virginia Hasn't Always Been for Lovers: Interracial Marriage Bans and the Case of Richard and Mildred Loving.* Carbondale: Southern Illinois Press, 2004. Examines the *Loving* case in the context of laws banning interracial marriage and includes the personal recollections of *Loving* attorneys, as well as those of a member of the Loving family who had previously maintained public silence on the issue.

Romano, Renee. *Race Mixing: Black-White Marriage in Postwar America.* Gainesville: University of Florida, 2006. Traces the history of interracial marriage since 1940, when 31 states banned the practice.

Wallenstein, Peter. *Tell the Court I Love My Wife: Race, Marriage, and Law—An American History.* New York: Palgrave, 2004. Focuses on a history of the *Loving* case.

World Wide Web

"LovingDay." http://www.lovingday.org. The site is dedicated to the celebration of interracial relationships and includes a history of the *Loving* case.

"The *Loving* Decision: 40 Years of Legal Interracial Unions." http://www.npr.org/templates/story/story.php?storyId=10889047. Includes a timeline of the *Loving* case, a summary of the story, and a link to the 2007 *All Things Considered* NPR radio segment on the case.

Multimedia Source

Mr. and Mrs. Loving. Platinum Disc, 1996. DVD and VHS. This compelling movie based on the *Loving* case stars Timothy Hutton and Lela Rochon.

89. Martin Luther King Jr. Is Assassinated (1968)

The murder of Martin Luther King Jr. in 1968 sent shock waves through the United States. It set off riots by blacks in cities and served as an ugly bookend to the civil rights movement of the 1960s.

By 1968, King had begun to focus on the economic advancement of African Americans. In April, he traveled to Memphis to offer support to predominantly black sanitation workers who were striking for better pay. As King stood on the balcony of a motel, a shot felled him. News of the killing of the apostle of nonviolence resulted in an outpouring of shock and anger across the country. African Americans in more than 100 cities rioted in response to the assassination in the days afterward. In 1969, James Earl Ray, an escaped convict, pleaded guilty to the murder of King. Ray received 99 years in prison and died behind bars. There has been a continuing debate since Ray's conviction over whether he pulled the trigger and whether he acted alone.

TERM PAPER SUGGESTIONS

1. Upon the murder of Robert F. Kennedy in 1968, a black woman lamented that all the good men were being killed. Discuss the impact of the murder of Martin Luther King Jr.

2. Consider the various theories about King's murder. Does it seem plausible that James Earl Ray acted alone?

3. Malcolm X argued that revolution by definition is bloody and that the civil rights revolution could not be an exception. Does King's violent end demonstrate that nonviolence failed as a strategy?

4. Trace the history of the civil rights movement after King's death. Had his moment passed, or could King still have made a substantial contribution to African American life?

5. Discuss the conspiracy theories that always appear when a prominent political leader is killed. Do these theories reflect a cynical age filled with distrust of the government?

ALTERNATIVE TERM PAPER SUGGESTIONS

1. Create a Web site that pays tribute to Martin Luther King Jr.

2. Create a Web site that examines several of the theories of King's murder.

SUGGESTED SOURCES

Primary Sources

Carson, Clayborne, ed. *The Autobiography of Martin Luther King, Jr.* New York: IPM in Association with Warner Books, 1998. Written with the cooperation of the King family, this is the best biography of King.

King, Coretta Scott. *My Life with Martin Luther King, Jr.* New York: Holt, Rinehart and Winston, 1969. King's life as seen through the eyes of his wife.

Secondary Sources

Oates, Stephen. *Let the Trumpet Sound: The Life of Martin Luther King, Jr.* New York: New American Library, 1985. A solid and readable biography of King.

Posner, Gerald. *Killing the Dream: James Earl Ray and the Assassination of Martin Luther King, Jr.* New York: Harvest, 1999. Examines evidence uncovered in the years since King's murder, Ray's history, and the steps leading to the killing.

Ray, John Larry, and Lyndon Barsten. *Truth at Last: The Untold Story Behind James Earl Ray and the Assassination of Martin Luther King, Jr.* New York: Lyons Press, 2008. A book written by the brother of King's assassin immediately raises some questions about objectivity. This work uses flimsy evidence to argue that Ray did not murder King.

World Wide Web

"The King Center." http://www.thekingcenter.org/. A memorial established by the King family to honor the work and legacy of Martin Luther King Jr.; includes a King chronology.

"The Martin Luther King, Jr. Research and Education Institute." www .kinginstitute.info.. The largest online archive of King-related documents, including photocopies and scans of papers owned by other institutions.

Multimedia Sources

Martin Luther King, Jr.: The Man and the Dream. New York: A&E Entertainment, 2004. Stellar biography of King.

Who Killed Martin Luther King? New York: Clarendon Entertainment, 2008. The King family has long harbored doubts that James Earl Ray killed Martin Luther King Jr. This film was made with their support.

90. Kerner Report Is Issued (1968)

President Lyndon B. Johnson formed the National Advisory Commission on Civil Disorders on July 28, 1967 to identify the underlying causes of the riots that swept through U.S. cities in the late 1960s. In 1968, the commission issued its findings, commonly called the Kerner Report after the chair of the committee, Illinois Governor Otto Kerner, It famously declared that "Our Nation is moving toward two societies, one black, one white—separate and unequal." It blamed white society and white institutions for creating this inequality and maintaining it.

The Kerner Report did not see racial polarization as inevitable. It urged national action to create new attitudes, new understanding, and new will toward racial changes. The commission recommended that Congress pass federal open housing legislation to cover the sale and rental of homes, thereby stopping a common form of racial discrimination that led to segregated neighborhoods. It urged Congress to remove artificial barriers to employment and educational opportunities. In response, Congress passed the Civil Rights Act of 1968 that banned racial discrimination with respect to housing.

Thirty years later, several scholars examined whether the Kerner Report had resulted in any long-lasting improvements for African Americans. Instead, they discovered that African Americans as a whole were worse off than in 1968 and that the division between the haves and the have-nots had grown.

TERM PAPER SUGGESTIONS

1. Use the conclusions of the Kerner Report about the causes of urban unrest in the 1960s and 1970s to assess the state of race relations and racial equity in your town or city.

2. Compare and contrast the Kerner Report with the state of black America today.

3. A black rioter in the Los Angeles section of Watts in 1965 stated that the riot was successful because whites were paying attention to blacks in the cities. Discuss whether riots are a successful form of protest.

ALTERNATIVE TERM PAPER SUGGESTIONS

1. Start a personal blog to report on your community's vital signs in terms of healthy race relations, efforts to combat poverty, and government responsiveness to the needs of citizens.

2. Create a Web site that uses a map with hypertext to identify and describe the major race riots of the 1960s.

SUGGESTED SOURCES

Primary Sources

The Kerner Report: The 1968 Report of the National Advisory Commission on Civil Disorders. New York: Pantheon, 1968. This is a copy of the report aimed at the general public with an introduction by journalist Tom Wicker.

Ritchie, Barbara. *The Riot Report: A Shortened Version of the Report of the National Advisory Commission on Civil Disorders.* New York: Viking, 1969. A condensed version of the official report that was designed for the general reading public.

Secondary Sources

Harris, Fred R., and Roger W. Wilkins, ed. *Quiet Riots: Race and Poverty in the United States.* New York: Pantheon, 1988. Considers the Kerner Report 20 years later.

Rueter, Theodore, ed. *The Politics of Race: African Americans and the Political System.* Armonk, NY: M.E. Sharpe, 1995. Contains one essay that examines the history of the Kerner Report.

Urban America and the Urban Coalition. *One Year Later: An Assessment of the Nation's Response to the Crisis Described by the National Advisory Commission on Civil Disorders.* New York: Praeger, 1969. An appraisal of the nation's racial environment by two civil rights organizations.

World Wide Web

Briggs, Vernon M., Jr. "Report of the National Advisory Commission on Civil Disorders: A Review Article." *Journal of Economic Issues* 2 (1968): 200–210. http://digitalcommons.ilr.cornell.edu/hrpubs/51/. The full text of this discussion of the Kerner Report is here.

"The Kerner Commission—40 Years Later." http://www.pbs.org/moyers/journal/03282008/profile.html. Contains the video of journalist Bill Moyer's interview with Fred Harris, one of the last living members of the original Kerner Commission. The site includes a blog, a link to the commission report, and recommended readings.

"The Kerner Commission Report and the Failed Legacy of Liberal Social Policy, by Stephen Thernstrom, Fred Siegel, and Robert Woodson, Sr.: Heritage Lecture #619." http://www.heritage.org/Research/PoliticalPhilosophy/hl619.cfm. Contains the transcript of a panel lecture held at the Heritage Foundation on March 13, 1998. The speakers, all well-respected conservative scholars, are critical of the policy initiatives that grew out of the 1968 report.

"Kerner Plus 40: An Assessment of the Nation's Response to the 1968 Report of the National Advisory Commission on Civil Disorders." http://www.kernerplus40.org/. Offers a summary of a 2008 joint project undertaken by the Annenberg School for Communication at the University of Pennsylvania and North Carolina A&T State University to determine how the nation has responded to the Kerner Commission's recommendations.

"The Millennium Breach: The American Dilemma, Richer and Poorer: In Commemoration of the Thirtieth Anniversary of the National Advisory Commission on Civil Disorders." http://www.eisenhowerfoundation .org/frames/the_millenium_book.html. In 1998, the Milton Eisenhower Institute and the Corporation for What Works released an update of the Kerner Report. It found that the economic situation for minorities had significantly worsened.

"A Nation Divided." http://www.pbs.org/newshour/bb/race_relations/ jan-june98/commission_3-2.html. Contains the transcript of a March 2, 1998 *NewsHour* episode that evaluated the state of racial equality 30 years after the Kerner Report.

"Revolution '67." http://www.pbs.org/pov/pov2007/revolution67/. Contains a video clip from *Revolution '67* and a video update of the racial situation in Newark, New Jersey in 2007.

Multimedia Source

Revolution '67. Los Angeles: California Newsreel, 2007. DVD. Focuses on the six-day Newark, New Jersey riot in mid-July 1967 that helped prompt the formation of the National Advisory Commission on Civil Disorders.

91. President Richard Nixon Promotes a Southern Strategy (1968)

In the 1960s, a new brand of political conservatism emerged that attacked the gains that African Americans had made. Richard Nixon and the leadership of the Republican Party promoted a "southern strategy" of opposition to black protests and civil rights in 1968 as means of winning voters who had historically voted for the Democrats.

While the Republican Party had long focused on anti-communism, a strong national defense, and a limited role for the federal government in domestic affairs, it began to challenge civil rights demonstrations and liberal Supreme Court decisions along with anti-Vietnam War protests and feminism in the 1960s. The South had a very long history of hostility to racial change. President Lyndon B. Johnson, a native Texan, recognized as much when he signed the Civil Rights Act of 1964 and commented, "I think we just delivered the South to the Republican Party." While Nixon did not explicitly condemn the gains made by blacks, he did so in a roundabout way. Nixon opposed "activist" judges who ordered southern schools to integrate, he voiced support for "law and order," and he backed a traditional hierarchy. Once in the White House, he appointed Supreme Court justices who were expected to interpret the Constitution narrowly, to limit government intervention to protect individual rights. He also opposed court-ordered busing as a means of integrating public schools.

Nixon spent two terms in the White House partly because he courted the votes of Americans uncomfortable with the pace of racial change. Other members of the Republican Party, including senators and governors, followed Nixon's southern strategy to win and hold political offices. In the 1970 elections, Republicans used the southern strategy to take several congressional seats from Democrats, although the party of the president typically loses seats in midterm elections. In 2005, Ken Mehlman, the Republican National Committee chair, publicly apologized to a national convention of the National Association of the Advancement for Colored People for the southern strategy. He said that using race as a wedge issue to appeal to white southern voters had been "wrong."

TERM PAPER SUGGESTIONS

1. Trace the history of opposition to civil rights in the years after the passage of the 1964 Civil Rights Act.

2. Examine the controversy over busing as a way to achieve integration. Many black parents, as well as white ones, opposed sending their children on long rides to schools where teachers might not welcome or respect them.

3. Discuss Richard Nixon's opposition to civil rights.

4. Trace the history of the Republican Party's involvement with civil rights.

ALTERNATIVE TERM PAPER SUGGESTIONS

1. Create a Microsoft PowerPoint presentation that explains conservative opposition to civil rights in the years after passage of the 1964 Civil Rights Act.

2. Create a map on the Web that shows the political history of southern states from 1960 to the present. Focus on elections for U.S. senatorial and U.S. presidential elections. Is there a substantial switch from the Democratic to the Republican Party?

SUGGESTED SOURCES

Primary Source

"Nixon Presidential Library and Museum." http://nixon.archives.gov/. Includes
a virtual library of documents, photos, and online exhibits.

Secondary Sources

Aistrup, Joseph A. *The Southern Strategy Revisited: Republican Top-Down
Advancement in the South.* Lexington: University Press of Kentucky,
1996. Aimed at political scientists, this is a study of the long-term success
of Nixon's strategy.

Black, Conrad. *Richard M. Nixon: A Life in Full.* Jackson, TN: Public-
Affairs, 2008. This is a 1,050-page book by a journalist who
defends the southern strategy as a principled stand against northern
hypocrisy.

Black, Earl, and Merle Black. *Politics and Society in the South.* Boston: Harvard
University Press, 2005. The authors explains the emergence of the New
South with particular attention to the decline of the Democratic Party
in the region.

Black, Earl, and Merle Black. *The Rise of Southern Republicans.* Boston: Belknap,
2003. This is the best and most readable study of how the South turned
in the 1960s from its historic loyalty to the Democratic Party to become
a stronghold of Republicans.

Kalk, Bruce H. *The Origins of the Southern Strategy.* Lanham, MD: Lexington
Books, 2001. Details the rise of the two-party system in South
Carolina in the mid-twentieth century, as a new southern base became
the core of the Republican Party's presidential campaign strategy after
1968.

Key, V. O. *Southern Politics in State and Nation.* Knoxville: University of
Tennessee Press, 1984. The characteristics of each state are covered in
separate chapters before Key analyzes the politics of the region.

Kotlowski, Dean J. "Nixon's Southern Strategy Revisited." *Journal of Policy
History* 10, no. 2 (1998): 207–38. Contains a good summary of the
significance of the southern strategy.

Perlstein, Rick. *Nixonland: The Rise of a President and the Fracturing of America.*
New York: Scribner, 2008. Explores how Nixon created a dividing line
in American political life by contrasting riots and display of unrest with
law, order, and respect for a traditional hierarchy.

Sanders, Randy. "Rassling a Governor: Defiance, Desegregation, Claude Kirk,
and the Politics of Richard Nixon's Southern Strategy." *Florida Historical*

Quarterly 80, no. 3 (Winter 2002): 332–59. A readable account of the effects of the southern strategy upon a state gubernatorial election in Florida.

Small, Melvin. *The Presidency of Richard Nixon.* Lawrence: University Press of Kansas, 2003. The University Press of Kansas has published a series of excellent studies on the foreign and domestic politics of the presidents. This is one of the best books on the Nixon presidency.

Sweeney, James R. "Southern Strategies: The 1970 Election for the United States Senate in Virginia." *Virginia Magazine of History and Biography* 106, no. 2 (Spring 1998): 165–200. A very readable account of how the southern strategy helped the Republicans in the 1970 midterm elections.

World Wide Web

"American President: Richard Milhous Nixon." http://millercenter.org/academic/americanpresident/nixon. This site, created by the Miller Center of Public Affairs at the University of Virginia, contains in-depth essays on Nixon as well as biographical details.

"The Republican Party and African Americans: The Real Story." http://www.h-net.msu.edu/~hns/articles/2000/082900a.html. This article, by David Greenberg of History News Service, provides a history of modern Republican Party views on race.

"The Way Down South." http://www.thenation.com/doc/20070212/moser. This essay by Bob Moser appeared in the January 25, 2007 issue of *The Nation.* Moser recounts his experiences as a southern white boy learning about Nixon's southern strategy for the first time alongside his father in 1972. He also analyzes the success of the strategy.

92. *Roots* Is Televised (1977)

The *Roots* miniseries, based on the book of the same name by African American novelist Alex Haley, became a sensation when it aired on television in January 1977. The broadcast fueled interest in black history and is credited with giving the wider American public a greater sympathy for the struggles of African Americans.

ABC television did not expect that *Roots* would attract much of an audience because of the subject matter. Haley traced his ancestors from

Africa, across the Atlantic, and into slavery in America. He did not shy away from addressing the brutality of slavery or the racism that blacks endured. ABC showed the entire series over one week, essentially to get the show over and done with. To the great surprise of television executives, an average of 66 percent of American households watched some portion of *Roots.* About 130 million Americans watched the show. *Roots* won one of the largest audiences for a drama in the history of television. Restaurants and bars lost sales when the program aired because patrons went home to watch it. Bartenders kept customers only by switching from basketball and hockey games to *Roots.* Black parents named their children after characters in the show, particularly favoring the lead character of Kunta Kinte.

The broadcast of the miniseries led to a debate about the effects of television. The program aired a year after the nation's bicentennial fueled interest in American history and prompted many African Americans to start genealogy projects. While the absence of birth certificates for slaves makes it difficult for African Americans to trace their roots, Haley debunked the myth that it was impossible for blacks to do. The program also sparked interest in the general history of African Americans on the part of both whites and blacks.

TERM PAPER SUGGESTIONS

1. Examine the portrayal of African Americans on television in the past and in the present. How has the image of the African American male changed in the past decades?
2. Analyze the effect of media stereotypes of black men and women through the twentieth century. Who is Mammy and who is Sambo?
3. Explore how the characters in *Roots* were shaped by the histories of their ancestors.

ALTERNATIVE TERM PAPER SUGGESTIONS

1. Create a chapter of a graphic novel that features panels relating to the involvement of one of your family members with one of the major topics in African American history, perhaps World War II, the civil rights movement, or Hurricane Katrina. (You may want to use "Comic Life" software available from the Plasq.com Company.)
2. Trace your genealogy as far back as you can reach. Write a paper explaining how the history of your family connects with African American history.

SUGGESTED SOURCES

Primary Source

Haley, Alex. *Roots.* Garden City, NY: Doubleday, 1976. Perhaps the best novel about the African American past and certainly the most influential.

Secondary Sources

Fishbein, Leslie. "*Roots*: Docudrama and the Interpretation of History." In *American History, American Television: Interpreting the Video Past.* Edited by John E. O'Connor. New York: Ungar, 1983. Each generation interprets the same facts differently. This essay explores how the creators of the miniseries interpreted the black past.

Gonzalez, Doreen. *Alex Haley: Author of Roots.* Hillside, NJ: Enslow, 1994. A good biography of Haley for secondary school students.

Gray, Herman. *Watching Race: Television and the Struggle for "Blackness."* Minneapolis: University of Minnesota Press, 1995. Examines what it means to be African American on television.

Shirley, David. *Alex Haley.* New York: Chelsea House, 1994. The standard biography of the author.

Williams, Sylvia B. *Alex Haley.* Edina, MN: Abdo and Daughters, 1996. A solid biography of Haley.

Woll, David. *Ethnic and Racial Images in American Film and Television.* New York: Garland, 1987. Shows how poor images of blacks in movies and on television have had a destructive impact upon public views about African Americans.

World Wide Web

"Alex Haley." http://www.museum.tv/archives/etv/H/htmlH/haleyalex/haleyalex.htm. A biography of the writer that emphasizes his work on *Roots.*

"*Roots:* U.S. Serial Drama." http://www.museum.tv/archives/etv/R/htmlR/roots/roots.htm. This site, created by the Museum of Broadcast Communication, contains an essay on the reception and significance of the miniseries as well as a cast listing.

Multimedia Sources

Alex Haley. Los Angeles: California Newsreel, 1987. VHS and DVD. Includes one of the few in-depth conversations with Haley recorded before his 1992 death. Haley discusses the creation of *The Autobiography of Malcolm X* and the quest for identity that yielded *Roots.*

Color Adjustment. Los Angeles: California Newsreel, 1991. VHS, DVD, 16 mm.
Traces 40 years of racial myths and stereotypes on television.

Ethnic Notions. Los Angeles: California Newsreel, 1987. DVD. This is a stun-
ning, Emmy-award documentary by Marlon Riggs that links media stereotypes to antiblack prejudice.

Roots—Anniversary Edition. Los Angeles: Warner Home Video, 2007. 4 DVDs.
Popular 1977 miniseries about the history of an African American
family.

93. Michele Wallace Publishes *Black Macho and the Myth of the Superwoman* (1978)

In *Black Macho and the Myth of the Superwoman,* City University of New
York English Professor Michele Wallace attacked the male supremacist
bias of 1960s and 1970s African American politics. She argued that the
Black Power movement that attempted to empower blacks only empowered black men. Women remained marginalized, unable to develop a
political strategy to take control of their own lives.

Wallace grew up in New York City as the daughter of black feminist
artist Faith Ringgold. She noticed that as the civil rights movement
advanced, the status of black women did not. Searching for an explanation for the hostility facing black women, she looked at America's history
of racism. Wallace found that blacks had been systematically deprived of
their own African culture. While slavery and segregation were enormously
damaging, blacks were also hurt by integration and assimilation that
denied them the knowledge of their history of struggle and the memory
of their own cultural practices. In the process of assimilation, integration,
and accommodation, African Americans took on white cultural attitudes
and values in regard to sexuality and gender. As a result, black men
became sexist and misogynistic and black women became self-hating.
In hating black women, black men hated themselves. They had accepted
the negative stereotypes about the black race.

At the time that Wallace wrote her book, the significance of black
women as a distinct category was routinely erased by the way in which
the women's movement and the black movement chose to set their goals
and recollect their histories. In 1978, no one discussed racial oppression
and women's oppression at the same time. Partly as a result of Wallace's
work, black women are now seen both as black and as women.

TERM PAPER SUGGESTIONS

1. At the time of the publication of Wallace's book, Maulana Karenga, the founder of Kwanzaa, commented that "Books like 'Black Macho' and plays like 'For Colored Girls' only help to divide us, while flattering the white oppressor." Explore this criticism.

2. Analyze Wallace's book. Does her evidence convince you that black men accepted negative stereotypes about the black race?

3. Many black women refuse to identify as feminists because they define feminism as a white woman's movement that excludes women of color. They also argue that, as black women, they have more in common with black men than with white women. Explore how Wallace challenges both of these views as a black feminist.

ALTERNATIVE TERM PAPER SUGGESTIONS

1. As a feminist scholar, Wallace believes in using the personal to illustrate the political. Use the same strategy and create a Microsoft PowerPoint presentation that uses family photographs to illustrate the African American past.

2. Create a play that examines some of the issues facing modern-day black women.

SUGGESTED SOURCES

Primary Sources

"Black Macho and the Myth of the Superwoman." http://books.google.com/ books?id=9uAslh9KnQsC&dq=michele+wallace+black+macho+and+the +myth+of+the+superwoman&pg=PP1&ots=c4Jkbk6imW&sig=RnIg f4UylgcYLBFcZJV5e0fM7Gg&hl=en&sa=X&oi=book_result&resnum =1&ct=result#PPR9,M1. A limited number of pages of this book can be downloaded from Google.

Wallace, Michele. *Black Macho and the Myth of the Superwoman.* New York: Dial Press, 1978. Wallace's landmark work.

Secondary Sources

Byrd, Rudolph P., and Beverly Guy-Sheftell, eds. *Traps: African American Men on Gender and Sexuality.* Bloomington: Indiana University Press, 2001. Explores a black man's place in black feminist criticism as well as the patriarchy's exploitation of black women.

Carson, Clayborne, Emma J. Lapsansky-Werner, and Gary B. Nash. *The Struggle for Freedom: A History of African Americans.* New York: Pearson Longman, 2007. One of the best general histories of African Americans.

Collins, Patricia Hill. *Black Sexual Politics: African Americans, Gender, and the New Racism.* New York: Routledge, 2005. Essentially the successor book to Wallace's work, Collins explores how images of black sexuality have been used to oppress blacks.

Collins, Patricia Hill. *From Black Power to Hip Hop: Racism, Nationalism, and Feminism.* Philadelphia: Temple University Press, 2006. The best history of modern black feminism.

Estes, Steve. *I Am A Man!: Race, Manhood, and the Civil Rights Movement.* Chapel Hill: University of North Carolina, 2005. Examines male attitudes toward the civil rights movement and the Moynihan Report that blamed the collapse of the black family on female-headed households.

Robnett, Belinda. *How Long? How Long?: African-American Women in the Struggle for Civil Rights.* New York: Oxford University Press, 1997. A history of the civil rights movement from the perspective of black women.

Rosen, Ruth. *The World Split Open: How the Modern Women's Movement Changed America.* New York: Viking Penguin, 2000. One of the best histories of the women's movement.

Shange, Ntozke. *For Colored Girls Who Have Considered Suicide When the Rainbow Is Enuf.* New York: Scribner, 1997. Poetic history of what it means to be a black woman in America.

World Wide Web

"Critical Noir: Taking One for the Team—Michele Wallace." http://www.blackvoices.com/entmain/music/critno10604/20050302. This 2005 essay, by Mark Anthony Neal of BlackVoices, discusses the criticism that Wallace faced for exposing sexism with the African American community.

"Michele Wallace." http://www.blackculturalstudies.org/wallace/wallace_index.html. Contains a brief biography of Wallace, links to a review of the book and Wallace's other works, and the full text of Wallace's essay "To Hell and Back: On the Road with Black Feminism in the 60s & 70s."

"Michele Wallace: An Interview." http://www.vdb.org/smackn.acgi$tapedetail? MICHELEWAL. Provides a link to the video of a 1991 interview with Wallace.

"Sifting through Generations: Michele Wallace Explores Personal and Political Experiences." http://cjournal.concordia.ca/journalarchives/2005-06/

mar_23/006565.shtml. This essay for *Concordia Journal* reports on a lecture that Wallace delivered after going through her family photographs for information about the African American past.

Multimedia Source

For Colored Girls Who Have Considered Suicide/When the Rainbow Is Enuf. New York: WNET, 1982. This is a PBS television adaptation of the play with Alfre Woodard and Lynn Whitfield in the starring roles.

94. *Bakke* Case (1978)

The *Bakke* case involved the question of how to include African Americans in areas where they had traditionally been excluded because of racial discrimination. *Bakke* essentially put affirmative action on trial. The case is regarded as the most important civil rights decision since the end of segregation, as well as one of most complicated ever heard by the U.S. Supreme Court.

Affirmative action programs arose as a means of addressing the long-standing exclusion of minorities from certain educational and professional opportunities. Allan Bakke, a 35-year-old white man, had twice applied and been rejected for admission to the University of California Medical School at Davis. The school reserved 16 places in each entering class for 100 "qualified" minorities, as part of its affirmative action program. Bakke's grade point average (GPA) and test scores exceeded those of any of the minority students admitted instead of him. Bakke sued the university on the grounds that he had been discriminated against on account of his race. He sought color-blind admissions procedures.

Bakke's claim of reverse discrimination struck a chord among many whites who thought that unqualified African Americans were being unfairly promoted. The claim also angered blacks who charged that white men had long benefitted from unofficial racial preferences and that affirmative action was necessary to permit blacks to advance. His case was argued before the Supreme Court on October 12, 1977 in *Regents of the University of California v. Bakke*.

The Court had to decide whether the University of California had violated both the Fourteenth Amendment's Equal Protection Clause and the Civil Rights Act of 1964 by using admission criteria based upon race.

The Court ordered Bakke's admission to medical school with its decision on June 26, 1978. Four justices agreed that any racial quota system violated the law and four justices declared that the Civil Rights Act permitted affirmative action. Justice Lewis Powell agreed that Bakke had been discriminated against, and his vote ordered the medical school to admit Bakke. While Powell also ruled that the school's use of racial quotas violated the Fourteenth Amendment, he also offered the opinion that the use of race is permissible as one of several admission criteria. The Court managed to pacify both white Americans hostile to affirmative action and blacks who supported it.

TERM PAPER SUGGESTIONS

1. In 1996, the U.S. Supreme Court ruled in *Hopwood v. Texas* that the University of Texas could not use affirmative action to determine admissions to its law school. In 2003, the Court ruled that the University of Michigan could use affirmative action to determine admissions. Compare and contrast the *Bakke* case with the *Hopwood* case and the University of Michigan cases.

2. Examine the use of affirmative action as a means of repairing the damage from centuries of discrimination based upon race. Is it an effective method for advancing African Americans?

3. Some African Americans, notably Supreme Court Justice Clarence Thomas, oppose affirmative action. Examine why some blacks do not support this method of addressing discrimination.

4. Trace the history of the *Bakke* case. What were the arguments of supporters and opponents of affirmative action?

ALTERNATIVE TERM PAPER SUGGESTIONS

1. Create a Web page that explains affirmative action, opposition to it, and major Supreme Court cases related to it.

2. Write an editorial for a newspaper that either supports or opposes affirmative action programs.

SUGGESTED SOURCES

Primary Source

Regents of the University of California v. Bakke (No. 7811) 18 Cal.3d 34, 553 P.2d 1152, Affirmed in Part and Reversed in Part. http://www.law .cornell.edu/supct/html/historics/USSC_CR_0438_0265_ZS.html.

This page, provided by the Legal Information Institute of the Cornell University Law School, reprints the *Bakke* decision as well as the opinions of the dissenting justices.

Secondary Sources

Ball, Howard. *The Bakke Case: Race, Education, and Affirmative Action.* Lawrence: University Press of Kansas, 2000. This is a very readable explanation of affirmative action as well as a good introduction into the process by which Supreme Court justices decide cases and write opinions.

Banfield, Susan. *The Bakke Case: Quotas in College Admissions.* Berkeley Heights, NJ: Enslow Publishers, 1998. Aimed at secondary school students, this book presents an overview of discrimination in America, the evolution of civil rights, and the basic principles of affirmative action.

Dreyfuss, Joel. *The Bakke Case: The Politics of Inequality.* New York: Harcourt, 1979. Aimed at students, this book focuses on the political history of the case.

Fleming, John E., Gerald R. Gill, and David H. Swinton. *Case for Affirmative Action for Blacks in Higher Education.* Washington, DC: Howard University Press, 1978. This book, published by a historically black university in the immediate wake of *Bakke,* argues in support of affirmative action.

McPherson, Stephanie Sammartino. *The Bakke Case and the Affirmative Action Debate: Debating Supreme Court Decisions.* Berkeley Heights, NJ: Enslow, 2005. Aimed at young adults, this is a solid introduction to the *Bakke* case.

Stefoff, Rebecca. *The Bakke Case: Challenge to Affirmative Action* New York: Benchmark, 2006. A basic account of the case in a book aimed at secondary school students.

Stohr, Greg. *A Black and White Case: How Affirmative Action Survived Its Greatest Legal Challenge.* New York: Bloomberg, 2004. Stohr, a legal reporter, provides a detailed look at the 2003 U.S. Supreme Court decision upholding the University of Michigan law school affirmative-action program.

World Wide Web

"The *Bakke* Case and Affirmative Action, 1978." http://www.pbs.org/wgbh/amex/eyesontheprize/story/22_bakke.html. This site, part of the American Experience *Eyes on the Prize* series, includes a summary of the case, a video explaining the case, a newspaper editorial about the case, and links to related pages on equal opportunity and legislation in support of affirmative action.

"*Regents of the University of California v. Bakke.*" http://www.oyez.org/
cases/1970-1979/1977/1977_76_811/. Oyez: Supreme Court Media is
a site that provides summaries of U.S. Supreme Court cases. The
page lists the participating attorneys, provides the votes of the justices,
and summarizes the case. Links allow visitors to listen to the oral arguments, hear the announcement of the opinion, and obtain the full written opinion.

Multimedia Source

Eyes on the Prize, 1954–1985. Blackside, 1990. VHS. The "Keys to the Kingdom" chapter focuses on the *Bakke* case. A transcript of the video, which
includes comments from people involved with the case, can be found at
http://www.pbs.org/wgbh/amex/eyesontheprize/about/pt_207.html.

95. Black Miami Residents Riot over Police Brutality (1980)

By the 1970s, most Americans thought that race riots were a feature of
the past. In 1980, the black sections of Miami exploded in the worst race
riot since the 1960s. The riot came in response to an incident of police
brutality, but it reflected deep anger at persistent police mistreatment as
well as neglect of the black community by political leaders.

As a result of Jim Crow legislation and widespread racism, many
Miami blacks were clustered in the predominantly-black communities
of Overtown and Liberty City. Long shut out of power by whites, blacks
found themselves losing political and economic ground in the 1970s to
the large numbers of Cuban immigrants who had poured into Miami
since the 1960s. By 1979, Liberty City had a 50 percent unemployment
rate. The McDuffie incident triggered an explosion that had been building for some time.

In the early morning hours of December 17, 1979, former U.S. Marine
and current insurance salesman Arthur McDuffie attempted to elude
police by taking them on a high speed chase. The police claimed that
McDuffie died when he crashed his motorcycle. However, the coroner
disputed this claim, finding that McDuffie died of multiple skull fractures
caused by a blunt instrument. In the subsequent trial, a police officer tes-
tified that four officers had beaten McDuffie with their flashlights when

he forcefully resisted arrest. An all-white jury in Tampa acquitted the police after a brief deliberation.

Miami officials did not anticipate widespread anger at the verdict. Black political leaders called for a silent protest march in front of the police headquarters and courthouse. About 5,000 people turned out to march. The moderates quickly lost control of the situation as the crowd began to shout, "We want justice!" Within the hour, rioting had erupted in black Miami. In Liberty City, rioters dragged three white men from their truck and beat them to death. A Cuban man was seized and burned alive. White Miamians then retaliated, seemingly with the approval of the police, by killing several blacks. In the aftermath of the riot, little changed despite promises to fix the underlying causes of the revolt. Miami suffered smaller race riots in 1982 and 1989.

TERM PAPER SUGGESTIONS

1. Trace the history of racial conflict between minorities in Miami in the 1970s or Los Angeles in the 1990s.
2. Compare and contrast the Miami riot of 1980 with the Los Angeles riot of 1992.
3. Police brutality is a long-standing complaint in black communities. Investigate ways in which police officials have tried to remedy this problem.

ALTERNATIVE TERM PAPER SUGGESTIONS

1. Assume that you are a newspaper reporter in May 1980. Write an editorial proposing peaceful solutions to the concerns of Miami blacks.
2. Create a Microsoft PowerPoint that traces the history of race riots in the twentieth century. What are the commonalities and differences?

SUGGESTED SOURCES

Secondary Sources

Burris, John L. *Blue v. Black: Let's End the Conflict Between the Cops and Minorities.* New York: St. Martin's, 1999. Argues that neither side has benefitted from the clashes between police and African Americans.

Dunn, Marvin. *Black Miami in the Twentieth Century.* Gainesville: University Press of Florida, 1997. A wonderful study of race relations in a southern city that covers the 1980 riots.

Gale, Dennis E. *Understanding Urban Unrest: From Reverend King to Rodney King.* Thousand Oaks, CA: Sage, 1996. Examines the underlying causes of riots, including the Miami revolt.

Harris, Daryl B. *The Logic of Black Urban Rebellions: Challenging the Dynamics of White Domination in Miami.* Westport, CT: Praeger, 1999. One of the few scholarly studies of the motivations of rioters in the post-civil rights era.

Porter, Bruce, and Marvin Dunn. *The Miami Riot of 1980: Crossing the Bounds.* New York: Lexington Books, 1984. One of the best studies of the riot.

Portes, Alejandro, and Alex Stepick. *City on the Edge: The Transformation of Miami.* Los Angeles: University of California Press, 1994. Covers the history of Miami from the time of the Spanish, but the focus is on the impact of the migrations of Cubans, Haitians, and Nicaraguans in the 1970s and 1980s upon Anglo and African Americans.

Skolnick, Jerome H., and James J. Fyfe. *Above the Law: Police and the Excessive Use of Force.* New York: Free Press, 1993. This is a study of police violence that includes a historical context of policing and the changing styles of police work. The authors examine the causes of abusive behavior and explore remedies.

Vaca, Nicolas Corona. *The Presumed Alliance: The Unspoken Conflict Between Latinos and Blacks and What It Means for America.* New York: Harper, 2004. Examines the relationship between Latinos and African Americans, including the incident between a Latino police officer and an African American man that set off the 1982 Overtown riot.

World Wide Web

"Miami's Failures at Rebuilding after Riot." http://www.floridacdc.org/members/overtown/riots.htm. This 1993 *Los Angeles Times* essay by Miles Corwin, on the Overtown Collective site, compares the Miami riot with the 1992 Los Angeles race riot.

"Overtown Chronology" and "Overtown Community." http://www.library.miami.edu/archives/ohp/Overtown/Chronology.html and http://www.library.miami.edu/archives/ohp/Overtown/Index.html. These two sites are part of the University of Miami Oral History Program. The chronology provides a history of black Miami. The community section includes an essay and two interviews that focus on the history of the black community, not the riot.

96. Jesse Jackson Runs for President (1984)

Longtime civil rights activist Jesse Jackson ran for the presidency of the United States in 1984. In doing so, he became the first African American man to mount a serious bid for the White House. His campaign promised to show the political power of blacks and to raise awareness of the issues facing the poor.

Jackson's candidacy grew out of his experiences as an advocate for the poor. Born to an unwed teenage mother in 1941, Jackson noted that he never spent a night under the roof with his natural father. He broke his family's pattern of poverty by graduating from college. Along the way, he became a civil rights activist in North Carolina and spent time in jail for participating in protests. In March 1965, he joined Martin Luther King in Selma. As a leader in King's Southern Christian Leadership Conference, Jackson organized economic boycotts in Chicago to expand black opportunities. In 1971, he founded Operation People United to Serve Humanity (PUSH) and continued to use economic boycotts. By 1980, Jackson had emerged as a major black leader. In 1983, he announced his bid for the presidency. Jackson was not the first black person to seek the White House. Shirley Chisholm, the first African American woman elected to Congress, had become the first African American to seek the Democratic nomination for president in 1972.

Jackson strongly objected to the policies of Republican President Ronald Reagan, who had cut federal programs that helped the poor. However, he also sharply criticized the Democratic Party for not giving priority to the concerns of African Americans. He expected that his candidacy would force the Democrats to be more responsive to black issues. Although a strong campaigner, Jackson made several public relation blunders that cost him support. He received about 3.5 million votes and 300 delegates but lost the nomination to Jimmy Carter's vice president, Walter Mondale. Jackson ran again for the presidency in 1988. By March, he had the lead in popular votes and delegates, but he soon lost ground to the eventual nominee, Michael Dukakis. He has since devoted himself to defusing ethnic tensions in Africa and encouraging American black parents to become more involved with the education of their children.

TERM PAPER SUGGESTIONS

1. Jesse Jackson and Barack Obama are the only two African American men to mount major presidential campaigns. Compare and contrast the two political leaders.

2. Jackson's forceful criticisms of Ronald Reagan helped him become the most influential black political figure of the 1980s. Examine these criticisms. How did Jackson believe that blacks had suffered under Reagan's policies, and what solutions did he propose?

ALTERNATIVE TERM PAPER SUGGESTIONS

1. Political cartoons have been used as weapons since the first contested presidential election in 1800. Draw 10 cartoons accompanied by appropriate explanations that either support Jackson's positions or criticize his presidential candidacy.

2. Jackson is famed as one of the best orators to emerge from the civil rights movement. Create a speech that pays tribute to Jackson's accomplishments and urges voters to support his presidential candidacy.

3. When Jackson ran for the presidency in 1984, famed civil rights activists Coretta Scott King and Andrew Young argued privately that he would damage the prospects of a liberal white candidate with a better chance to defeat Reagan. Backers of Jackson advised that his candidacy would enable African Americans to gain enough power within the Democratic Party to force its support of policies beneficial to blacks. Write a newspaper editorial that either urges Jackson to abandon his campaign or urges him to pursue it.

SUGGESTED SOURCES

Primary Source

Democratic National Convention: Jesse Jackson, 1984. Washington, DC: National Archives and Records Administration, 2008. This 51-minute historical recording presents Jackson's speech about his candidacy.

Secondary Sources

Bruns, Roger. *Jesse Jackson: A Biography.* Westport, CT: Greenwood Press, 2005. Ideal for school assignments, this readable biography doubles as a reference book on Jackson.

Clemente, Frank. *Keep Hope Alive: Jesse Jackson's 1988 Presidential Campaign.* Boston: South End Press, 1999. Good account of the failed 1988 campaign.

Frady, Marshall. *Jesse: The Life and Pilgrimage of Jesse Jackson.* New York: Simon and Schuster, 2006. A well-written biography of Jackson by a man who followed Jackson for years and had extensive access to him.

Hertzke, Allen D. *Echoes of Discontent: Jesse Jackson, Pat Robertson, and the Resurgence of Populism.* Washington, DC: Congressional Quarterly Press, 1993. Interesting comparison of populist beliefs common to politicians on the right and the left.

Reed, Adolph L. *The Jesse Jackson Phenomenon: The Crisis of Purpose in Afro-American Politics.* New Haven: Yale University Press, 1986. Reed argues that Jackson's 1984 candidacy hurt the development of a viable black political movement.

Timmerman, Kenneth. *Shakedown: Exposing the Real Jesse Jackson.* Washington, DC: Regnery Press, 2002. This is a controversial biography by a Republican activist that portrays Jackson as an extortionist of American businesses. With the ready availability of balanced biographies of Jackson by Frady and Bruns, this is a poor choice as a sole reference.

World Wide Web

"The Pilgrimage of Jesse Jackson." http://www.pbs.org/wgbh/pages/frontline/jesse/. A wonderful site about Jackson, this site contains a video interview with biographer Marshall Frady, interviews with Jackson's friends and advisors, and audio excerpts of Jackson's speeches to the 1984 and 1988 Democratic National Conventions. A Jackson chronology is also included.

"RainbowPUSH Coalition." http://www.rainbowpush.org/. The official site of the organizations founded by Jackson.

Multimedia Sources

America Beyond the Color Line. PBS Paramount, 2004. DVD. In this documentary, historian Henry Louis Gates examines the state of black America at the start of the new century. He speaks with Jackson and includes coverage of inner-city Chicago with the East Coast, Deep South, and Hollywood.

Jesse Jackson. Educational Video Network, 2004. DVD. This is a short (13-minute) biography of Jackson.

97. Clarence Thomas Is Appointed to the U.S. Supreme Court (1991)

African American political conservatives and the issue of sexual harassment of African American women all took center stage when President George H. W. Bush appointed Clarence Thomas to serve on the U.S. Supreme Court on October 23, 1991. The Thomas confirmation hearings focused attention on gender relations within the black community and challenged black solidarity.

Thomas filled the "black seat" on the Court that had previously been held by Thurgood Marshall, one of the best-known and most respected civil rights attorneys of the twentieth century. At first glance, Thomas did not appear to have the stature of Marshall. Born in 1948 in Georgia, Thomas attended divinity school and earned a law degree from Yale University in 1974. He served as the assistant attorney general of Missouri and worked for Monsanto before joining the Reagan Administration in 1981 as the assistant for civil rights in the U.S. Department of Education. He then worked alongside Anita Hill as chair of the U.S. Equal Employment Opportunity Commission from 1982 to 1990. When Bush nominated Thomas for the Supreme Court, he had spent only a year as a judge, serving on the U.S. Court of Appeals for the District of Columbia Circuit. He did not have Marshall's reputation for legal brilliance or a reputation as a supporter of civil rights.

Thomas ran into serious difficulties during his nationally televised confirmation hearings in October 1991. He faced charges of incompetence, indifference to racism, and, most famously, sexual harassment. Hill alleged that Thomas had behaved inappropriately from 1981 to 1983 and threatened to ruin her professionally if she went public with his misconduct. Many women viewed the hearings as a referendum on sexual harassment. Thomas sought the support of the black community by charging that the hearing had become an attempt at a "high-tech lynching for uppity blacks." African American women were told that they were betraying the race by prioritizing gender solidarity over black solidarity. Thomas won Senate confirmation, but only by the slimmest margin (52 to 48) of any Supreme Court nominee in American history.

In the years since the hearings, many women have credited Hill for prompting a new awareness of sexual harassment. The sight of an articulate, composed black female law professor being questioned about her mental state by a group of unsympathetic men because she charged harassment struck too close to home for female viewers who had themselves been subjected to harassment. In the next congressional elections, an unprecedented number of women were elected, perhaps not coincidentally.

TERM PAPER SUGGESTIONS

1. In *Black Macho and the Myth of the Superwoman* in 1978, Michele Wallace argued that the Black Power movement that attempted to empower blacks only empowered black men. Consider Wallace's claims with respect to Clarence Thomas and Anita Hill. Did the civil rights movement only empower black men?

2. Compare and contrast Clarence Thomas's view of his confirmation hearings with Hill's account.

3. Review the Thomas hearings. Discuss whether you would have voted to confirm Thomas.

4. Research the history of the Supreme Court and civil rights. How significant a role has the Court played in advancing the concerns of blacks?

5. Research the history of the Supreme Court and women's rights. How significant a role has the Court played in advancing the concerns of women?

6. Discuss the divisions in the black community over Thomas and Hill.

7. Thomas supports a strict constructionist view of the Constitution. Explore what this means.

ALTERNATIVE TERM PAPER SUGGESTIONS

1. Write an editorial that either supports Thomas's confirmation or opposes it. Explain your reasoning.

2. Presidents typically appoint one or two Supreme Court justices during their time in the White House. Write an opinion piece for a newspaper that urges the president to appoint a justice in the mold of Thomas or a justice with an entirely different judicial philosophy. In your article, review Thomas's decisions.

SUGGESTED SOURCES

Primary Sources

Hill, Anita. *Speaking Truth to Power.* New York: Anchor, 1998. Hill's version of the Thomas confirmation hearings.

Miller, Anita, ed. *The Complete Transcripts of the Clarence Thomas-Anita Hill Hearings: October 11, 12, 13, 1991.* Chicago: Academy, 1994. National Public Radio reporter Nina Totenberg explains in the introduction that the hearings were as much about Hill and Thomas as the way that the Senate Judiciary Committee performed its job. The transcripts show the rude treatment of Hill by senators as well as a reluctance to question Thomas. The book includes the transcript of an interview with Angela Wright by counsel for the Judiciary Committee. Wright, Thomas's former director of public affairs at the Equal Employment Opportunity Commission, also charged Thomas with sexual harassment.

Thomas, Clarence. *My Grandfather's Son: A Memoir.* New York: Harper, 2007. Thomas's autobiography includes his view of his confirmation hearings.

United States Congress Committee on the Judiciary. *The Complete Transcripts of the Clarence Thomas-Anita Hill Hearings.* Chicago: Academy Chicago Publishers, 1994. Contains the full and official record of the hearings.

Secondary Sources

Chrisman, Robert, and Robert L. Allen, eds. *Court of Appeal: The Black Community Speaks Out on the Racial and Sexual Politics of Clarence Thomas vs. Anita Hill.* New York: Ballantine Books, 1992. Interesting examination of the conflict over Thomas and Hill.

Cooper, Armin A. *The Prince and the Pauper: The Case Against Clarence Thomas, Associate Justice of the U.S. Supreme Court.* Bloomington, IN: Author-House, 2001. This is a self-published book that is hostile towards Thomas.

Flax, Jane. *The American Dream in Black and White: The Clarence Thomas Hearings.* Ithaca, NY: Cornell University Press, 1999. Aimed at advanced readers, this book includes discussions of feminist, political, and psycho-analytic theory.

Foskett, Ken. *Judging Thomas: The Life and Times of Clarence Thomas.* New York: Harper, 2005. Good study of Thomas and his natural law philosophy that relies on a mixture of secondary sources and interviews.

Gerber, Scott Douglas. *First Principles: The Jurisprudence of Clarence Thomas.* New York: New York University Press, 2002. An excellent review of Thomas's opinions, his legal thinking, and his place in the Supreme Court.

Holzer, Henry Mark. *The Keeper of the Flame: The Supreme Court Opinions of Justice Clarence Thomas 1991–2005.* Bangor, ME: Booklocker.com, 2006. Presents all 327 judicial opinions that Thomas rendered over this time span.

Marcosson, Samuel. *Original Sin: Clarence Thomas and the Failure of the Constitutional Conservatives.* New York: New York University Press, 2002. Interesting examination of the narrow reading of the Constitution supported by Thomas. Marcosson places Thomas in the position of having to concur or dissent in the Supreme Court case *Loving v. Virginia* that involved whether a state could prohibit marriage between blacks and whites.

Merida, Kevin, and Michael Fletcher. *Supreme Discomfort: The Divided Soul of Clarence Thomas.* New York: Broadway, 2008. A biography that examines how Thomas's conservatism has made him a pariah in the black community.

Meyer, Jane, and Jane Abramson. *Strange Justice: The Selling of Clarence Thomas.* New York: Plume, 1995. This account of Thomas's confirmation to the Supreme Court and the accompanying smear campaign against Hill received nominations for two major book awards.

Morrison, Toni, ed. *Race-ing Justice, En-Gendering Power: Essays on Anita Hill, Clarence Thomas, and the Construction of Social Reality.* New York: Pantheon, 1992. This is a collection of essays marked by Judge A. Leon Higgonbotham's open letter to Thomas that points out how Thomas has benefitted from the civil rights legislation that he opposes as a strict constructionist.

Smitherman, Geneva, ed. *African American Women Speak Out on Anita Hill-Clarence Thomas.* Detroit: Wayne State University Press, 1995. This is a collection of essays that includes scholarly examinations of the dispute as well as personal reflections about the controversy.

Thomas, Andrew Peyton. *Clarence Thomas: A Biography.* New York: Encounter, 2002. This is a 672-page biography of Thomas that is likely to be the best available until passions cool about the justice and a more objective work can be produced.

World Wide Web

"Anita Hill—Clarence Thomas Hearings." http://www.museum.tv/archives/etv/H/htmlH/hill-thomash/hill-thomas.htm. An excellent summary of the hearings as well as their significance to black history.

"Clarence Thomas." http://www.oyez.org/justices/clarence_thomas/. A good biography of Thomas with links to his financial disclosure records and photographs.

"Clarence Thomas: Recent Decisions." http://www.law.cornell.edu/supct/justices/thomas.bio.html. Provides a short biography of Thomas as well as his latest judicial opinions.

"Justice Clarence Thomas." http://www.supremecourthistory.org/history/supremecourthistory_history_current_thomas.htm. A biography of Thomas by the Supreme Court Historical Society.

98. Jury Acquits Los Angeles Police Officers in the Beating of Rodney King and Rioting Ensues (1992)

When a jury of 10 whites, 1 Asian, and 1 Latino acquitted police officers of wrongdoing in the beating of black motorist Rodney King on April 29, 1992, the city of Los Angeles erupted. Violence swept through the predominantly black section of South Central as rioters looted stores, burned buildings, and attacked whites trapped in the riot zone. The Los Angeles riot resulted in the deaths of 52 people, most of whom were black; 2,383 serious injuries; and property damage of about $1 billion from some 500 fires. The episode became the worst race riot since the 1960s.

On March 3, 1991, 25-year-old King sped down the 210 freeway in Los Angeles. A man with a quick temper often fueled by excessive drinking, he had been arrested for assaulting his estranged wife and had served time in prison for robbery. When the California Highway Patrol (CHP) attempted to pull King over for speeding, he feared that his probation would be revoked. He then made the poor decision to attempt to evade the police, eventually hitting 115 miles per hour. Eventually forced to stop and ordered to exit his vehicle, King stepped out to meet several Los Angeles police officers who had come to offer assistance to the CHP. Some of the officers decided that King was resisting arrest. As George Holliday videotaped the scene unbeknownst to the police, Sgt. Stacey Koon shot King twice with a TASER gun, and several cops beat him savagely with their baton. Holliday gave the tape to the media and the scene played repeatedly on television nationwide.

The history of police mistreatment of African Americans in Los Angeles helped to create a wave of enormous outrage at the King incident. However, many people expected that the evidence of the videotape would prove that the police had abused their authority. When the police officers were acquitted, many residents of South Central believed that they simply could not get justice because of their race. In response, they rioted. King tried to calm the situation by going on television to famously ask, "Can we all just get along?"

King recovered from the beating and won $3.8 million in damages from the City of Los Angeles. He would struggle over the next few years to get his life together before finally moving to suburban Los Angeles to live quietly with his family. Los Angeles also found it difficult to rebound from the riot.

TERM PAPER SUGGESTIONS

1. Describe the conditions in Los Angeles that gave rise to the riots. Be sure to include both poverty and police mistreatment.

2. Trace the history of the Los Angeles riots. What changed as a result of the violence?

3. Compare and contrast the Overtown riots of 1980 with the Los Angeles riots of 1992.

4. The National Advisory Commission on Civil Disorders formed in response to the race riots of the 1960s. The commission's report can be found at http://www.pbs.org/moyers/journal/03282008/profile.html. Examine whether the problems identified by the commission in 1968 contributed to the 1992 riots.

ALTERNATIVE TERM PAPER SUGGESTIONS

1. Assume that you are a community leader during the 1992 riots. Prepare a podcast speech that seeks to restore calm to South Central Los Angeles.

2. Using the Web, research South Central Los Angeles today. Create a Web page that provides an update on the area that suffered the most from the 1992 riots.

SUGGESTED SOURCES

Primary Sources

"Famous American Trials: Los Angeles Police Officers' (Rodney King Beating) Trial." http://www.law.umkc.edu/faculty/projects/ftrials/lapd/lapd.html. This is easily the best site on the Rodney King case. It contains the Holliday videotape, a chronology, key figures, a use of force chart, police transmissions, King's arrest record, a trial transcript excerpt, and links to related sites.

"George Holliday's Rodney King Beating Video." http://www.multishow.com.ar/rodneyking/. This is Holliday's page, and it contains his video that shocked the nation.

"Rodney King." http://www.youtube.com/watch?v=ROn_9302UHg. The videotape of the assault can be seen on YouTube.

Secondary Sources

Cannon, Lou. *Official Negligence: How Rodney King and the Riots Changed Los Angeles and the LAPD.* Boulder, CO: Westview Press, 1999. Good discussion of the significance of the Los Angeles riots.

Deitz, Robert. *Willful Injustice: A Post-O.J. Look at Rodney King, American Justice, and Trial by Race.* Washington, DC: Regnery Press, 1996. Argues that prosecutorial misconduct resulted in a federal court finding that the two L.A.P.D. officers violated King's civil rights.

Delk, James. *Fires and Furies: The L.A. Riots: What Really Happened.* Palm Springs, CA: Etc, 1994. Good exploration of the riots.

Geller, Laurence, and Peter Hemenway. *Last Chance for Justice: The Juror's Lonely Quest.* N.P.: NCDS Press, 1997. Fascinating discussion of the breakdown of the jury system. The authors examine the evidence presented to the King juries to determine the role played by pretrial publicity, whether people of color received unequal justice, whether the verdicts could be correct given the evidence presented, and how jury trials could be improved.

Koon, Sgt. Stacey, and Robert Deitz. *Presumed Guilty: The Tragedy of the Rodney King Affair.* Washington, DC: Regnery Gateway, 1992. Koon, a former L.A.P.D. officer convicted of violating King's civil rights, continues to protest his innocence.

Owens, Tom, and Rod Browning. *Lying Eyes: The Shocking Truth Behind the Corruption and Brutality of the LAPD and the Beating of Rodney King.* New York: Avalon, 1994. This book makes a charge that has been repeated since at least the 1940s—that the L.A.P.D. violates the civil rights of suspects of color.

World Wide Web

"Hate-Motivated Violence: The Rodney King Case." http://www2.ca.nizkor.org/hweb/orgs/canadian/canada/justice/hate-motivated-violence/hmv-006-00.html#6-1. Good essay on the case from a Canadian perspective.

"The L.A. Riots: 15 Years After Rodney King." http://www.time.com/time/specials/2007/la_riot/article/0,28804,1614117_1614084,00.html. A short article in *Time* magazine that reviews the incident and provides an update on King.

"PBS Online Forum: Lou Cannon Discusses the King Case." http://www.pbs.org/newshour/authors_corner/jan-june98/cannon_4-7.html.

The author of one of the best books on the King case reviews the incident.

"Rodney King's Legacy." http://www.courttv.com/archive/casefiles/rodneyking/. Provides the transcript of an interview with Lou Cannon, author of *Official Negligence: How Rodney King and the Riots Changed Los Angeles and the LAPD.*

Multimedia Source

The Rodney King Case: What the Jury Saw in California v. Powell. Los Angeles: Court TV, 1992. VHS. Originally shown on cable television's *Court TV,* this program contains highlights of the trial of L.A.P.D. Officer Lawrence Powell pulled from over 150 hours of television coverage. It contains the Holliday video as well.

99. Welfare Reform Act (1996)

By 1990, growing conservatism in the United States prompted Democratic politicians to join Republicans in attacking the existing social welfare programs. Many of these programs served African Americans, historically the poorest segment of American society. When Bill Clinton campaigned for the presidency in 1992, he vowed to "end welfare as we know it." In 1996, Clinton ended the 61-year American tradition of guaranteeing cash assistance to the poor by signing the Personal Responsibility and Work Opportunity Reconciliation Act, also known as the Welfare Reform Act.

The old system of welfare emerged during President Franklin D. Roosevelt's New Deal as a response to the Great Depression. The federal government offered aid to the poor—mostly women with children—without regard to the details of their personal circumstances and with no time limit. As the decades passed, the welfare state and the legacy of the New Deal came under increasingly heavy attack. The long-term tendency of the media to connect welfare with blacks placed African Americans in the category of undeserving poor in the minds of many whites. By the 1980s, President Ronald Reagan regularly gave speeches that included attacks upon black "welfare queens" who collected food stamps yet drove Cadillacs. Many Americans came to believe that the poor collected welfare to avoid working and that black women bore more children to get an increase in their welfare benefits. Democratic policymakers worried that a culture of dependency had become embedded in the ghettos, encouraging poor Americans to rely upon the government to take care of all of their needs and to teach their children to do the same.

The Welfare Reform Act had bipartisan support. It broke from precedent by pushing poor women to get jobs regardless of their childcare responsibilities. The law contained "strong work requirements, a performance bonus to reward states for moving welfare recipients into jobs, state maintenance of effort requirements, comprehensive child support enforcement, and supports for families moving from welfare to work—including increased funding for child care and guaranteed medical coverage."

TERM PAPER SUGGESTIONS

1. Trace the history of poor relief in the United States in the twentieth century.

2. Prior to the twentieth century, the poor were widely viewed as being responsible for their own poverty. The title of the 1996 legislation seems to indicate a return to this old attitude. Examine the changing attitudes of the American public to welfare.

3. Several scholars and policymakers, including Martin Gilens, argue that stereotypical images of African Americans as shiftless and lazy are at the root of efforts to reform welfare to reward the "deserving" poor. Research the images of the poor in the media from 1980 to the present.

ALTERNATIVE TERM PAPER SUGGESTIONS

1. Interview someone who has received financial assistance from the government. Write a paper that sets that person's experiences within the wider context of government policy to help the poor.

2. Assume that you are giving a presentation to a community group. Create a Microsoft PowerPoint presentation that explains all the forms of assistance available to poor individuals in your community.

SUGGESTED SOURCES

Primary Sources

Eitzen, D. Stanley, and Kelly Eitzen Smith, eds. *Experiencing Poverty: Voices from the Bottom.* Belmont, CA: Thomson Wadsworth, 2003. One of the few books to include oral histories by people experiencing poverty after the passage of the 1996 welfare reform legislation.

"1996 Personal Responsibility and Work Opportunity Reconciliation." http://www.sourcewatch.org/index.php?title=1996_Personal_Responsibility_and

_Work_Opportunity_Reconciliation_Act. Provides a copy of the legislation and links to related documents, such as the U.S. Department of Health and Human Services September 1996 Administration Fact Sheet for an overview of provisions in the act.

"Public Law 104–193—AUG. 22, 1996." http://www.fns.usda.gov/FSP/rules/Legislation/pdfs/PL_104-193.pdf. Provides the original text of the legislation.

United States. *Personal Responsibility and Work Opportunity Reconciliation Act of 1996.* Washington, DC: Government Printing Office, 1996. Provides the full text of the legislation.

Secondary Sources

DeParle, Jason. *American Dream: Three Women, Ten Kids, and a Nation's Drive to End Welfare.* New York: Viking, 2004. Traces the lives of three women and their children in Wisconsin as the 1996 welfare reform bill passes through Congress and Wisconsin conducts its own reform.

Gilens, Martin. *Why Americans Hate Welfare: Race, Media, and the Politics of Antipoverty Policy.* Chicago: University of Chicago Press, 2000. Shows that most Americans support governmental assistance to the poor who actively seek employment yet oppose it for those who are perceived as lazy. Gilens analyzed racial stereotypes to show that race lies at the root of opposition to welfare programs.

Hays, Sharon. *Flat Broke with Children: Women in the Age of Welfare Reform.* New York: Oxford University Press, 2004. Reports that single mothers are often pushed into jobs that have no stability or possibility for advancement and are encouraged to marry men who can support them.

Trattner, Walter I. *From Poor Law to Welfare State: A History of Social Welfare in America.* New York: Free Press, 1998. This book, now in its sixth edition, is the standard history of poor relief in the United States.

World Wide Web

"Welfare Reform in America: A Clash of Politics and Research, Diana Zuckerman, Ph.D." http://www.center4research.org/poverty3.html. Reprints an essay that first appeared in the Winter 2000 issue of the *Journal of Social Issues* about how political pressures resulted in the 1996 legislation, despite doomsday predictions and almost no solid information about the law's likely impact.

"Welfare's Changing Face." http://www.washingtonpost.com/wp-srv/politics/special/welfare/welfare.htm. Reprints a July 1998 *Washington Post* special report on welfare reform with links to editorials and key news stories.

Multimedia Sources

Historic Poverty Films on DVD: 1948–1967. Quality Information, n.d. DVD. This is a collection of six short films relating to poverty. The 1956 film *Poverty in Rural America* and the 1967 film *With No One to Help Us,* about welfare mothers in Newark who organize to protest price gouging, are particularly informative.

1967 Welfare, Poverty, Food Stamps & Financial Aid Documentary. Quality Information, n.d. DVD. Contains the film *With No One to Help Us.*

100. Hurricane Katrina Devastates New Orleans (2005)

After several days of spinning in the Gulf of Mexico, Hurricane Katrina made landfall on August 29, 2005. The resulting devastation in Mississippi and Louisiana shocked the country. The catastrophic breaching of the levees in New Orleans led to the deaths of about 1,700 people, many of them black. When government help failed to materialize for days, many charged that officials were permitting a "chocolate city" to die.

On August 24, a storm began to brew in the waters off of the Bahamas. Wal-Mart started to ready supplies for an expected rush to its stores for hurricane supplies. On August 25, the storm became a Category 1 hurricane named Katrina. It hit Florida, killing 18 people and causing $600 million in property damage. The storm lost strength while over Florida but began gaining power as it moved into the warm waters of the Gulf of Mexico. On August 26, hurricane forecasters predicted that Katrina would hit either Mississippi or Louisiana in three days. The governors of Mississippi and Louisiana declared civil emergencies, while the Red Cross and Salvation Army began to organize relief efforts. On August 27, Mayor Ray Nagin of New Orleans asked citizens to evacuate and designated the Superdome as a hurricane shelter. About 100,000 people did not evacuate. President George W. Bush declared a federal state of emergency in Louisiana. On August 28, Katrina became a Category 5 hurricane, the most dangerous type of storm. The head of the National Hurricane Center warned Bush and Federal Emergency

Management Agency (FEMA) Chief Michael Brown that the levees protecting New Orleans from flooding might be breached by Katrina. On August 29 at 4 A.M., Katrina began to breach the levees of New Orleans. Flooding continued for days. The storm hit the city at 6:10 A.M. and knocked out electricity. Further levee breaches caused catastrophic flooding in New Orleans. FEMA was advised by officials of the National Weather Service, the Transportation Security Administration, and the Department of Homeland Security that the levees had been breached. FEMA staff in New Orleans advised Brown that people were trapped by the rising waters. By August 30, about 80 percent of New Orleans was under water, 200,000 homes had been destroyed, and about 15 percent of the New Orleans police had abandoned their posts.

Bush came under extremely heavy criticism for the slow response of the federal government to the disaster in New Orleans. The Royal Canadian Mounted Police actually arrived in New Orleans to offer aid before the federal government showed up. Bush claimed that no one predicted the failure of the levees. One week after the storm, victims were still being rescued from rooftops. By the start of October, more than 40,000 people were still living in shelters, awaiting temporary housing. Recovery efforts cost about $1 billion per day, and Katrina is estimated to be the nation's most expensive disaster.

TERM PAPER SUGGESTIONS

1. Louisiana State Representative Karen Carter commented, "I thought I lived in America until shortly after Katrina." Explore what Carter meant.
2. Racism is not just a psychological matter. It can also be seen in the structure of politics and in economics. Discuss the role played by racism in the response to Katrina in New Orleans.
3. Compare and contrast the response to Katrina with the response to another hurricane, perhaps Betsy or Ike.

ALTERNATIVE TERM PAPER SUGGESTIONS

1. Create a Web site that charts the progress of Katrina and the progress of recovery from the storm.
2. Create a photo montage of images of New Orleans before and after the storm with accompanying commentary. Address the current state of recovery.

SUGGESTED SOURCES

Primary Source

Editors of *Time* Magazine. *Time: Hurricane Katrina: The Storm That Changed America.* New York: Time-Life, 2005. Contains oral histories and photographs that were originally printed in *Time*.

Secondary Sources

Brinkley, David. *The Great Deluge: Hurricane Katrina, New Orleans, and the Mississippi Gulf Coast.* New York: Morrow, 2006. A typically engaging and well-researched book from one of the nation's best historians.

Dyson, Michael Eric. *Come Hell or High Water: Hurricane Katrina and the Color of Disaster.* New York: Basic Books, 2006. Argues that the failure to offer timely aid to Katrina's victims is indicative of deeper problems in race and class relations.

Hartman, Chester, and Gregory D. Squires, eds. *There Is No Such Thing as a Natural Disaster: Race, Class, and Hurricane Katrina.* New York: Routledge, 2006. A scholarly examination of the social implications of Katrina.

McKinney, Louise. *New Orleans: A Cultural History.* New York: Oxford University Press, 2006. A good history of the city before the storm struck.

Troutt, David Dante, ed. *After the Storm: Black Intellectuals Explore the Meaning of Hurricane Katrina.* New York: New Press, 2007. Explores the political and social response to Katrina.

World Wide Web

"City of New Orleans Falling Deeper into Chaos and Desperation." http://transcripts.cnn.com/TRANSCRIPTS/0509.02/ltm.01.html. CNN reporter Soledad O'Brien's coverage of New Orleans on September 2, 2005.

"Global Flood Watch." http://www.onthemedia.org/yore/transcripts/transcripts_090905_global.html. This September 9, 2005 episode of NPR's *On the Media* reviews coverage of Katrina in Europe and Asia.

"Katrina Timeline." http://thinkprogress.org/katrina-timeline/. Lists events associated with Katrina from August 26, 2005 to August 2006.

"LBJ and the Response to Hurricane Betsy, by Kent B. Germany." http://tapes.millercenter.virginia.edu/exhibits/betsy/. Introduces the 1965 Hurricane Betsy and includes both transcripts and audiotapes of President Lyndon B. Johnson's quick response to the storm.

"Mayor to Feds: Get Off Your Asses." http://edition.cnn.com/2005/US/09/02/ nagin.transcript. A transcript of reporter Garland Robinson's interview with New Orleans Mayor Ray Nagin.

"Special Edition: Hurricane Katrina." http://transcripts.cnn.com/TRAN SCRIPTS/0509/01/acd.01.html. A transcript of a Septembe 1, 2005 episode of *Anderson Cooper 360 Degrees*.

"Timeline: How the Hurricane Crisis Unfolded: A Day-by-Day Look at How the Crisis Has Unfolded in New Orleans, after the City Was Battered by Hurricane Katrina." This is a BBC site that has news coverage of each day of Katrina from August 28 to September 9, 2005. It also includes video clips of people fleeing New Orleans and of the hurricane striking the city, pictures of the devastation, and interviews with those residents who stayed in New Orleans.

"Transcript of Audio of President Johnson in New Orleans Following Landfall of Hurricane Betsy, September 10, 1965." http://www.lbjlib.utexas.edu/ johnson/AV.hom/Hurricane/audio_transcript.shtm. The Lyndon B. Johnson Library and Museum provides transcripts of Johnson's remarks upon and leaving New Orleans after Hurricane Betsy had struck. Johnson also spoke with several residents of the city, and those conversations are also transcribed on this site.

"What Katrina Teaches About the Meaning of Racism." http://understanding katrina.ssrc.org/Gilman/. This essay by Nils Gilman is a good introduction to the complexity of racism.

"The White House Katrina Report: A Failure of Initiative." http://www.white house.gov/reports/katrina-lessons-learned/. This is a 520-page study of the government's response to Hurricane Katrina.

Multimedia Sources

National Geographic—Inside Hurricane Katrina. Washington, DC: National Geographic Video, 2005. Focuses on the devastation caused by Katrina.

When the Levees Broke: A Requiem in Four Acts. New York: HBO, 2007. DVD. Spike Lee's documentary won the George Polk Award for television documentary. In the DVD, Lee's director's commentary discusses how his perspective on individuals featured in the film shaped the design of the film.

Index

About the Author

CARYN E. NEUMANN is Visiting Assistant Professor of History at Miami University of Ohio.